The Economics of
New Technology in
Developing Countries

The Economics of
New Technology in
Developing Countries

Edited by

Frances Stewart
Jeffrey James

Frances Pinter (Publishers), London
Westview Press, Boulder, Colorado

© Frances Stewart and Jeffrey James 1982

First published in 1982 by
Frances Pinter (Publishers) Limited
5 Dryden Street, Covent Garden, London WC2E 9NW

Published in 1982 in the United States of America by
Westview Press, 5500 Central Avenue,
Boulder, Colorado 80301
Frederick A. Praeger, Publisher

ISBN 0–86531–281–8

Library of Congress Catalog Card Number: 82-80429

British Library Cataloguing in Publication Data

The Economics of new technology in developing
    countries.
    1. Technology–Social aspects–Underdeveloped
    areas
    I. Stewart, Frances II. James, Jeffrey
    303.4'83   T14.5

ISBN 0–86187–216–9

Typeset by Anne Joshua Associates, Oxford
Printed by SRP, Exeter

Contents

Preface

This book is the outcome of a Development Studies Association Workshop on Technology that we convened in Queen Elizabeth House in March 1980. In one form or another, many of the essays were first presented at that workshop. In addition, we are pleased to include some by authors who did not attend the workshop.

Two of the essays (Forsyth, McBain and Solomon; James and Stewart) have been published in journals. We are grateful to *World Development* and *Oxford Economic Papers* for permission to use them.

J. J. and F. S.

1 Introduction

FRANCES STEWART and JEFFREY JAMES

In the 1960s and 1970s most research on technology in poor countries was directed at the question of the labour or capital intensity of production technique (sometimes described as the 'neo-classical' question[1]). But recently, largely as a result of the findings of such research, the focus has changed quite radically. There is not a single new focus, but rather a new set of directions. In general, the new perspectives[2] are concerned with technology in a *dynamic* setting, with attention on how technology changes over time, whereas previously the major concern was the *static* question of choice out of a given set of techniques.

This set of essays consists of a wide range of examples of the new concerns. Because the areas covered are departures, the approach, as represented here and elsewhere, tends to be rather experimental and the coverage incomplete. The collection of essays raises questions as much as it provides answers: but in so doing it provides a comprehensive introduction to the major new topics which are of substantial concern to those working on issues of technology and development.

THE NEO-CLASSICAL QUESTION

The neo-classical question was concerned with choice of technique — defined in terms of labour or capital intensity — out of a given set of technical alternatives in order to produce a given product. The initial focus of the research was theoretical rather than empirical: the aim was to identify the optimum technique, from the point of view of LDC objectives, especially those of employment creation and economic growth. The initial view[3] that LDCs should choose labour intensive techniques in order to make efficient use of their abundant factor (labour) and economise on their scarce factor (capital), was challenged by those[4] who saw that the choice of technique helped determine the savings rate and that giving weight to the generation of savings as an objective would tend to lead to more capital intensive choice of techniques. This is illustrated in Diagram One, where, with certain assumptions, technique B maximises the surplus. In so far

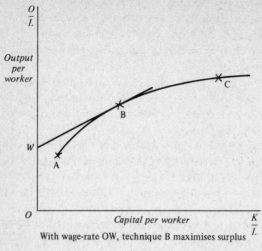

With wage-rate OW, technique B maximises surplus

Diagram One

as employment growth depends on output growth, the more capital intensive technique would lead to a higher rate of growth of employment, so
that after some time the more capital intensive technique would actually
involve a higher level of employment than the more labour intensive technique. However, it was soon pointed out that a number of rather restrictive
and unrealistic assumptions were necessary for this outcome. The model
assumes that each technique pays the same wage rate; that all savings are
reinvested; and that the government cannot ensure the desired savings rate
in some other way (e.g. through general taxation) than through the choice of
technique. Each of these assumptions has been challenged empirically
and theoretically, whilst the emergence of a dualistic economy in many
countries, with its associated problems of underemployment and poverty,
has re-created emphasis on the need for labour-intensive technologies.

While at a theoretical level debate was focused on criteria for establishing the 'optimum' technique out of a given 'well-behaved'[5] set of alternative
technologies, at an empirical level research has been concentrated on
establishing the extent to which there does exist a set of technically
efficient alternatives,[6] as against the technological determinist view that
the choice is very limited.[7] This is of course of critical importance to
the significance of criteria for choice of technique, since if there exists
only one or two possible technologies for each industry, the question
of choice of technique for such industry becomes of limited significance,
and the major choice becomes one of industrial composition.

A very substantial amount of research was devoted to the empirical question; the conclusions of this research have been summarised in a number of places.[8] Dahlman and Westphal succinctly sum up the main conclusion: 'It is now well established that there is scope for choosing between techniques with differing levels of labour intensity and productivity, but that the scope for choice is by no means uniform.' Three of the essays in this book further develop investigation into the neoclassical question, each with a rather different approach from the main body of work on the static question.

Charles Cooper's essay is concerned further to explore the question of criteria for choice of optimum technique. He takes the Dobb–Sen approach to the question of choice of technique and applies it to choice of technique in the capital-goods sector. He assumes a planned economy with abundant labour supply and limited investible surplus. Under these assumptions for any real wage rate a certain amount of labour can be employed in the capital-goods sector. Choice of technique in that sector is defined as consisting of the allocation of that limited labour between the sector which makes machines for the consumption sector and the sector which makes machines for the investment sector (i.e. machines to make machines for the consumption sector). The criterion of choice is to maximise output of machines for the consumer-goods sector. Cooper shows that, using this criterion, the optimum technique in the capital-goods sector depends purely on the technical conditions of production and not at all on the level of real wages. The optimum choice may be the capital-intensive or the labour-intensive technique depending on the technical conditions. Cooper's conclusion accords with, and in part explains, two important facets of the real world: first, as often observed, capital-goods industries are neither uniformly capital-intensive, as is sometimes supposed, nor uniformly labour-intensive. Secondly, the Cooper analysis lends support to the view that different factor intensity may be appropriate in different sectors of the economy: one aspect of this conclusion is the 'walking on two legs' strategy. While these glimpses of reality lend authority to the model, it needs to be noted that it rests on some very simplified assumptions, the removal of which may undermine the conclusions.

First, it assumes that workers in the sector making machines to make machines do so totally unassisted by machines. This is of course incorrect: the nature of the machines they need could affect the conclusions. Secondly, there is the assumption of a given wage rate which does not vary with technique. If the wage rate varies with technique, then the total employment affordable in the investment sector will depend in part on the technique chosen. These are both probably rather trivial qualifications and are unlikely to affect the major conclusions of the model. Of greater significance is the way it ignores time in a curious way, despite the fact that using a more capital intensive technique in the capital goods sector is essentially a way of increasing the 'roundaboutness' of production, extending the time period of production with the eventual result (it is normally assumed) of increasing consumption. This is the way the question is treated in the Feldman/Domar and Mahalanobis models. Another way of expressing this point is that the criterion of maximising machines for consumption is only unambiguous if time is ignored. If by devoting more resources to machines to make machines, the amount of machines to make consumption goods is reduced in the short term, but increased in the long term, then time preference becomes critical.

The other two essays on the static question are mainly empirical. Forsyth *et al.* (Chapter 3) attempt to develop the concept of *technical rigidity* by investigating the physical/chemical properties of production in different industries. They identify eight 'fundamental physical barriers to the substitution of labour for capital', including the use of high or low process temperature, the application of fluid pressure on materials in process and so on. They then develop an 'Index of Technical Rigidity' (ITR) for various industries based on how many of the eight barriers apply in any one industry. They thus attempt to give a technical, as against economic or historical, explanation to technological determinism. Applying their measure to industries in a number of countries they show a rather complex picture; while the ITR helps to explain substitution (or its absence) in some industries, in some countries, the effects are not uniformly in the expected direction. Their empirical work shows that scale is very important in determining factor use, particularly in industries with high ITR. In general, they find considerable factor substitution in the developing countries they looked at, in comparison with UK factor use. Technical change, they suggest, will tend to reduce the scope for substitution by increasing scale of production.

The chapter represents an interesting attempt to apply physical and chemical 'laws' to the question of choice of technique. One can question the precise details of the barriers chosen and also the way the index is constructed. In particular, adding up the barriers may not be the most appropriate approach (as they admit) since a barrier is an on/off concept. If a barrier is operative, then adding another one should not make a difference. However, in practice, many of these barriers are not fully operative in this sense: that is by additional effort/investment or by allowing more skills, or by permitting variation in product standards, the barriers may be avoided. Moreover, the barriers represent the historical way in which technology has developed. With a different historical path (e.g. more emphasis on small-scale techniques in research and development) the nature of the barriers in being today would be different. Hence the barriers are not entirely the product of iron physical laws, but are also products of human endeavour and organisation. It is, therefore, not surprising that the ITR did not always work in the expected way in reality. Despite these qualifications, the attempt to give physical clothes to 'technical rigidity' is pioneering and offers promising avenues for future work.

Enos' chapter is not so much concerned with the nature of choices facing developing countries, but with how they make these choices – the selection mechanisms. He suggests that the production function approach to choice is fundamentally misleading, in focusing attention on the wrong set of variables – on choice of technique as the main issue in technology transfer and on factor prices as the main selection mechanism. But in the case examined – petrochemicals – the question of choice of technique never arose: all countries wanted the most modern technique for producing a standard product. In South Korea, each of the thirteen patented processes for the manufacture of polyethelene and six for the manufacture of VCM had virtually identical input requirements: in terms of Diagram One, which illustrates the production function approach, each was on the same point on the production function. The real choice then became how to select among near identical techniques and the terms of the technology transfer contract. In the South Korean case, the government's aims are described as being first, to minimise foreign exchange cost, and to maximise the rate of output; and secondly, to ensure eventual Korean control and mastery of the technology. In the case of the other countries cited (where actual evidence produced is slight), the objectives and criteria were very different: the major objective is argued to be the maximisation of benefit to particular individuals and groups: 'what is sought in the developing country is not so much a production of goods as an assignment of benefits; and what is employed in the seeking is not so much a technology as a political process'. He concludes that developing countries choose beneficiaries rather than techniques.

Inevitably, the example chosen – a high technology industry – means that there is less potential choice of technique (in Forsyth *et al.*'s categorisation the ITR is high). It is unlikely – in its extreme form – that the Enos thesis can be generalised to other industries, where there is more choice. But many studies have supported the view that the selection mechanisms are much broader than simply relative prices;[9] that the Enos factor – the private beneficiaries of decisions – is an important aspect in many countries, especially for large investment decisions, is undoubtedly true. But most studies of choice of technique suggest there are other factors of influence as well.[10] One question is left unanswered in the Enos chapter: why do South Korea's objectives vary so sharply, according to him, from that of every other developing country? It is necessary to explore this question before the conclusions gain operational significance.

X-EFFICIENCY

The static choice of technique literature is concerned with (one dimension of) efficiency of resource allocation: it implicitly assumes (see Diagram One) that for any given investment, each technique is associated with a unique amount of labour, of capital and of output. In fact, as Harvey Leibenstein (1966) long ago pointed out, any particular production process may be operated with greater or lesser efficiency, so that there is not a unique quantity of factor use or level of output associated with any particular process, but each will vary according to all sorts of factors. He named the phenomenon X-efficiency and quite a few investigations showed that the potential increase in output from raising X-efficiency could often exceed the potential from increasing allocational efficiency. Empirical investigations, which looked at actual techniques in use (as against those which took their 'facts' from engineering brochures and 'best practice' techniques in developed countries) also revealed the very significant variations in efficiency with which techniques were operated. In so far as these variations are systematically associated with the nature of the techniques (e.g. in being greater for less for 'machine paced' techniques as Hirschman (1958) suggested), then the phenomenon becomes highly relevant to the question of choice of technique. In addition, in so far as X-efficiency is amenable to improvement by policy changes, by concentrating such changes on labour-intensive techniques LDCs can increase the relative productivity of these techniques and therefore the profitability from their use. This could become a significant way of influencing choice of technique.

Curiously, apart from investigations of the 'Hirschman' hypothesis,[11] the question of extent and causes of X-efficiency and how it is related to choice of technique has been generally neglected. Pack's essay begins to fill that gap. He takes data on the textile industry in Latin America in 1950 and attempts to explain variations in X-efficiency of particular techniques. He decomposes the differences into those due to differences at the level of the national economy, those at the industry level, those at the firm level and those at the task level. If responsibility for differences in X-efficiency can be attributed to the various levels, strong policy conclusions will emerge. Pack found, on the 1950 evidence, that worker inefficiency (or task-level differences) were a relatively small element in explaining differences in X-efficiency; differences due to differences in efficiency at the level of the national economy and of industry were of greater significance. Differences in X-efficiency were found to vary with technology, but not consistently since among spinning plants the older technologies (less capital intensive and automated) were less efficiently operated than the new, in relation to best practice operation, but among weaving technologies the opposite conclusion held.

LEARNING AND TECHNICAL CHANGE

One reason why the productivity of particular techniques may vary is that accumulation of experience among managers, the work force, suppliers and so on, will tend to raise productivity over time. Thus a general explanation of the differences in productivity between DCs and LDCs using the same technology is that in the DCs there has been a much longer accumulation of experience. Increases in productivity associated with accumulation of experience can again be associated with different levels: the learning may occur at each of Pack's four levels. In his chapter Pack ignores the time/learning dimension, perhaps because he only has the data for a particular point in time. But elsewhere he has forcefully drawn attention to the phenomenon.[12] The chapters by Dahlman and Westphal and that by Bell are primarily concerned with changes in productivity arising from the accumulation of experience.

Dahlman and Westphal introduce the concept of *technological mastery* which they define 'as operational command over technological knowledge'. 'Mastery manifests itself in the ability to use knowledge effectively, and is achieved by the application of technological effort.' They apply the concept to four broadly defined categories of activities: production engineering; project execution; capital goods manufacture; and research and development. The first two categories, especially the first — production engineering — are related to the X-efficiency concept: in these categories Dahlman and Westphal attribute differences in productivity with particular techniques to the accumulation of technological mastery. The four categories are thought to be interlinked, with technological mastery at any stage contributing to mastery at others. Experience is believed to be a major source of technological mastery. They cite the example of an integrated steel mill in Brazil where the plant's capacity was effectively doubled over seven years with very little additional investment and no increase in the work force.[13] Similar results have been found by the Katz project.[14]

The concept of technological mastery has important theoretical and practical implications. It overlaps, but is not identical with, the concept of X-efficiency. Technological mastery is one powerful explanation of differences in X-efficiency, but there are other explanations (e.g. the competitive structure of the economy, managerial efficiency) and we need empirical tests to investigate their relative importance. Technological mastery is in part — but not wholly — the outcome of experience. But it is also (see the discussion of Bell *et al.* below and the Katz (1978) studies) a matter of the other conditions in the economy, the industry and the firm (e.g. the extent of skill availability, the need for adaption of technology). The existence of technological mastery as a significant phenomenon has a number of implications for choice of technique and choice of project, as well as for general economic policies.

Looking again at the initial postulate of a range of technologies, shown in Diagram One, we see that it has to be amended substantially to allow for X-efficiency and technological mastery. The existence of X-inefficiency means that in any economy the choice is not the production function shown, implicitly assumed to be uniform for all circumstances, but rather a series of points which are under the line by a varying and (usually unknown) extent, showing the actual relationships, rather than the engineering or best practice ones. This is indicated in Diagram Two. The learning/

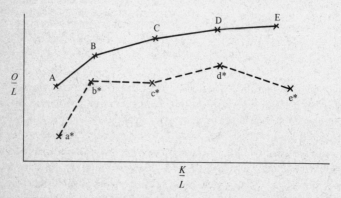

ABCDE shows choice using 'best practice' techniques; a*b*c*d*e* shows actual choice in an economy allowing for X-efficiency.

Diagram Two

technological mastery phenomenon introduces an important new dimension. The actual positions now depend not only on various aspects of each economy, industry and firm at a point in time, but on the accumulation of experience which is a function chiefly (although not exclusively) of the time that has occurred (and the experience accumulated) in the use of a particular technique. Hence there will be a different range of choice (or a different production function) as time proceeds, but these differences will not be simply a function of time, but also of the choice initially made and therefore the experience accumulated. According to this view, the points in Diagram Two are moving over time, depending on which choice was made. At time period 2 the choice could be aa′ or ee″ depending on whether technique a* or technique e* was chosen at the time period 1

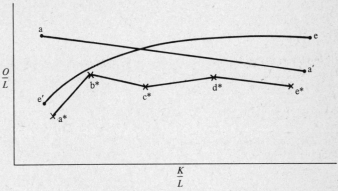

a*b*c*d*e* shows the potential choice at period 1. aa′ shows the choice at period 2 if technique a* is chosen at period 1; ee′ shows the choice at period 2 if technique e* is chosen at period 1.

Diagram Three

(as shown in Diagram Three).[15] In addition, there could be a general change in the productivity of every technique due to the fact that experience accumulated in the economy as a whole may raise the productivity of every technique.

Diagram Three has probably greatly exaggerated the experience factor in contributing to technical change and X-efficiency. Much depends on how significant the phenomenon is and how far it is technique specific, and does not carry over to other techniques. Clearly we need more empirical research to investigate this. None the less, any degree of learning alters the considerations relevant to choice of technique because the learning phenomenon also has to be taken into account. In so far as the learning is internal to a firm and foreseen by it, it can be expected to be taken into account in the firm's own decisions. But in so far as the benefits are not fully captured by the particular firm, or are not foreseen by a firm when taking a decision, then public intervention will be required. The learning phenomenon also lends support to policies of protection of local activities. Learning has always been a justification for 'infant industry' protection. In addition, where the learning is related to the accumulation of experience in developing technology, it gives justification for protecting local technological efforts and for selecting the mode of technology transfer in the light of these effects. Dahlman and Westphal explore how this has been successfully pursued in the case of South Korea. Technology has been acquired from abroad in arms-length contracts, in which the aim has been to maximise local assimilation and mastery of the imported technology.

Bell, Scott-Kemmis and Satyarakwit's chapter contrasts strongly with that of the other chapters in this section because they describe a case where virtually no learning took place. They identify two types of 'process-related' technological change: evolutionary change which 'might be effected over time in an existing production system' or intra-vintage technical change: and technical change which takes the form of introducing new production systems (inter-vintage technical change). Their study examines production of galvanised sheet steels in three lines in a firm in Thailand. One of the lines was imported from Japan in 1961 and the other two were locally built in 1964 and 1968. Between 1968 and 1973 there was *no* improvement in performance in the three lines and in some cases productivity declined. Comparisons between the three lines show no improvements in the later lines, as compared with the earlier one. 'Over a period of at least about nine years this infant industrial firm did not improve any of four important aspects of the production efficiency.' There was thus neither intra- nor inter-vintage technical change.

The example shows that learning is not automatic, not simply a function of time of use of a particular technique; other factors are also necessary. Two are noted by Bell *et al.*: first, the firm needs to devote resources to the learning process; secondly, the external environment needs to be conducive to technical change. While Dahlman and Westphal and others have pointed to the potential significance of learning and technical change, the Bell example emphasises that we need much more empirical research in order to identify those conditions in which this learning is likely to occur and those in which it is not.

THIRD WORLD TECHNOLOGY

There is a strong case for Third World countries developing their own capacity to create technology.[16] This is partly to enable them to use imported technology more efficiently, because imported technology is rarely well adapted to Third World circumstances and its efficiency can often be markedly increased by local adaptation. Secondly, local technological development is necessary for the development of more appropriate techniques and products, since technology imported from advanced countries tends to be increasingly inappropriate — capital-intensive, large scale and producing sophisticated products. Thirdly, the development of local technological capacity reduces dependence on advanced countries, permitting countries to strike a better bargain for imported technology, as well as contributing to objectives of independence and self-reliance. Fourthly, the development of local technological capacity can lead to comparative advantage in this area and significant export earnings. The chapters by Lall, Morehouse and Biggs *et al.* as well as Dahlman and Westphal, are concerned with different aspects of the process of building up Third World technology capacity.

The Dahlman and Westphal chapter (as noted above) is concerned with the first aspect of creating Third World technology — the way in which technological mastery contributes to raising the efficiency of production. Lall's essay is largely concerned with the fourth aspect: that is how the accumulation of experience in technology has led to quite substantial technology exports in some LDCs, notably India. These technology exports are significant as a general indicator that quite significant technical accumulation has taken place in India. This provides a powerful supplement to case-study material, which by its nature is confined to very few examples. In addition, it indicates that the technological capacity created has produced results which are of value at a world level, and not simply in the protected environment of a single country. The evidence of the technology exports is also important in supporting the conclusion that comparative advantage is a dynamic phenomenon and static advantage at any one time may be no guide to a country's potential, lending support to the case for 'infant industry' protection during a learning period. In Lall's view, strong protection for local technological development was essential for its success in India and has been justified by the results.

The evidence of flourishing technology exports for some countries suggests that, for these countries at least, the 'no learning, no local technical change' of Bell *et al.* is not widely applicable, and the learning stories of Dahlman and Westphal and the Katz studies are more typical. But the Bell case study remains as a powerful reminder that technical change cannot simply be assumed, it is necessary to investigate the conditions in which local technological accumulation flourishes. Studies of technology exports alone cannot do this: they need to be supplemented by investigations of what lies behind the technological developments, which are evidenced by the rising technology exports.

Morehouse's chapter is a case study of the development of local technology: he traces the story of the Swaraj tractor in India and shows that production based on the local technology has become as efficent as production based on imported technology, while it has also involved generally more appropriate factor use. The study shows that the development of local technology is an infant industry, requiring protection and support in the initial period, but one that does grow up, in this case in a quite short period, so that it becomes rapidly competitive with foreign sources.

It is often argued that the structure of research and development in LDCs is unsuited to generating technological capacity:[17] it is argued that it is too formal, with insufficient links with local industry. Lall's paper shows that as a general condemnation of Indian research and development (R&D) this proved incorrect. No doubt the efforts could have been much more efficiently deployed but eventually there have been results. The tractor case also is an illustration of successful development in a government laboratory, confounding the usual conclusions.

Statements about the efficacy, or lack of it, of R&D efforts tend to be based on rather casual observation. Biggs' chapter is an example of a much more systematic appraisal of R&D systems.[18] He contrasts an 'ideal' system, with appropriate two-way links between R&D institutions and local producers and international scientists, with the normal system which is riddled with 'imperfections', and where dominant influences on R&D often produce a type of research which is totally dysfunctional, or which is functional only coincidentally. Biggs contrasts three schools of thought about the direction of technological change in LDCs: the view that it is 'induced' by the prevailing factor prices,[19] the view that it is the outcome of dominant class interests,[20] and the view (of which his study is an example) that it is determined by interest groups and arrangements in the R&D institutions. While the institutional dimension represented here is obviously of importance — and indeed is the main way in which governments and the international community try to influence technical change — it could be argued that the institutions are themselves the product of other factors, and not therefore really an independent influence or instrument of policy. On the one hand, the class interest school would argue that the nature of R&D institutions in any situation reflects prevailing class interests. The dysfunctional nature of R&D institutions then, from the point of view of achieving relevant results for poor rural producers, is no accident of institutional design, but the outcome of dominant interests at both national and international levels. On the other, the induced innovation school would argue that the way institutions function depends on the market structure and prices they face. The institutional school might accept both these comments, in large part, but would claim some independent influence arising from the power and ambitions of the scientific community itself. All three schools of thought may be formally consistent: institutions may respond to factor prices, but the relevant factor prices may be shaped by the dominant classes. The evidence would then support each view — which often does seem to be the case. The major difference then is in belief as to which influence forms the prime mover. Views on that are largely a matter of judgement: it is difficult to devise empirical tests which could decide.

It is interesting to compare the type of approach to R&D, represented by all three schools, with the other approaches illustrated in this book. While the other essays describe the technological developments in particular cases, a broader approach is needed to see how the particular cases fit into the macro-picture and to understand the influences on the direction and usefulness of R&D. Formally, the work of Biggs and of the other schools he describes have been almost exclusively related to agriculture. Application of a similar approach to industrial R&D could produce similar and significant results.

PRODUCTS

The final section of the book is concerned with products. This area has been neglected in research on technology. The initial choice of technique model was concerned with choice of technique for a *given* product. Empirical research into choice of techniques soon revealed that variations in technique often involved variations in products, while changing the product composition of output offered more potential for changing factor proportions than changing choice of technique. In addition, it became evident that choice of product is of major significance in its own right, independently of the consequences for factor proportions. The nature of products available determines how a society meets its needs. Product development in advanced countries designed to meet the needs of relatively rich consumers often produces 'inappropriate' products for poor countries, being of excessively high standards, embodying unnecessary characteristics for much poorer people. The net result is that the expensive imported products can often only be consumed by a minority of the people in LDCs, and the remainder have very few products.[21] The two essays on this topic further explore the issue of products.

The first chapter — James and Stewart — looks at the welfare impact of new products in LDCs. It uses the Lancaster framework to show that new products often tend to be inegalitarian in impact, and may sometimes (especially if old products are withdrawn) actually lead to overall welfare losses. In an examination of eight cases, one case (soap) is shown to have purely negative effects (on choice, on distribution and on production technology), while in the other cases, the results are mixed. More case studies are needed. It is argued that LDCs should have an active products policy, so as to reduce the undesirable effects of new products.

The second essay looks at the question of product standards, which is one important part of a products policy. It is sometimes suggested that LDCs should have the same product standards as in rich countries, while in reaction to this, others suggest that LDCs should have no product standards. James examines the origin and justification of product standards in rich countries and shows that the justification for having *some* standards, applies at least as much, if not more in poor countries. But he argues that different standards are appropriate, because rich country standards embody excessive standards, which mean that, when applied in poor countries, only a minority can afford the products, and the remainder either receive no products at all, or totally unregulated products (like illegally produced beer). Thus the majority suffer from the imposition of developed-country standards. In this respect, the question of standards is a special case of the general impact of advanced country products in LDCs.

CONCLUSION

As this introduction has indicated, the essays in this book cover a very large area. They are both examples of and pointers to the major new approaches to technology in developing countries.

NOTES

1   See extended definition of the 'neo-classical question' in Stewart (1977) p. 18.
2   Rosenberg (1976), from an economic historian's point of view, deals with many of the topics dealt with here.
3   E.g. Kahn (1951).
4   See Galenson and Leibenstein (1955); Dobb (1956–7); Sen (1968).
5   A 'well behaved' set of techniques is defined as occurring where the production function is continuous and exhibits a diminishing marginal rate of substitution between the factors.

6 I.e. a set in which any technique which uses more of one factor to produce a given output uses less of another factor, as compared with other techniques.
7 See Eckaus (1955).
8 See Bhalla (1975); Stewart (1977; chapter Eight); White (1978).
9 For a description of various non-conventional selection mechanisms see for example Lecraw (1979); Stewart (1977); Winston (1979).
10 Ibid.
11 See for example Teitel (1981).
12 See Pack (1974).
13 Dahlman and Fonseca (1978).
14 The IDP/ECLA Research directed by Katz. Preliminary results are summarised in Katz (1978).
15 This type of phenomenon was described by Atkinson and Stiglitz (1969) as 'localised technical progress'.
16 The arguments for creating Third World technological capacity are developed in Stewart (1981).
17 See for example USAID (1972) and some examples in Ranis' Introduction to Beranek and Ranis (1978).
18 See also his other work (referred to in the references to his chapter) and Clark (1980).
19 Binswanger and Ruttan (1978).
20 Griffin (1974).
21 See Stewart (1977) for more extended discussion.

REFERENCES

Atkinson, A. B. and Stiglitz, J. B. (1969). A new view of technological change, *Economic Journal*, LXXIX, 3, pp. 573–578.
Beranek, W. and Ranis, G. (1978). *Science and Technology and Economic Development*, Praeger.
Bhalla, A. S. (1975). *Technology and Employment in Industry*, ILO.
Binswanger, H. P. and Ruttan, V. W. (1978). *Induced Innovation: Technology, Institutions and Development*, Johns Hopkins,
Clark, N. (1980). The economic behaviour of research institutions in developing countries – some methodological points, *Social Studies of Science*, 10, 1, pp. 75–93.
Dahlman, C. J. and Fonseca, F. V. (1978). From technological dependence to technological development: The case of the Usiminas Steel Plant in Brazil, IDB/ECLA/UNDP/IDRC Regional Program of Studies on Scientific and Technical Development in Latin America, Working Paper, No. 21. Buenos Aires, ECLA.
Dobb, M. (1956–7). Second thoughts on capital intensity of investment, *Review of Economic Studies*, XXIV, pp. 33–42.
Domar, E. (1957). *Essays in Economic Growth*, Oxford University Press, London.
Eckaus, R. S. (1955). The factor proportions problem in underdeveloped areas, *American Economic Review*, XLV, 4, pp. 539–565.
Galenson, S. and Leibenstein, H. (1955). Investment criteria, productivity and economic development, *Quarterly Journal of Economics*, LXIX, pp. 343–370.
Griffin, K. (1974). *The Political Economy of Agrarian Change*, Macmillan, London.
Hirschman, A. (1958). *The Strategy of Economic Development*, Yale University Press.
Kahn, A. E. (1951). Investment criteria in development programs, *Quarterly Journal of Economics*, LXV, pp. 38–61.
Katz, J. (1978). Technological change, economic development and intra and extra regional relations in Latin America, IDB/ECLA/UNDP/IDRC Regional Program

of Studies on Scientific and Technical Development in Latin America Working Paper, no. 30, Buenos Aires, ECLA.

Lecraw, D. J. (1979). Choice of technology in low wage countries: A non neo classical approach, *Quarterly Journal of Economics*, XCIII, pp. 631–654.

Leibenstein, H. (1966). Allocative efficiency vs. X-efficiency, *American Economic Review*, LVI, pp. 392–415.

Mahalanobis, P. C. (1953). Some observations on the process of growth in national income, *Sankhya*, **12**.

Pack, H. (1974). The employment output trade off in LDCs — a micro economic approach, *Oxford Economic Papers* **26**, 3, pp. 388–404.

Rosenberg, N. (1976). *Perspectives on Technology*, Cambridge University Press.

Sen, A. K. (1968). *Choice of Techniques* (3rd Edn), Basil Blackwell, Oxford.

Stewart, F. (1977). *Technology and Underdevelopment*, Macmillan, London.

Stewart, F. (1981). Arguments for the generation of technology by LDCs, *The Annals*, **458**, pp. 97–109.

Teitel, S. (1981). Productivity, mechanisation and skills: A test of the Hirschman hypothesis for Latin American industry, *World Development*, **9**, 4, pp. 355–371.

USAID (1972). The role of the research institute in industrial growth, in *Appropriate Technologies for International Development*, United States Agency for International Development, Washington, DC.

White, L. J. (1978). The evidence on appropriate factor proportions in less developed countries: a survey, *Economic Development and Cultural Change*, **27**, 1, pp. 27–59.

Winston, G. (1979). The appeal of inappropriate technologies: self inflicted wages, ethnic pride and corruption, *World Development*, **7**, 7, pp. 835–845.

PART I STUDIES ON CHOICE OF TECHNIQUE

2 Sectoral capital intensities

CHARLES COOPER

This chapter examines A. K. Sen's analysis of choice of techniques in the capital-goods sector.[1] Sen considers a model in which a range of techniques of differing capital intensities is available in both capital- and consumer-goods sectors. The appropriate choice for each sector is then to be worked out by constrained maximisation of the planner's objective function. However, the solution to this choice of techniques problem is left implicit in a set of simultaneous equations.

We shall show that by adding a little more 'structure' to the problem, it is possible to discuss the choice of techniques in this two-sector model more explicitly and without undue restrictiveness. The extra 'structure' consists of assumptions about the form of the production function in the capital-goods sector.

The chapter is primarily concerned with choice of techniques in the capital-goods sector when the availability of investible surplus is limited. In Section II, we examine the case where only one kind of machinery (or technique) exists in the consumer-goods sector, but where two alternative efficient techniques are available in the capital-goods sector to produce it. In Section III, the assumption of one kind of consumer-goods machinery is retained, but we allow for a full range of technical alternatives in the capital-goods sector. In each case, given the assumptions of the model, the optimal technique of production in the capital-goods sector turns out to depend *only* on technical conditions of production. In particular, it is independent of the level of real wages. The level of employment in the capital-goods sector is independent of choice of techniques and is determined simply by the availability of surplus and the real wage.

In Section IV, the analysis is extended somewhat to discuss the case where a range of techniques exists in the consumer-goods sector. Section V contains the main conclusions.

II

The basic model is identical to Sen's. We assume a planned economy in which labour is abundant. There is one final output: a composite consumer good produced in the C-sector. It is produced by workers using C-machines. The workers are paid a real-wage w, measured in units of this composite consumer good. The investible surplus is the amount of composite consumer good produced in excess of the wage bill in the C-sector. The whole of the surplus is used to support workers in the capital-goods sector — at the wage-rate w.

The capital-goods sector is divided into two: the I-sector where workers use I-machines to produce C-machines for use in the consumer-goods sector; and the J-sector, where workers unassisted by machinery, make I-machines. Other assumptions of the simple model are retained (Sen, 1968; p. 12): there is no depreciation, constant returns to scale prevail in all sectors, no account is taken of gestation lags or technical progress.

In order to highlight the issue of choice of technique in the *capital-goods* sector, we assume initially that there is only one kind of C-sector machine, i.e. only one production technique exists in the C-sector, but that different types of I-sector machine exist to produce this C-sector machine. The choice of techniques problem is reduced to the selection of an appropriate I-machine from these alternatives. Again in the interests of simplifying the problem, assume initially that there are only two types of I-sector machine.

These different types of I-sector machine are distinguished by differences in capital intensity. The concept of capital intensity used reflects the fact that the model equates capital to 'stored-labour', in the style of the labour theory of value. Hence if in a given period of time, l_j workers are required in the J-sector to produce a particular kind of I-sector machine, which provides employment for l_i workers in the I-sector, the capital-intensity of this I-sector machine is defined as $b = l_j/l_i$. It measures the amount of labour-time needed in the J-sector (where direct unassisted labour is the only input to production), to provide employment for one worker in the I-sector. The ratio differs between I-sector techniques.[2]

It is assumed that the surplus available at the beginning of each period is the binding constraint on the growth of the economy. This surplus consists of the excess output of the composite consumption good in the C-sector, after C-sector workers have received their wages. The assumption that the availability of surplus for investment is constrained is critical to the choice of technique in the capital-goods sector. Suppose that an amount S of surplus is available at the beginning of the period. It follows that $S/w = L$, workers can be employed to make capital-goods, i.e. to make machinery in the J- and I-sectors. In other words, the level of employment in the capital-goods sectors is determined entirely by the availability of surplus output from the C-sector and the level of real wages. It does *not* depend on the choice of techniques in the capital-goods sector under our assumptions about economic organisation.

In fact, it is easy to show that the decision about which technique should be used in the I-sector to make C-sector machines is essentially about the allocation of the L workers who can be supported out of the C-sector surplus between the J- and I-sectors. Suppose that the two techniques available in the I-sector have capital-intensities of b and b^* respectively. Then there are two ways[3] of allocating the available labour-time L: either support l_j workers in the J-sector producing machines which employ l_i workers in the I-sector, such that $l_j/l_i = b$; or support l_j^* workers in the J-sector producing machines which employ l_i^* workers in the I-sector, such that $l_j^*/l_i^* = b^*$; and $l_i + l_j = l_i^* + l_j^* = L$. We assume $b^* > b$ in the following.

The obvious question is: on what grounds must the choice between these two 'allocations', corresponding to the alternative I-sector techniques, be made. The answer is straightforward. Recall that, by assumption there is only one type of C-machine available. It is immediately clear that the only consideration which is relevant to the efficient use of the available surplus is that it should be applied so as to produce the largest possible output of new C-machines from the I-sector. This criterion must determine the choice between the two I-sector techniques which are available.

However, the criterion by itself does not lead to any *a priori* conclusions about which of the I-sector techniques should be used. Diagrams One and Two demonstrate that either the more capital-intensive I-sector technique or the less capital-intensive might maximise the output of C-machines from the sector, depending on the technical conditions of production.

In Diagram One, we take advantage of the fact that only one type of C-sector machine, with a fixed ratio of workers per machine, is produced in the I-sector. Consequently, output of these machines in the I-sector can be measured in terms of L_c, the number of workers that can be employed in the C-sector. L_c is measured on the right-hand horizontal axis in Diagram One. The L_i axis measures number of workers employed in the I-sector. Using these units we can represent the two I-sector techniques by the 'productivity lines' p_i and p_i^* whose slopes measure the output per worker (measured in terms of C-sector jobs created) for the b and b^* techniques in the I-sector. The diagram is drawn so that both techniques are technically efficient. Output per worker, p_i for the less capital-intensive b technique, is less than p_i^*, for the b^* technique, but if one were to make the same total investment in the b^* technique as in the b technique (i.e.

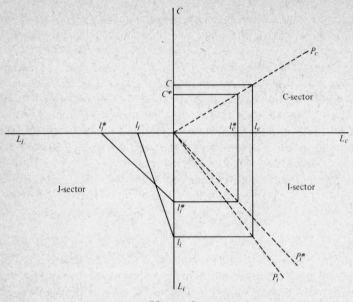

Diagram One

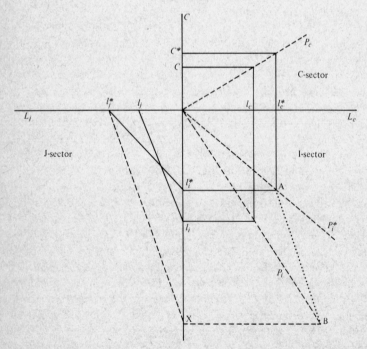

Diagram Two

allocate the same amount of J-sector labour time to producing each type of I-sector machine), total output would be less with the b^* technique than with the b technique. This is not shown on the diagram but can be demonstrated by a simple construction.

However, the central point of the analysis is that the restriction on the surplus available necessarily implies that we *cannot* invest the same amount of J-sector labour-time in each technique. Suppose we decide to invest the whole surplus in the b technique. We would then allocate l_j workers to the J-sector (shown in bottom left quadrant of Diagram One) in order to produce machines which employ l_i workers in the I-sector, such that $l_i + l_j = L$ and $l_j/l_i = b$. In this case, as indicated in Diagram One, output of machinery for the C-sector is sufficient to employ l_c workers there, and given our choice of units, we can write

$$l_c = l_i \cdot p_i$$

Alternatively, the whole surplus may go into the b^* technique. In this case l_j^* workers are employed in the J-sector and l_i^* in the I-sector. Once again, $l_i^* + l_j^* = L$ and $l_j^*/l_i^* = b^*$, and by assumption $b^* > b$, as shown in Diagram One. The full deployment of the surplus to produce the more capital-intensive b^* technique for use in the I-sector requires a larger investment of J-sector labour time (l_j^*), than with the b technique. In this case, total output of machines for the C-sector is sufficient to employ l_c^* workers there and

$$l_c^* = l_i^* \cdot p_i^*.$$

Now, as drawn in Diagram One, $l_c > l_c^*$, and it is plain that the less capital intensive b technique will allow a larger output of C-machines than the b^* technique. Consequently, in this case, the b technique is to be preferred. It will allow a larger increment in consumer goods output ($C > C^*$ in Diagram One), and a larger amount of surplus and employment growth in the C-sector than the b^* technique.

However, the main point of the analysis is that this result is by no means general. Diagram Two shows that it is quite consistent with all the assumptions we have made that the more capital-intensive b^* technique should turn out to be the appropriate choice in the I-sector. The diagram follows the same logic as Diagram One. The b and b^* techniques are both technically efficient (as shown by the configuration of the production function AB, drawn for a constant investment of l_j^* labour-time in the J-sector). The only difference between the two cases is that the gain in labour productivity in moving from the less capital-intensive b technique to the b^* technique, is greater in Diagram Two than in Diagram One. This change in the relative positions of p_i^* and p_i is such that $l_c^* > l_c$ in Diagram Two and in this case the more capital-intensive b^* technique should be used in the I-sector.

Plainly, as a general rule, the more capital-intensive b^* technique should be used in the I-sector, if $l_c^* > l_c$; in other words, if

$$p_i^* \cdot l_i^* > p_i \cdot l_i.$$

Now dividing both sides of this condition by L and noting,

$$\frac{l_i}{L} = \frac{l_i}{l_i + l_j} = \frac{1}{1 + b}$$

and similarly

$$\frac{l_i^*}{L} = \frac{1}{1 + b^*}$$

we can re-write the condition as

$$\frac{p_i^*}{1 + b^*} > \frac{p_i}{1 + b}$$

In other words, the more capital-intensive technique will be favoured in the I-sector, provided that labour productivity p_i^* increases sufficiently as the capital-intensity of production goes from b to b^*. In principle, either technique could turn out to be appropriate in the I-sector. The choice depends strictly upon the technical conditions of production.

III

It is helpful to extend this result to a more general case in which a full range of technically efficient production techniques exists in the I-sector, all other assumptions of Section II being retained.

Recall that only one type of C-machine is produced in the I-sector. Consequently, we can measure the physical output of the I-sector as

$$y = A \cdot n = l_c$$

where A = number of C-sector workers employed per machine,
n = number of machines produced in I for C, and as before
l_c = total number of C-sector workers employed.

Now suppose that a continuum of efficient techniques exists in the I-sector and that they can be represented by a production function

$$y = f(l_i, l_j). \tag{1}$$

We make some conventional assumptions about this production function, i.e. it is continuous; partial first differentials of y with respect to l_i, l_j are positive and corresponding partial second differentials are negative; and it is assumed that the production function is linear homogeneous. It is plain that l_j in (1) measures the amount of (unassisted) labour-time required in the J-sector to produce I-machines which will employ l_i labour-time in the I-sector. Thus l_j is a labour-time measure of 'capital input'.

Once again, we assume that the surplus available at the beginning of the period is constrained, so that given the real wage the total numbers of workers that may be employed in capital goods production is fixed, i.e.

$$\frac{S}{w} = L = l_i + l_j. \tag{2}$$

It is clear that the 'choice-rule' of section II remains applicable. The choice of technique in the I-sector must be such as to maximise the output of machines for the C-sector. Analytically, the appropriate technique in the I-sector is such that $y = f(l_i, l_j)$ is maximised subject to the constraint (2). To solve this use the Lagrangian

$$\phi(l_i, l_j) = f(l_i, l_j) - \lambda(l_j + l_i - L),$$

from which it is plain that the conditions for the (constrained) maximum are simply,

$$\frac{\partial f}{\partial l_i} = \lambda = \frac{\partial f}{\partial l_j} \tag{3}$$

at which point the marginal rate of substitution of l_j for l_i, along an isoquant y_0, is -1. The result (3) is straightforward enough: given the constraint on surplus, the labour available for the J- and I-sectors must be allocated between them in such a way that output of C-machines for use in the consumer-goods sector cannot be increased by moving workers from the J-sector to the I-sector, or vice versa. The capital intensity of the optimum I-sector technique will then be determined by $l_j/l_i = b$.

The form of this constrained maximisation is extremely familiar of course, but its interpretation requires a little care. It is set out in Diagram Three. Here the constraint arising from the limited availability of surplus is shown as the line $L = l_i + l_j$, which has a negative slope of unity (with respect to the l_i, l_j axes). This constraint must not be confused with the cost curves of neoclassical analysis. The isoquant y' gives the constrained maximum level of output of C-machines in the I-sector. The I-sector

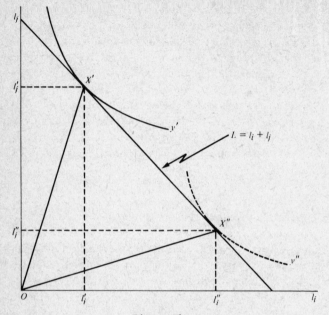

Diagram Three

production technique which allows this maximum output to be reached is indicated by the point of tangency at X', where y' has a slope of -1, and condition (3) is met. The technique is specified by the slope of the ray $OX' = l'_j/l'_i = b'$, its capital intensity. $L = l'_j + l'_i$ gives the allocation of workers between the J- and I-sectors. Once again it is clear that the capital-intensity of the optimal technique in the I-sector, depends entirely on the technical conditions of production. For example, if the production function had the configuration y'' instead of y', the optimal I-sector technique would have a capital-intensity $l''_j/l''_i = b''$, which is much less than b'.

The relationship to the linear model of section II can be indicated as follows. From (1) we can write

$$y = f(l_i, l_j) = l_i \cdot g\left(\frac{l_j}{l_i}\right). \tag{4}$$

From (3), we know that the optimal I-sector technique is such that $\partial y/\partial l_i = \partial y/\partial l_j$. Using (4) we have

$$\frac{\partial y}{\partial l_i} = g\left(\frac{l_j}{l_i}\right) - \frac{l_j}{l_i} \cdot g'\left(\frac{l_j}{l_i}\right) = g(b) - b \cdot g'(b) \tag{5}$$

$$\frac{\partial y}{\partial l_i} = g'\left(\frac{l_j}{l_i}\right) = g'(b) \tag{6}$$

where primes indicate differentiation with respect to the argument of the function. From (5) and (6), the condition for optimality can be written as

$$g'(b) = g(b)\,\frac{1}{1+b}$$

or

$$\frac{\partial y}{\partial l_j} = \frac{g(b)}{1+b} = \frac{\partial y}{\partial l_i}$$

and noting that $g(b) = p_i$, the condition can be written as

$$\frac{\partial y}{\partial l_j} = \frac{\partial y}{\partial l_i} = \frac{p_i}{1+b}$$

which is precisely similar in form to the 'choice criterion' in section II. Now it is easy to show that if $p_i/(1+b)$ *increases* with b, the level of capital-intensity, then $\partial y/\partial l_j > \partial y/\partial l_i$ and the output of C-machines can be increased by moving workers from the I-sector to the J-sector and adopting a more capital-intensive I-technique. This corresponds to the result in section II.

The analysis has shown up some special aspects of choice of technique in the capital-goods sector, under the assumptions we have made about economic organisation and structure. Under these assumptions the level of employment in the capital-goods sector is independent of the choice of technique in the sector and depends only on the availability of surplus and the real wage rate. The choice of techniques in the I-sector for production of any given type of C-sector machine is dictated solely by the efficiency requirement that the maximum number of C-sector machines must be produced given the surplus available. The question of *which* I-sector technique (and corresponding allocation of labour time between the J- and I-sectors) will ensure this depends only upon the technical conditions of production. It is independent of considerations like the level of real wages (which plays a critical role in the choice of techniques in the C-sector). Real wages only affect matters by determining the number of workers L, who may be employed in the capital-goods sector: a low real wage makes it possible to employ more workers in capital-goods production for a given amount of consumer-good surplus. However, so long as production functions in the I-sector are linear homogeneous, the real wage will not affect the choice of techniques itself: the optimum I-sector technique could be labour-intensive even though real wages are 'high', or capital intensive even though the real wage is 'low' — and increases or decreases in the real wage will not affect technical choice.

Matters are not greatly changed if the assumption of linear homogeneity is dropped and the possibility of economies of scale permitted. In this case, the capital intensity of the optimum I-sector technique will depend on the scale of capital goods production, i.e. on the absolute amount of surplus available. However, the principles of technical choice in the I-sector remain unchanged: *given* the number of workers available L, and hence the attainable scale of production, optimal capital intensity in the I-sector will still depend solely on technical conditions of production. The level of real wages *can* affect choice of techniques in the I-sector in this case, but only by a roundabout and unfamiliar route. Lower real wages will allow a larger number of workers to be employed in capital-goods production and so increase the scale of output. Changes in the scale of output may then affect the choice of technique in the I-sector.

IV

The analysis can be extended to deal with the case where a number of techniques exist in the C-sector for making the consumer goods. Each of these n techniques may be thought of as constituted by a different type of C-machine. We assume that the n types of C-machine are technically efficient and each is distinguished from the others *inter alia* by its capital-intensity. The capital-intensity of a C-machine may be unambiguously defined as

$$a' = \frac{L}{l'_c}$$

where L is defined as before as the total employment in the production of capital goods — constrained by the surplus available; and l'_c is the maximum amount of C-sector employment generated when the particular C-machine in question is produced with the optimal I-sector technique for making it.

Clearly, for each of the n different C-machines available there will exist a production function like (1) specifying the different I-techniques for making it. The whole set of I-sector production functions is given by

$$y^k = f^k(l_i, l_j); \qquad k = 1, \ldots, n$$

but there is no reason to anticipate any systematic relationship between these n production functions.

It is clear that the analysis of Section III applies to the production of any particular C-machine. In other words, given a constraint on the amount of surplus available, the optimal I-sector technique for producing the kth C-machine is determined solely by technical conditions of production, independently of the real wage rate — and, if I-sector production functions are linear homogeneous, independently of the absolute amount of surplus available. Thus for each of the n different kinds of C-machine available, there exists a *single technique* in the I-sector which will be used to produce it.

Consequently, in this model, the 'choice of techniques problem' only really arises in relation to the C-sector. Given the level of real wages and the configuration of the C-sector production function (made up of the n different types of C-machine), technical choice in the C-sector will proceed in terms of the usual 'trade-offs'. A 'surplus-maximising' C-sector technique will exist which will give the highest attainable rate of growth of employment and output — at the expense of present employment and output. Similarly there will be an 'output maximising' C-sector technique of lower capital intensity giving the highest level of output immediately attainable and the highest (efficient) level of employment — at the cost of lower surplus and growth rates. In most cases, a socially optimal C-sector technique will be chosen with a capital intensity lying in the range between the surplus- and output-maximising techniques, and reflecting the relative importance attached to present employment and output *vis-à-vis* the growth of employment and output in the planner's 'objective function'. Once the C-sector technique is chosen in line with these criteria, the I-sector technique which is to be used to produce the corresponding type of C-machine is uniquely determined.

It will be evident from this discussion that there is no reason to expect any systematic relationship between the capital-intensities of the n C-sector techniques, and the capital-intensities of the I-sector techniques which are to be used in their production. Thus, in C-sector terms, the capital-intensity of the surplus-maximising type of C-machine will be greater than the capital-intensity of the output-maximising machine; but it is quite possible that in I-sector terms, the capital intensity of the I-technique to be used for making the surplus-maximising C-machine will be *less* than the capital intensity of the I-technique to be used for making the output-maximising C-machine.

It is also clear that changes in policy could produce shifts in capital intensities which are, at first sight, counter-intuitive. Suppose, for example, that planners are resolutely committed to high growth and hence to the use of surplus-maximising techniques in the C-sector. Suppose, in addition, that the real wage is allowed to rise from one period to another. The rise in the real wage will normally imply that a more capital-intensive type of C-machine will be chosen in order to maximise surplus in the C-sector. However, this newly determined and more capital-intensive, surplus-maximising, C-sector machine may well be produced optimally by an I-technique of lower capital-intensity than that used before. Despite the rise in real wage, the optimal capital intensity in the I-sector may fall, conceivably sharply.

V

The following main conclusions come out of the discussion of 'sectoral capital intensities' in the two-sector planned economy specified by Sen.

First, since availability of investible surplus is the binding constraint on the growth of the economy, the 'choice of technique' in the I-sector (where workers may use I-machines of varying capital-intensity to produce machines for the consumption-goods or C-sector), is determined by the need to maximise the output of C-machines for the surplus available.

Secondly, the I-sector technique which accomplishes maximum output of any given C-machine is uniquely defined by technical conditions of production. Assuming that the various I-sector machines are made by un-assisted labour in the J-sector, their capital-intensities can be measured by the amount of labour time required in the J-sector to provide employment on machinery for one worker in the I-sector. The capital-intensity of the optimal I-sector technique is independent of the real wage, and (assuming a linear homogeneous production function) also independent of the scale of output. It depends only on the shape and position of the I-sector production function. This result follows from the assumption that the surplus is constrained, so that it is only possible to support a limited amount of labour in capital goods production, (and this labour has to be allocated between the I- and J-sectors).

Thirdly, there is a uniquely defined optimal I-sector technique for making any particular C-sector machine. Consequently, the choice of technique in the I-sector is simply determined by the choices made in the C-sector. However, there is no reason to anticipate any 'well-behaved' relationship between the capital-intensities of the various C-sector machines and the capital intensities of the I-machines used to make them. Optimal production of C-sector machines of low capital-intensity may require highly capital-intensive I-sector techniques. As a hypothetical example, the optimal technique for manufacturing hand-looms might be a highly automated assembly line.

At one level, the analysis points to a well-known, but often forgotten, point. Even if employment and output maximisation have overwhelming weight in the 'objective function', it does not follow that labour-intensive techniques are to be used in all sectors. Inter-sectoral considerations are always likely to require the use of highly capital-intensive techniques in some parts of the economy — most probably in machine-making. A 'walking-on-two-legs' strategy need not reflect an arbitrary technological compromise; it may be the coherent outcome of an output- and employment-maximising plan.

However, a more surprising result of the analysis, is the fact that under the particular planned-economy assumptions which are made, the choice of technique in the capital-goods sector turns out to be so rigidly dependent on technical conditions of production, and quite independent of the real wage.

ACKNOWLEDGEMENTS

I am indebted to Clive Bell, Jeffrey James, Amartya Sen, Frances Stewart and Roy Turner for comments on earlier drafts of this paper.

NOTES

1 Sen, A. K. (1968). *The Choice of Techniques* (3rd edn.), Chapter III, Basil Blackwell, Oxford.
2 The definition assumes that the number of I-sector workers needed per machine is technically fixed — an assumption which is retained throughout.
3 Formally, linear combinations of these allocations are also possible. However, as will appear, such combinations are only of interest in a special case.

3 Technical rigidity and appropriate technology in less developed countries*

DAVID J. C. FORSYTH, NORMAN McBAIN, and
ROBERT F. SOLOMON

1. INTRODUCTION

The issue

It is widely asserted that the favourable impact on unemployment of the growth of manufacturing in less developed countries (LDCs) is greatly weakened by the capital-intensive nature of the technology used. Eckaus (1955), in a seminal article published some two decades ago, emphasised the importance of 'technical rigidity' (i.e. intrinsic inflexibility of factor proportions) as a barrier to large-scale absorption of labour in LDC manufacturing. Subsequent discussion of the technology–labour absorption issue, while acknowledging the possible validity of Eckaus' view, has centred on the more optimistic hypothesis that the choice of 'excessively' or 'inappropriately' capital-intensive technology is due to some distortion in the mechanism used to transfer technology from industrialised countries to LDCs or to aberrations in the choice-of-technology process itself.[1] A large number of alternative explanations have been suggested, the most popular being distorted factor prices in LDCs,[2] 'satisficing' behaviour in the presence of monopoly power,[3] and the 'high-technology' predilections of multinational corporations.[4]

The outcome of this unresolved issue has considerable significance for policy. If 'distortions' and 'aberrations' of various sorts are, in fact, responsible for widespread 'inappropriate choice' of technology, then the problem is potentially susceptible to direct corrective policy measures designed to push technology choices closer to the labour-intensive sectors of production functions. However, if all opportunities for factor substitution are, in fact, taken, and if underlying technical rigidity is the root cause of the still 'undesirably' high capital intensity in LDCs, then no adequate response to current difficulties is possible which runs in terms

*This article first appeared in *World Development*, vol. 8, pp. 371–398 (1980).

of 'correction' of price signals and consequent movements along existing production functions, for even a full adjustment to a competitive optimum will fail to create an adequate number of modern-sector jobs within an acceptable time period. In this event, the need for a new technology strategy would be urgent. One possibility would be a deliberate con-centration on 'high technology' and an all-out 'dash for growth' — but a much more likely response, given the current pessimism regarding the prospects for growth in many LDCs, would be an acceptance of the need to concentrate on 'basic needs' and to reject modern production tech-nology and associated 'Western' concepts of allocative efficiency.

This view of the conclusions to be drawn from alternative findings on the investment behaviour of manufacturers in effect stands the con-ventional wisdom on its head. The 'failure' of modern industrialisation to deliver the promised employment (and associated benefits) can be excused only if opportunities for substituting labour for capital have not been taken thus far — but may in the future through suitable policy tuning. And the previously comforting conclusion that 'factor substitution is alive and well in development countries'[5] may now be seen as reflecting *adversely* on the ability of industrialisation programmes to have any great impact on the central problem of unemployment.

Despite two decades of intensifying debate, the precise nature and extent of the appropriate technology problem is still uncertain. This study is intended to cast light on the central issue of the degree to which LDC manufacturers have, in fact, responded to the factor substitution opportunities inherent in fundamental technological possibilities.

Analysis

For the most part, empirical work on the choice of technology in LDCs has either made use of estimated production functions, or has involved very detailed and explicit analysis of a small number (usually two) of alternative technologies for given industries. Unfortunately, it is now widely accepted that there are very serious problems with regard to both accurate estimation and interpretation of conventional econometric production functions in the present context and it does seem that this form of analysis is incapable of telling us much about the appropriate technology issue.[6] (Particularly unsatisfactory is the circularity inherent in the attempt to assess the extent to which LDC investors take full advantage of flexibility in factor proportions when that flexibility is defined in terms of their choices.) At the same time, the direct comparison of alternative technologies is laborious, and given the very large number of industries to be considered and the smallness of the resources available for this kind of research, it seems unlikely that *general* conclusions of universal validity can be arrived at in this way. Furthermore, virtually all of the examples of this genre look at *existing* technologies, rather than at all currently *feasible* technologies, and attempts to broaden the analysis have proved so complex as to be impossible to apply across a broad range of manufacturing and at the 'establishment' level of aggregation.

An engineering-based approach

It is the contention of the authors of this chapter that the contribution of technological rigidity to the 'appropriate-technology problem' has not yet been satisfactorily analysed[7] and that an adequate treatment of this fundamental factor is not possible without direct reference to the engineering characteristics of manufacturing processes. Indeed, in the absence of separate sets of information on the degree of rigidity — or flexibility — inherent in the relevant industries' technologies, it is not possible to compare actual with potential choices in order to assess the extent to which current factor intensities exhaust the potential for labour–capital substitution.

In this chapter an 'index of technical rigidity' (ITR) is constructed on the basis of a study of the characteristics of manufacturing subprocesses in a large sample of industries. The index summarises an engineering-based assessment of the opportunities for substituting labour for capital in manufacturing subprocesses. A major advantage of this approach is that it focuses attention on *feasible techniques*, given the state of technical knowledge, rather than on available techniques or techniques actually in use. The opportunities for labour–capital substitution are seen as depending on the incidence of certain 'technical barriers' (that is, functions that cannot readily be performed manually). It is shown that by attacking the analysis of factor substitution via a careful consideration of the engineering characteristics of different technologies we bypass many of the conceptual and estimation problems which bedevil the attempt to analyse actual technologies using conventional production functions.

The ITR has many obvious applications (for example, as a device for rapid screening of industries under consideration as effective job-creators in LDCs) and is readily extended beyond the industries listed in Appendix 2. For purposes of the present analysis, however, the index is used simply to generate a classification of narrowly defined product groups in terms of the inherent barriers to the use of labour. This information on the nature of the technology of the production process provides the basis for a case-study analysis of the technology problems faced by four LDCs — Ghana, the Philippines, Turkey and Malaysia. We adopt the approach of examining the degree of adaptation of techniques used in the industrial-ised world — represented by the UK — by producers in these LDCs in order to focus attention on the situation in which, despite different factor availability, there may be a failure to adopt techniques which exploit the use of inputs with low opportunity costs.[8]

The concept of technological rigidity is discussed in Section 2 and this is followed in Section 3 by a detailed account of the technology classification. The data base and the econometric strategy employed in evaluating the nature and extent of the technology problem are presented in Section 4, the results of the analysis are given in Section 5, and discussed in Section 6. Conclusions and policy implications are set out in Section 7. The ITR itself is tabulated in Appendix 2.

2. THE 'RIGIDITY' OF MANUFACTURING TECHNOLOGIES

The notion of 'rigid' techniques has been used by writers on technology/labour absorption problems in LDC manufacturing in three distinct ways. First, rigidities have been associated with the basic case in which, given the state of technical knowledge, only one (or a very small number of) manufacturing process(es) is (are) known to be capable of producing a particular good.[9] Secondly, as a refinement of the first case, it is asserted that, since technical innovation is often aimed at improving product quality, even where a range of techniques is available for making a given product, the close specification of product quality may eliminate all but one technique of production from contention. Rigidities are thus associated with the demand for high-quality, modern, 'inappropriate products'.[10] Both these forms of rigidity relate to *inherent rigidities* imposed by basic technological constraints which can only be removed, if at all, by a shift in engineering know-how which will enable labour to undertake the relevant operations. Distinct from these forms of rigidity are *rigidities imposed by the availability of techniques*. These relate not only to inherent rigidities but also to the source of capital goods used in the LDCs. Thus, rigidities have been related to unadapted techniques imported by foreign firms,[11] the general dominance of imported capital goods and the difficulties of establishing an indigenous capital-goods sector,[12] the technological gap between advanced and poor nations,[13] and the 'extinction' of vintage techniques.[14] Rigidities imposed by availability relate not only to inherent rigidities but also to rigidities derived from the economic conditions relevant to the selection, of techniques for commercial development from methods that are technically feasible.[15]

The distinctions drawn amongst these forms of rigidity are important in providing a perspective to our view of the technology problems faced by LDC manufacturing. We seek to examine the extent to which inherent technical rigidities and the restrictions on the availability of capital goods each contribute to the determination of the choice of technique of production used in LDC manufacturing.

The classification of techniques

The approach adopted here to assessing inherent technical rigidities is that of deriving a classification of technologies by building on the foundation of the engineering characteristics of production processes. Although this approach seems fairly obvious — indeed, necessary — it has hitherto been almost wholly ignored by economists. Isolated attempts have been made to identify certain features of technology which might increase or reduce 'rigidity' but these attempts have been fairly restricted in number and, with few exceptions,[16] have been made on a non-rigorous and *ad hoc* basis.[17] The usefulness of classifications of technology has clearly been more evident to engineers, although the rationale behind their efforts has naturally been other than that which we discuss in this chapter.[18]

We may conveniently view any production process as involving a number of stages in each of which the application of human labour may face natural limitations. Within this context we may consider inherent technological rigidities that arise from such limitations and become apparent in both the *nature* of the process and the *scale* of operations.

Technological rigidity and the nature of the process

If, given the stock of knowledge, the use of (for example) very high temperatures is required in the production of a given good, this will, in some processes, act as an *'absolute' (technical) barrier* to the application of human effort. In most cases, however, the use of high temperatures is a means of vastly increasing the productivity of processes rather than being 'absolutely' necessary; that is, it constitutes a *'relative' (technical) barrier* to the use of human effort.

In the case of absolute barriers the only feasible techniques are those intensive in mechanized, non-human effort. In the more general case of relative barriers the feasible techniques will be 'dominated' by those techniques employing the non-human effort. Such conditions will give rise to what may be termed a 'dominated production function' — illustrated in Figure 1. The circles in the figure represent factor input combinations for producing a given level of output using techniques of production which are feasible but which do not take advantage of the high-temperature

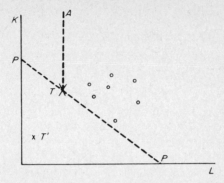

Figure 1. Technical barriers and domination of the production function

process. The latter requires the use of some form of non-human effort and this implies additional capital expenditure, taking us to a point like *T*. The effective isoquant is then *ATP*. Thus, *T* dominates all techniques at relative prices greater than those implicit in the slope of the line *PP*. Given the separation of the mechanised technique *T* from the others shown in the figure, it will dominate for all cases but that of very cheap labour; that is, we have 'relative domination'. If the productivity gains stemming from the use of the high-temperature process are sufficiently great a point like *T'* will arise as the representation of the mechanised technique. Here we have 'absolute domination', as technique *T'* dominates all other techniques at *all* relative factor price ratios. Either way, the net effect of the enormous increase in productivity stemming from mechanisation leads to 'one-way' factor substitution. So long as the machine-intensive techniques dominate the labour-intensive techniques, price signals will not be able to shift the system towards the latter (at least in the short run; in the long run, movements in relative factor prices may influence the form that innovation takes).

When such relative, or absolute, domination of the production structure occurs, the *technical barriers* to the use of human effort will act as barriers to the adaptation of production techniques.[19]

Technical rigidity and scale

A number of barriers to the substitution of human effort for capital are directly related to scale, e.g. the inability of men to operate at high speed or with indivisible large or heavy objects. In addition to such straightforward scale effects a number of basic physical laws may serve to cause some machine-intensive techniques to dominate at large scales.[20] Where an absolute technical barrier exists, or there are overwhelming productivity gains to overcoming a relative technical barrier, capital investment in the mechanized means of overcoming the barrier will be required. Thus, there will be a close association between those industries in which there are absolute or relative technical barriers and the degree of mechanisation. Further, in those industries which are highly mechanised, advantage may be taken of the natural laws relating the rate of output to scale to reap the benefits of economies of scale.

This discussion suggests two testable hypotheses — that it is in those industries in which technical barriers exist that scale economies are important, and that, in these same industries, the dominance of the production function (more specifically, the range of the function dominated) becomes greater at increased scale as the significant productivity gains to the mechanised techniques are reaped at high rates of output. Thus, the range of large-scale viable techniques in industries characterised by many technical barriers may be expected to be much smaller than in other industries with fewer barriers, and in the same industry at a lower scale. These possibilities are examined in conjunction with the broader investigation of the appropriate technology issue below.

3. AN INDEX OF TECHNICAL RIGIDITY

The scheme used here to classify technologies focuses on those characteristics which affect the degree of rigidity of their factor proportions. The starting point of the analysis was a search for fundamental barriers to manual operation of the various subprocesses[21] of some 181 industries known to operate currently in LDCs, these industries being narrowly defined in terms of product. As far as possible the search for 'barriers' was carried out with reference not just to the relatively restricted range of plant and machinery actually available to businessmen, but rather to the somewhat broader range of techniques which could be designed given the current state of engineering knowledge, and which were capable of producing output of a more or less comparable standard (though some variation in product quality was allowed.)

The criteria

In all, eight fundamental physical barriers to the substitution of labour for capital were identified. In the interests of brevity these are simply listed below; more detail on each barrier is presented in Appendix 1. The barriers are associated with:

1. the use of high, or low, process temperatures;

2. the presence of fluids (liquids or gases);
3. the application of fluid pressure on materials in process;
4. the need for high-speed operation;
5. the achieving of close manufacturing tolerances;
6. the application of electrical power and of high load factors;
7. the handling of indivisible, heavy materials; and
8. the presence of special hazards.

The technology classification

The principle on which the technology of a particular product was characterised was that of 'scoring' in terms of the existence of the barriers discussed above. On the basis of an engineering-based assessment of the *feasible* production methods in a given industry it was possible to indicate which, if any, of the barriers were important given the state of contemporary scientific and engineering knowhow. Each product group was then 'scored' to yield the ITR, defined as the number of technical barriers important in the processes feasible for the making of the relevant product. (The ITR may take values 0–8, the higher values indicating the rigid techniques so far as the substitution of labour for capital is concerned.) All technologies were examined at the disaggregated, subprocess level, though it was not feasible to mount really intensive investigations into the production methods used in each and every industry covered in this study. (Indeed, such probing would defeat one object of the present approach which is to provide a quick indicator of flexibility of factor proportions.)

It is necessary to note that the scoring procedure used to aggregate the technical index is open to one fairly obvious line of criticism. Simple adding up of the barriers may not adequately account for the relative impact of any one barrier on the production process, and more than one barrier may affect the same subprocess — which could imply some double counting. Furthermore, it may be the case that one barrier is sufficient to render the whole technology rigid, particularly where the production process is closely integrated. In short, the barriers, as measures of rigidity of technique, may not be additive in all cases. At the end of the day our indices are defended as providing a simple, relatively available index of factor substitutability that combines the virtues of simplicity and ease of construction with a genuine engineering input.[22]

Our classification of 181 industries — selected for their general importance in LDC manufacturing — is presented in full in Appendix 2.

4. TECHNICAL BARRIERS AND THE ADAPTATION OF TECHNIQUES

The ITR and production function analysis

We may adopt the useful heuristic device of setting our analysis in the context of a CES production function. The CES function is taken as a representation of the 'abstract technology'[23] generated by a given stock of technical knowledge. Since the function relates to all feasible efficient techniques derived from a given stock of knowledge its parameters are internationally stable. The CES function is given by:

$$V = \gamma[\delta K^{-\rho} + (1-\delta)L^{-\eta}]^{-\nu/\rho} \tag{1}$$

where δ, ρ, ν, γ are, respectively, the distribution, substitution, returns-to-scale and efficiency parameters; V, K and L represent, respectively, the rate of value added and inputs of capital services and labour services; the elasticity of factor substitution (σ) is given by:

$$\sigma = 1/(1+\rho)$$

Since the ITR has been constructed on the basis of an assessment of the opportunities for factor substitution there is a natural correspondence between the ITR and σ. In particular, let us postulate a systematic relationship between σ and ITR [the exact form of the relation is, for the moment, unimportant; one obvious possibility is for low (high) values of σ to be associated with high (low) values of ITR].

Under competitive conditions the real wage (W) is given by:

$$\frac{\partial V}{\partial L} = W \tag{2}$$

Combining equations (1) and (2) yields equation (3) where A is a constant term defined by the production function parameters:

$$\ln(V/L) = A + \sigma \ln W + (1 - 1/\nu)(1 - \sigma)\ln V \tag{3}$$

Taking V/L as our indicator of capital intensity we may examine the international adaptation of techniques as reflected in capital intensity. Adopting the subscripts H and L to refer to high-wage and low-wage economies, respectively, we derive from equation (3):

$$\ln(V/L)_L = \ln(V/L)_H + \ln(W_L/W_H) + (1 - 1/\nu)(1 - \sigma)\ln(V_L/V_H) \tag{4}$$

We assume $W_L < W_H$ and to isolate the effect of factor availability consider the constant returns to scale case ($\nu = 1$). Then equation (4) reduces to:

$$(V/L)_L = [(W_L/W_H)^\sigma](V/L)_H \tag{5}$$

and since $W_L/W_H < 1$ we see that the effect of increased factor substitutability (increased σ) is to 'rotate' the relation between the capital intensities in the two economies such that the shift to labour intensity in the low-wage economy is greatest for the product groups exhibiting the highest degree of substitutability. This we term the *'rotation effect'*.

Shifting attention to the impact of scale equation (4) gives a formal specification to our discussion of the scale effect in Section 2. Where the low-wage economy scale is lower, $\ln V_L/V_H$ is negative. In the presence of increasing returns to scale (which we have argued is likely in high-barrier, low-elasticity-of-substitution industries) the nearer σ is to zero the greater is the depression in the LDC capital intensity. Within the CES framework it is evident that for $\sigma > 1$ a lower scale will be associated with an increase in capital intensity. Factor substitutability thus has an effect on capital intensity differences in a scale dimension which we refer to as the *'scale effect'*.

Whilst the CES function is a useful heuristic device (and setting our analysis in this context aids comparison with previous studies) our empirical work is not, in fact, cast in the CES mould. We have, however, introduced the relationship between techniques used under different factor price regimes and, in particular, the *interaction* between factor substitutability and both capital intensity and scale differences. Shifting attention from the elasticity of substitution approach to the ITR, our empirical analysis is based on a relation analogous to equation (4), which in its most general form we write as:

$$VM_L = f(VU, SD, ITR) \tag{6}$$

where we take value added per man as our measure of capital intensity, and the capital intensity in the ith industry in the low-wage economy (VM) is expressed as a function of capital intensity in the ith industry in the high-wage economy (VU), the scale differential for the ith industry (SD) and the ITR for the relevant industry. Note that the form of this relation will be one in which the interaction between the ITR and VU and SD will be of prime importance.

The estimating equation

We examine the shifts in factor intensity between high-wage and low-wage environments within the context of a single-equation model. Consider the use of a binary variable D defined such that $D = 1$ for 'low'-ITR industries and zero otherwise. The exact definition of a 'low' ITR will be the subject of empirical investigation. The following variables are defined for each industry in our sample:

VM = value added per man in the low wage economy;

VU = value added per man in the UK;

SD = the difference in *average* plant size between the UK and the low-wage economy measured as value added per establishment in the UK — value added per establishment in the low-wage economy.

The value added data for the low-wage economies were converted into sterling at an appropriate rate, details of which are given below. Where appropriate, non-wage value added was used rather than value added. To simplify the present exposition we concentrate on the use of value added.

The following variables may now be defined:

$$VU(L) = VU \cdot D$$

$$VU(H) = VU(1 - D)$$

and interpreted as follows. $VU(L)$ will be non-zero for low-ITR observations and will thus give the value added per man in low-barrier industries. $VU(H)$ will give non-zero observations only for the high-barrier industries. Similarly:

$$SD(L) = SD \cdot D$$

$$SD(H) = SD(1 - D)$$

giving for the former non-zero observations for the scale differential in low-ITR industries and for the latter non-zero observations only in high-barrier industries.

The basic estimating equation may now be written as:

$$VM = b_0 + b_1 \ VU(H_1) + b_2 \ VU(L_1) + b_3 \ SD(H_2) + b_4 \ SD(L_2) + U \quad (7)$$

where b_i are parameters of the equation and U is a stochastic term. In equation (7) we have introduced $VU(H_1)$, $VU(L_1)$, $SD(H_2)$ and $SD(L_2)$ where the implication is that the definition of low ITR with respect to the VU variable (L_1) *may* be different from the definition of low ITR with respect to the scale differential. Equation (7) gives the operational form of equation (6) in which we have incorporated the interaction effects discussed in the previous sections.

The parameters of equation (7) may be related to our discussion of the rotation and scale hypothesis. Parameters b_1 and b_2 are *a priori* positive, the rotation hypothesis implies b_1 greater than b_2. The scale differential is measured such that when the low-wage economy operates at a lower scale SD is positive. Thus, b_3 and b_4 are *a priori* negative, the scale hypothesis implying that b_3 is less than b_4 (that is the *magnitude* of the scale effect is greater in high-barrier industries).

The rotation and scale hypotheses may be summarized: (a) rotation hypothesis: $(b_2 - b_1) < 0$; (b) scale hypothesis: $(b_4 - b_3) > 0$. It is convenient to recast equation (7) in an alternative form for the purposes of estimation. We have:

$$VU(H_1) = VU(1 - D) = VU - VU \cdot D = VU - VU(L_1)$$

and:

$$SD(H_2) = SD - SD(L_2).$$

Thus, equation (7) may be written:

$$VM = b_0 + (b_2 - b_1)VU(L_1) + b_1\ VU + (b_4 - b_3)SD(L_2) + b_3\ SD + U$$

$$(8)$$

Our two hypotheses are thus cast in terms of simple one-tailed tests on the parameters of equation (8).[24]

Data and empirical application

The empirical work reported here uses data on the UK as the high-wage economy. The low-wage economies investigated are Turkey, Ghana, the Philippines and Malaysia. Our data refer to the period 1967–1970 and are drawn from the statistical sources given in Appendix 3. Tables 1 and 2 present summary information on the nations and industries included in the study.

Table 1 gives an indication of the respective levels of industrialisation in the four LDCs. All four exhibit a *per capita* GDP in the range 13–16 per cent of the UK figure, but there is considerable diversity within the group both in the contribution made by manufacturing to GDP and in the rates of growth of *per capita* GDP achieved over the decade 1960–1970. Further, the rates of growth of value added in the manufacturing sector over the 1960s were well above the rates of growth of employment in manufacturing in all but West Malaysia.

On the basis of Sutcliffe's three tests for industrialisation[25] both Turkey and the Philippines are ranked high in the list of developing nations in which manufacturing predominates in a relatively large industrial sector (both pass two of the three tests). Malaysia, whilst having a relatively large industrial sector (comparable with Turkey and the Philippines in terms of proportion of GDP) has not developed the manufacturing sector to the same extent as the first two countries, and passes only one of

Table 1. Indicators of degree of industrialisation in the sample countries

Country	GDP per capita		Manufacturing as % of GDP, 1965	Employment in manufacturing (1965)		Annual rate of growth of value added in manufacturing 1960–1969	Annual rate of growth of numbers engaged in manufacturing 1963–1969
	Rate of growth 1960–1970	Level of US $		% of population	% of total employment		
Ghana	−0.4	256	2	4	9	10.6	8.1
Malaysia	3.1	208	10	2	6	8.6	10.5
Philippines	2.9	246	19	4	11	6.1	4.9
Turkey	7.1	257	15	3	7	14.5	7.9
UK	2.2	1579	35	16	35	3.2	

Sources: Ghana: *Industrial Statistics 1966–68* (Accra: CBS, 1970); West Malaysia: *Census of Manufacturing and Construction* (Kuala Lumpur: Department of Statistics, 1971); Philippines: *Economic Census of the Philippines, 1967* (Manila: Department of Commerce, 1970); Turkey: *Census of Industry and Business Establishments 1970* (Ankara: State Institute of Statistics, 1976); UK: *Census of Production for 1968* (London: HMSO, 1971).

Table 2. Industry and ITR coverage of data

	No. of observed industries	Observed industries as % of total manufacturing		Distribution of observed industries by ITR*			
		% of value added	% of employment	0/1	2	3	More than 3
Ghana	34	74	71	17 (50)	4 (12)	6 (18)	7 (20)
West Malaysia	50	56	60	24 (48)	10 (20)	8 (16)	8 (16)
Philippines	66	77	65	34 (51)	9 (14)	11 (17)	12 (18)
Turkey	54	73	65	29 (53)	10 (19)	7 (13)	8 (15)

*Figures in parentheses represent % of observations for relevant country.

Sutcliffe's tests. Ghana fails all three of the tests and in this sense must be considered as the least industrialised of our sample.

Table 2 gives summary information about the sample industries in the low-wage economies.

The measure of factor intensity used in the present study is based on value added per man. This measure may be affected by various market imperfections, but its use does have significant advantages in the present study. First (unlike measures based on stocks), it reflects the flow of capital services (both physical and human) into the production process. Secondly, data on value added per man are readily available in the required detail for the UK and a number of LDCs.[26]

None the less, there are important problems in the use of value added per man as an indication of factor intensity. The present study relies on international comparisons. Thus, we must be concerned with those factors which may act to distort value added per man as an indicator of factor intensity. We consider three major sources of distortion:[27] differences in statistical concepts, differing degrees of market protection, and the practice of fixing wages in the modern manufacturing sector above the shadow wage rate.

Clearly, strict international comparability cannot be expected in our data. It is worth noting in this context that our empirical method relies on the comparison of value added per man in *groups of industries* between countries. Since we are basically concerned with groups of industries rather than individual industries a certain amount of 'noise' in the data may be 'averaged out'.

Whilst we must accept the problems arising from differences in statistical concepts the problems related to the degree of protection and the control of wage levels can be faced in our empirical work. It is of heuristic value to consider total value added per man composed of R, the total reward to capital, and W, the total reward to labour. Thus:

$$VA/L = (R + W)/L$$

where VA denotes the rate of value added and L the rate of input of labour services. Thus:

$$VA/L = (R/L) + w$$

where w represents the wage rate. Value added per man thus incorporates the wage rate. Now consider the response to a fall in the wage rate (for example, as we move from a high- to a low-wage economy) where there is no change in technique of production. As w falls and the 'international price' of value added remains constant (where all goods are tradeable and there are no barriers to trade) the fall in w must be exactly offset by a change in R/L yielding the unchanged value added per man. Thus, no change in technique yields an unchanged value added per man. However, the assumption of perfect trade is not tenable. Thus, for example, where there is extensive protection in the low-wage economy there is no reason to believe that the fall in wage rates will be *exactly* offset. Highly protected industries may yield apparently higher levels of value added when valued at domestic prices.

In order to face this problem in the use of value added per man as an indicator of factor intensity, a crucial part of our empirical method is an analysis of the sensitivity of our results to the inclusion in our sample of highly protected industries.

The final point related to the use of value added per man is that this measure incorporates the wage rate. Under competitive conditions we might argue that since the wage rate reflects the marginal product of labour, a high wage rate (increasing the level of value added per man) reflects a return to human capital and thus is relevant to a measure of factor intensity. In a study of the manufacturing sector of low-wage economies where control of wage rates is an important phenomenon such an assumption is untenable. In order to check for the sensitivity of our results in this dimension we shift attention from value added per man to non-wage value added per man (R/L).

Thus, an important part of our empirical method is to analyse the sensitivity of our results to the inclusion of protected industries and the inclusion of the returns to labour in value added.

Finally, we must note that in order to estimate equation (8) we will have to employ some exchange rate to provide internationally comparable data. We thus run the risk of using an inappropriate rate of exchange which will yield estimates of $(b_4 - b_3)$ with *negative* bias.

5. RESULTS

Turkey

Table 3 presents basic results of the application of equation (8) to the Turkish data. The results are presented for the case for which $L_1 = L_2$, the low-barrier industries being defined as having at most two barriers. The sensitivity of the results to the inclusion of highly protected industries in the sample was checked by estimation of equation (8) first with, then without, observations taken from certain highly protected industries.

In the case of Turkey thirteen of the original fifty-four observations

Table 3. Principal results for technology choice in Turkey

	Value added per man						Non-wage value added per man					
	All industries			Highly protected industries excluded			All industries			Highly protected industries excluded		
Constant	-12,783.7 (-4.03)	382.34 (0.36)	349.7 (0.40)	-16,210.0 (-4.25)	971.30 (1.39)	383.4 (1.14)	-6709.0 (-3.06)	773.1 (1.76)	522.8 (1.59)	-8859.00 (-3.36)	608.20 (1.46)	265.2 (1.86)
$VU(L_1)$*			-0.50 (-1.70)			-0.43 (-3.67)			-0.29 (-1.03)			-0.40 (-2.99)
VU	7.46 (5.60)	0.95 (2.02)	1.08 (3.14)	9.45 (5.78)	0.42 (1.28)	0.94 (6.28)	8.11 (5.54)	0.39 (1.18)	0.73 (3.21)	10.63 (5.89)	0.30 (0.86)	0.95 (7.53)
$SD(L_2)$*			1.85 (6.54)			1.50 (11.12)			1.59 (6.33)			1.47 (15.66)
SD		-2.34 (-24.03)	-2.39 (-33.03)		-2.51 (-41.88)	-2.48 (-89.63)		-2.45 (-39.54)	-2.46 (-56.16)		-2.50 (-45.15)	-2.45 (-123.57)
$\bar{R}^2$	0.38	0.95	0.98	0.46	0.98	0.99	0.37	0.98	0.98	0.47	0.98	0.99

*$L_1 = L_2$; low-ITR industries have at most two barriers.

were considered to fall in the highly protected category. The selection of the highly protected industries was based on Kreuger's study of domestic resource costs in Turkey,[28] an industry being deemed highly protected if it exhibited negative value added at world prices or a relatively high domestic resource cost. On this criterion the following industries were deemed to be highly protected: alcoholic beverages, sugar, canned food, woollen textiles, paper, paper bags, cardboard, tyres, paints, motor vehicles, insulated cables, domestic electrical appliances, metal furniture.

It is evident from Table 3 that the variation in factor intensity in Turkish manufacturing is very closely related to the variation in factor intensity in UK manufacturing and the variation in the scale differential. This result is not sensitive to the use of value added per man or non-wage value added per man as an indicator of factor intensity. Similarly, it is not sensitive to the inclusion of highly protected industries. An outstanding feature of these results is the significance of the scale differential as an explanation of shifts to lower capital intensity in Turkey.

Turning specifically to the rotation and scale hypotheses, the trend of the results indicates considerable support for both hypotheses. It is particularly interesting to observe the degree to which the results on the rotation hypothesis are 'sharpened' (in terms of the t test of H_0: $b_2 - b_1 < 0$ and H_0: $b_4 - b_3 > 0$) when the data set is purged of the influence of the highly protected industries.

Finally, we may consider the sensitivity of our results to the definition of high/low barrier groups in terms of the number of technical barriers. Figures 2–5 examine the sensitivity of the rotation effect by relating the estimates of b_1 and b_2 to the definition of the low-barrier group (at most one barrier, at most two barriers, at most three barriers). It is evident that the significance of the rotation effect is more marked when we remove the protected industries from the data; the results are insensitive to the number of barriers defining the boundary. Our results also indicate that the scale effect is not sensitive to the definition of the low-barrier group in industries exhibiting at most three barriers.

Philippines

The results for the Philippines are presented in Table 4. The results presented are for the case in which L_1 is defined as at most three barriers, L_2 as at most two barriers. Selection of the highly protected industries was based on Power's study[29] of the structure of protection in the Philippines. Industries were classified as highly protected when they exhibited negative value added at world prices or exhibited high effective rates of protection in Power's study. On this criterion fifteen of the original

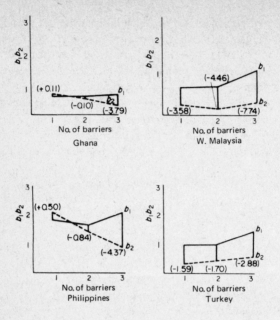

Figure 2. The 'rotation' effect — value added per man; all observations.

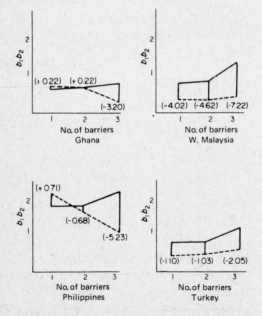

Figure 3. The 'rotation' effect — non-wage value added; all industries.

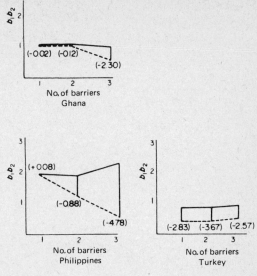

Figure 4. The 'rotation' effect — value added per man; highly protected industries excluded.

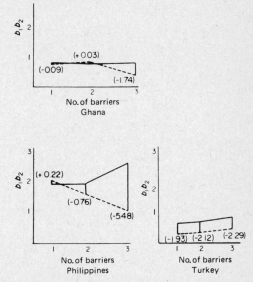

Figure 5. The 'rotation' effect — non-wage value added; highly protected industries excluded.

Table 4. Principal results for technology choice in the Philippines

| | Value added per man | | | | | Non-wage value added per man | | | | | |
	All industries		Highly protected industries excluded			All industries			Highly protected industries excluded		
Constant	−1841.97 (−2.99)	−587.75 (−0.94)	−2214.48 (−3.00)	−1998.47 (−2.58)	−747.89 (−1.08)	−632.12 (−1.80)	−476.90 (−1.32)	82.94 (0.26)	−880.64 (−2.07)	−611.35 (−1.43)	−25.56 (−0.07)
$VU(L_1)^*$		−1.03 (−4.37)			−1.24 (−4.78)			−1.49 (−5.23)			−1.58 (−5.80)
VU	1.89 (7.22)	2.06 (8.56)	2.01 (6.69)	1.96 (6.45)	2.30 (8.80)	2.07 (9.04)	1.97 (8.40)	2.53 (10.76)	2.18 (8.44)	2.02 (7.77)	2.62 (10.99)
$SD(L_2)^*$		0.20 (0.37)			0.22 (0.24)	.		−0.49 (−0.54)			−0.38 (−0.29)
SD	−0.23 (0.75)	−0.18 (−0.41)		−0.46 (−0.92)	−0.45 (−0.98)		−0.82 (−1.62)	0.26 (0.38)		−1.66 (−2.22)	−0.66 (−0.66)
$\bar{R}^2$	0.45	0.55	0.48	0.48	0.64	0.56	0.57	0.70	0.59	0.62	0.77

*L_1 – 'low' ITR (at most three barriers); L_2 – 'low' ITR (at most two barriers).

sixty-six industries were excluded as being highly protected; sugar, cocoa and chocolate, spinning and weaving of cotton, wooden boxes, metal furniture, fertilizers, bricks etc., paper stationery, leather tanning and finishing, household electrical appliances, batteries, electric lamps, motor vehicles, bicycles and motor cycles.

It is evident from Table 4 that the rotation hypothesis is confirmed[30] and that this confirmation is not sensitive to the inclusion of the protected industries or the use of the alternative indicators of factor intensity. The reader will note that the table presents results for the rotation effect with the low-ITR group defined as at most three barriers. Figures 2–5 demonstrate the sensitivity of the rotation effect to the definition of the low-ITR group. It is evident that, in contrast to the Turkish case, the very-low-ITR industries do not conform to our rotation hypothesis. The hypothesis is confirmed only as the low-ITR definition is broadened to include the industries with two or three barriers. This behaviour suggests a modified rotation effect in which it is the 'middle group' of industries, characterised by intermediate values of ITR, that show a significantly greater degree of rotation than those industries at *either* extreme of the ITR. The results of estimation using the non-wage value added data, where I indicates the intermediate industries with two or three barriers, are given below:

(a) All observations:

$$VM = -568.80 - 1.47VU(I) + 2.58VU - 0.95SD(L_2) + 0.09SD$$
$$(-5.64) \qquad (11.17) \quad (-1.05) \qquad (0.13)$$

$$\bar{R}^2 = 0.71$$

(b) excluding highly protected industries:

$$VM = -684.20 - 1.46VU(I) + 2.64VU - 1.19SD(L_2) + 0.61$$

$$\bar{R}^2 = 0.76$$

We note confirmation of the rotation effect for the intermediate barrier industries.[31] We will return to a discussion of this rotation effect in the intermediate group.

Finally, we may comment on the scale hypothesis. Table 4 indicates little direct support for $b_4 - b_3 > 0$. In no case do we obtain a significant coefficient for $SD(L_2)$ and there is also confusion as to the sign of the coefficient. Further analysis of the data does suggest the existence of collinearity problems. Consider, for example, the results using non-wage value added when all observations are used (the following results are not sensitive to the inclusion of the protected industries). Regressing the

Philippines non-wage value added per man on the scale differential variables above yields: [32]

$$VM = 1732 + 2.79SD(L_2) - 3.36SD \qquad \bar{R}^2 = 0.16; F = 5.84(2.63 \ df)$$
$$\quad (5.32) \quad (1.94) \qquad (-3.35)$$

Here we do pick up a significantly positive coefficient on $SD(L_2)$. The instability of the regression coefficients for the variables SD and $SD(L_2)$ is symptomatic of collinearity problems. Thus, we may argue that the evidence from the Philippines does provide some evidence in favour of the scale hypothesis.

Ghana

Table 5 presents results for Ghana. Suitable data on average plant size in Ghana were not available so our results relate only to the rotation effect. The rotation hypothesis does, however, account for between 57 and 68 per cent of the variation in the level of factor intensity depending on the measure of intensity and the data set used.

Information on the degree of protection of the industries in the Ghanaian sample was taken from Leith's[33] study of the effective rate of protection in Ghanaian industry for 1968. Eight industries were screened out as being highly protected: biscuits, confectionery, distilling, knitting mills, clothes, shoes, travel and hand bags, paints.

The results for Ghana follow closely those reported for the Philippines. The rotation hypothesis becomes significant as the definition of low-barrier industries is pushed to include three barriers. The results are not sensitive to the use of data on highly protected industries nor to the use of the alternative measures of factor intensity. As with the Philippines data, a modified form of rotation effect was estimated to yield:

$$VM = 221.7 - 0.54VU(I) + 0.78VU \qquad \bar{R}^2 = 0.58$$
$$\quad (1.12) \quad (-3.47) \qquad (6.65)$$

where all observations have been used, factor intensity taken as non-wage value added per man and I indicates the intermediate group of industries with two or three barriers.[34]

Again, we detect a significant rotation of the intermediate-ITR industries relative to *both high- and low*-ITR industries.

West Malaysia

Table 6 presents results for Malaysia. Information on the extent of protection of industry in Malaysia for the relevant time period was not available to the authors.

Table 5. Principal results for technology choice in Ghana

| | Value added per man | | | | Non-wage value added per man | | | |
	All observations		Highly protected industries excluded		All observations		Highly protected industries excluded	
Constant	-440.10	148.00	-902.80	-180.70	204.50	461.80	52.85	354.70
	(-1.16)	(0.42)	(-2.09)	(-0.36)	(0.89)	(2.12)	(0.20)	(1.15)
VU(L)*		-0.48		-0.41		-0.50		-0.42
		(-3.79)		(-2.30)		(-3.20)		(-1.74)
VU	0.77	0.84	1.00	0.95	0.62	0.74	0.78	0.78
	(5.30)	(6.83)	(6.04)	(6.13)	(4.96)	(6.37)	(5.35)	(5.62)
$\bar{R}^2$	0.47	0.62	0.60	0.67	0.43	0.56	0.54	0.59

*Low-barrier industries defined as having at most three barriers.

Table 6. Principal results for technology choice in Malaysia

	Value added per man			Non-wage value added per man		
	All observations			All observations		
Constant	421.43 (1.09)	469.23 (1.18)	686.10 (2.09)	455.40 (1.79)	519.89 (2.04)	513.30 (2.70)
$VU(L_1)$*			−0.61 (−4.54)			−0.72 (−4.62)
VU	0.37 (2.51)	0.38 (2.52)	0.70 (5.02)	0.40 (2.60)	0.43 (2.83)	0.83 (6.01)
$SD(L_2)$*			2.07 (4.06)			3.17 (5.74)
SD		−0.11 (−0.55)	−1.88 (−3.90)		−0.46 (−1.49)	−2.82 (−5.76)
$\bar{R}^2$	0.12	0.11	0.42	0.12	0.10	0.54

*$L_1 = L_2$ − low-ITR industries have at most two barriers.

These results follow the pattern of Turkey. The distinct rotation of the intermediate-barrier industries is not evident here. Considerable support is offered in favour of both the rotation and scale hypotheses. The evidence presented in Table 6 and Figures 2–5 indicates that our results are not sensitive to the definition of the low-barrier group or the alternative measures of factor intensity.[35]

One distinct feature of the results for Malaysia is the significance of the improvement in the fit of the model as the ITR is introduced into the equation. Thus, as the ITR is introduced, $\bar{R}^2$ increases from around 0.12 to around 0.70.

6. DISCUSSION OF RESULTS

The most striking aspect of the results presented above is the identification of a process of adaptation of technology in LDCs having both a scale dimension and what might be called a relative-price dimension (the rotation effect) − significantly related to our *a priori* measure of technical rigidity.

Several interesting features of the rotation effect have been observed. Figures 2–5 show a marked trend to an increasing degree of rotation (scale held constant) as the 'high'-barrier group is narrowed down to the 'very-high'-barrier group.[36] There appear to be two aspects to this behaviour. First, the upward drift in the b_1 coefficient in the charts reflects the increasing rigidity of the high-barrier industries. This appears to be a satisfactory explanation of the results for Malaysia and Turkey where the b_2 coefficients remain relatively stable. For the other two sample countries, however, the increasing gap between b_1 and b_2 is in part the result of a substantial fall in the b_2 coefficient as we move to the three-barrier upper boundary for the 'low'-ITR group.[37] The results on the modified rotation hypothesis confirm the notion that intermediate industries show a significantly greater adaptation than industries at *both* extremes of the ITR. The evidence from Malaysia and Turkey does imply that adaptation of the very-low-ITR industries is possible. The evidence here suggest that whereas the expected adaptation of technology takes place in 'intermediate' barrier industries in Ghana and the Philippines, full advantage is not taken of apparent possibilities for adaptation in the 'very-low'-ITR sector.

The estimates of the b_1 and b_2 coefficients themselves are of interest. Table 7 presents comparable estimates of the coefficients presented in Figures 2–5 for the case in which the low-ITR group includes industries

Table 7. Summary of factor intensity coefficients

Country	Coefficient for low-barrier group (b_2)	Coefficient for high-barrier group (b_1)
Ghana	0.38	0.84
West Malaysia	0.19	0.04
Philippines	1.03	2.06
Turkey	0.68	1.52

with at most three barriers. We use the results for all observations and value added per man as the measure of factor intensity on the basis that the results are not sensitive to the use of the alternatives discussed. Note that the estimated equations from which these results are taken yielded a significant constant term only for the case of Malaysia. Thus, for the other three countries the coefficients may all be considered comparable in terms of rays emanating from the origin. Given the presumed bias in estimation of these coefficients we can see that for Ghana and Turkey there is substantial adaptation in the low-barrier group as a whole (this is also the case for Malaysia). For the Philippines the low-barrier coefficient indicates substantially less adaptation than in the other countries. If we assume no measurement problems, the Philippines' factor intensity in the low-barrier industries appears to be almost identical to that in the UK. Given an overvaluation of the exchange rate some rotation will in fact be present. It does seem likely that the extent of adaptation is far less in the low-barrier Philippines sector than in our other sample countries. For the high-barrier group of industries there is some evidence of a shift to lower factor intensity at least in Ghana and perhaps in West Malaysia. For the Philippines and Turkey[38] the high-barrier industries show, in relation to the UK, what we may call 'reverse' rotation — shift to a higher level of factor intensity than prevails in the UK.

Thus, our results do indicate that in Ghana, West Malaysia and Turkey the technology adopted in the low-barrier industries does take advantage of technical possibilities to shift factor intensity to less capital-intensive techniques than are used in the UK. We cannot be certain of this conclusion for the Philippines. It appears that any process of adaptation there does not give rise to the substantial shifts from prevailing UK practice that is evident in the other countries. The fact that the Philippines is heavily dominated by the USA may imply that any process of adaptation starts from a base given by prevailing practice in the USA. Thus, whereas we have failed to detect any rotation relative to the UK this does not rule out the possibility of rotation relative to the USA. The fact remains that we have failed to detect a process of adaptation of factor intensity in the Philippines which clearly occurs in our other three sample countries. For the high-barrier industries we do find some evidence in our results for Turkey and the Philippines of the use of technologies with far higher factor intensities than are common in UK. Thus, for the high-barrier industries, at least for these two countries, there is considerable support for the notion of excessive capital intensity — with the use of modern technologies more capital intensive than those prevailing in the aggregate UK high-barrier sector.

The nature of the technology problem suggested by our results is rather more complex than this high capital intensity in the high-barrier, modern technology sector. Evidence from both Ghana and the Philippines reveals interesting rigidities in the putatively flexible technologies of the low-ITR (zero or one barriers) industries. Our results on the rotation of the 'intermediate-barrier' industries show that the shift to labour intensity in Ghana is significantly less and shifts to greater capital intensity (reverse rotation) in the Philippines is significantly greater, for industries at the extremes of the ITR relative to the intermediate industries. Thus, the problem of excessive capital intensity in these countries relates not only to the industries in which there exist technical barriers to the substitution of labour for capital but also to those industries in which such substitution is clearly available.

Our results on the impact of differences in the scale of operation between high- and low-wage economies on factor intensity are also reveal-ing. We find that such scale differences are very important in an explanation of shifts in factor intensity. Further, the interaction of the ITR with scale differentials shows that, as expected, it is in those industries characterized by technology rigidities that the trade-off between labour intensity and scale of operation is most important. That is, the 'traditional' view that high-technology industries offer little room for manoeuvre in terms of variation in factor proportions, is valid only for *given* levels of scale. Once scale is allowed to vary then even these industries display substantial variations in factor proportions. Indeed, the degree of adaptation related to differences in scale was found to be significantly greater in the industries characterised by many technical barriers than in the low-barrier group.

7. CONCLUSIONS

The above analysis suggests a number of interesting conclusions. The investigation of the engineering characteristics of a wide range of industries uncovers, as might be expected, the existence of considerable variation in the degree of '*a priori* rigidity'. This, in turn, implies that it is unlikely that intrinsic inflexibility of factor proportions is the principal cause of the low rates of labour absorption in LDC manufacturing. (This *general* conclusion broadens the industry-specific finding of the few detailed industry case studies currently available that a range of alternative tech-nologies does often exist.)

Going beyond this, we are now able to say that adjustment of factor proportions in LDCs to take account of the opportunities offered by 'flexibility' of technology is probably widespread. In our sample of four LDCs the tendency to install more labour-intensive technology where engineering circumstances permit is strong and clear-cut. It is not, of course, possible to demonstrate here that *full* advantage has been taken of each and every opportunity to substitute labour for machines (indeed, there is evidence of missed opportunities in the case of Ghana and the Philippines). But our analysis does offer strong support for the view that, across a wide range of manufacturing industry, LDC producers do select relatively labour-intensive technology where this is feasible in terms of the engineering characteristics of processes. At the same time, it is clear that the room for manoeuvre in this context is, in many industries, contracting as the optimal scale of operation increases.

These findings do not engender confidence in the view that simple 'cor-rective' policies — removal of factor price distortions, wider dissemination of information on available techniques, legislation on technology choice by multinational corporations and so on – can transform the employment situation by encouraging the 'appropriate' choice of technology. Rather, they suggest the pessimistic conclusion that such policies will have at best a marginal effect as adjustment of technology is already widespread in LDCs, and as the drift of innovation is tending to raise minimum economic levels of scale and, hence, increase technological rigidity. The inescapable corollary of this view is that, if employment creation rather than the attainment of allocative efficiency is the primary aim of policy, then more attention must be paid to developing indigenous labour-intensive methods of production.

ACKNOWLEDGEMENTS

We are grateful to Anthony Clunies-Ross, Charles Cooper and Howard Pack for helpful comments on an earlier draft of this chapter.

NOTES

1   The now very extensive literature on 'appropriate technology' is reviewed in Morawetz (1974).
2   As in Mason and Sakong (1971); Bruton (1972); and Little *et al.* (1970).
3   In one form or another this view is presented in Ranis (1975), White (1976), Wells (1973), and Morley and Smith (1974).
4   The capital-intensive bias of multinational corporations is noted in Sutcliffe (1971). A contrary view is expressed in Pack (1976), and Solomon and Forsyth (1977).
5   See for example, Nerlove (1967), and Morawetz (1976).
6   A number of straightforward comparisons of a limited range of techniques are presented in Bhalla (1975). Examples of the more complex form of analysis are given in Chenery (1953), and Boon (1964) – though both of these deal with individual subprocesses only; the application of a form of process analysis to complete 'factory specifications' has rarely been attempted – but see McBain (1977).
7   Given the considerable volume of research carried out in this field in recent years, the number of studies which attempt to assess the magnitude of the 'problem' is strikingly small – no doubt (though the point is rarely made) because this requires information on the range of technologies available for each industry. One notable attempt, which simply ignores the 'rigidity' issue, is made in Mason and Sakong (1971).
8   In this respect our approach resembles that used by Mason and Sakong (1971); and also by White (1976).
9   Eckaus (1955).
10   Stewart (1972).
11   Sutcliffe (1971).
12   Rosenberg (1976), especially Chapter 8.
13   Singer (1970).
14   Pack (1976).
15   Salter develops this point; see Salter (1966), pp. 14–15.

16   One exception is Morley and Smith (1974).

17   See, for instance, Pack (1976).

18   Examples of such classifications include: (i) the identifying of unit operations common to different branches of the chemical processing industries (Froust, 1960), and (ii) the classifying of components into cognate groups to identify possibilities for group processing (Burbridge, 1971).

19   Our view of the nature of technical progress is thus akin to that suggested in Rosenberg (1976; especially Chapter 4); and in Atkinson and Stiglitz (1969).

20   The nature of these laws is discussed later.

21   While it is probable that our concept of what constitutes a 'fundamental barrier' is to a degree conditioned by the nature of the existing regime of technology, which has evolved against the particular background of the now industrialized countries, it is our view that even in a counterfactual situation where the history of technology had followed a path more nearly suited to the current requirements of LDCs, most of the basic physical constants and fundamental laws of nature would have reasserted themselves in much the same way as they do in our 'technical barriers'.

22   For an earlier example of the use of an index constructed in this way see Adelman and Morris (1965).

23   The terminology is borrowed from Brown (1966).

24   One potential difficulty in the estimation of equation (8) is worth discussing at this point. The estimation of equation (8) is undertaken with the low-wage economy data on value added converted at some rate of exchange in order to give comparable data. When official exchange rates are used we must face the common problem that these rates in many LDCs may be grossly overvalued for the purposes of making meaningful international comparisons. Thus, *VM* may be overvalued and the observed scale differential may indicate a *smaller scale difference* than actually exists.

The overvaluation of *VM* will imply an upward bias in *the magnitude* of the estimated coefficients of equation (8). Such overvaluation will not affect the magnitude of the standard *t* statistic.

There is reason to believe that the undervaluation of *SD* will give rise to a *downward* bias in the estimation of the coefficients related to this variable. Since our major concern is to test if $(b_4 - b_3)$ is *significantly positive* the sensitivity of our results in this dimension need cause us no great concern.

25   Sutcliffe (1971).

26   In addition, there is some evidence suggesting that the value added per man variable is closely related to other measures of capital intensity where such measures are available. See, for example, Lary (1968), pp. 40–48.

27   See Lary (1968), pp. 58–61, for further discussion of these points.

28   Kreuger (1976).

29   Power (1971).

30   Further, this is not sensitive to very substantial shifts in the exchange rate.

31   Note that the scale effect still refers to the low/high classification.

32   L_2 is defined as in Table 3. The behaviour of the scale variables is reproduced when L_2 is defined to include the three-barrier industries in the low-ITR group.

33   Leith (1976).

34   This result is not sensitive to the exclusion of protected industries nor to the use of the alternative measure of factor intensity.

35   Similar results are obtained as L_2 is changed to include three-barrier industries.

36   Note, however, that when this high-barrier group is narrowed to those industries with four or more barriers we still have 15–20 per cent of our observations in the high group. Thus, the results are clearly not generated by the impact of a few 'special' industries.

37   In fact, as we include high-ITR industries in the low-ITR group we might expect b_2 to *increase*; which it does for West Malaysia and Turkey.
38   As we have used a 'realistic' exchange rate for Turkey the problem of bias in b_1 is perhaps less important than for the other countries.

REFERENCES

Adelman, I. and Morris, C. T. (1965). A factor analysis of the interrelationship between social and political variables and per capita Gross National Products, *Quarterly Journal of Economics*, **79**.

Atkinson, A. B. and Stiglitz, J. E. (1969). A new view of technological change, *Economic Journal*, **79**, 315.

Beyan, T. (1956). *The Theory of Machines*, 3rd edn, Longman, London.

Bhalla, A. S. (ed.) (1975). *Technology and Employment in Industry*, ILO, Geneva.

Boon, G. K. (1964). *Economic Choice of Human and Physical Factors in Production*, North Holland, Amsterdam.

Brockhurst, J. R. and Harker, J. H. (1973). *Process Plant Design*, Heinemann, London.

Brown, M. (1966). *On the Theory and Measurement of Technological Change*, Cambridge University Press, London.

Bruton, H. J. (1972). The elasticity of substitution in developing countries, Research Memorandum No. 45, Centre for Development Economics, Williams College.

Burbridge, J. L. (1971). *Production Planning*, Heinemann, London, pp. 390–407.

Central Bureau of Statistics (1971). *Industrial Statistics*, Government Printer, 1969, Accra.

Chenery, H. B. (1953). 'Process and production functions from engineering data', in W. Leontief (ed.), *Studies in the Structure of the American Economy*, New York.

Durrant, P. J. D. (1952). *General and Inorganic Chemistry*, 2nd edn. Longman, London.

Eckaus, R. S. (1955). The factor proportions problem in underdeveloped countries, *American Economic Review*, **45** 4, pp. 539–565.

Froust, A. *et al.*, (1960). *Principles of Unit Operations*, John Wiley, New York.

Henghein, F. A. (1969). *Chemical Technology*, Pergamon Press, Oxford.

Hume, K. J. (1951). *Engineering Metrology*, Macdonald, London, p. 72.

Jerome, H. (1934). *Mechanization in Industry*, National Bureau of Economic Research (NBER), New York.

Kreuger, H. (1976). *Foreign Trade Regimes and Economic Development: Turkey*, NBER, New York

Lary, H. B. (1968). *Imports of Manufacturers from Less Developed Countries*, NBER, New York.

Leith, C. I. (1976). *Foreign Trade Regimes and Economic Development: Ghana*, NBER, New York.

Lewitt, E. M. (1958). *Hydraulics and Fluid Mechanics*, 10th edn. Pitman, London.

Little, I. M. D., Scitovsky, T. and Scott, M. (1970). *Industry and Trade in Some Developing Countries*, Oxford University Press, London.

McBain, N. S. (1977). *The Choice of Technique in Footwear Manufacture in Developing Countries*, HMSO, London.

Mason, R. H. and Sakong, I. (1971). Level of economic development and capital-labour ratios in manufacturing', *Review of Economics and Statistics*, **53**, pp. 176–178.

Morawetz, D. (1974). Employment implications of industrialization in developing countries, *Economic Journal* **84**, 335, pp. 491–542.

Morawetz, D. (1976). Elasticities of substitution in industry: what do we learn from econometric estimates?, *World Development*, **4**, 1, pp. 11–13.

Morley, S. A. and Smith, G. W. (1974). Managerial discretion and the choice of technology by multinational firms in Brazil, Programme of Development Studies, Paper No. 56, Rice University.

Nerlove, M. (1967). Recent empirical studies of the C.E.S. and related production functions, in M. Brown (ed.), *The Theory and Empirical Analysis of Production*, NBER, New York.

Oziak, M. N. (1965). *Heat Exchange and Design*, John Wiley, New York.

Pack, H. (1976). The substitution of labour for capital in Kenyan manufacturing, *Economic Journal*, **86**, 341.

Power, I. H. (1976). The structure of protection in the Philippines, in B. Balassa (ed.), *The Structure of Protection in Developing Countries*, Johns Hopkins Press, Baltimore.

Pratten, C. E. (1971). *Economies of Scale in Manufacturing Industry*, Cambridge University Press, London.

Pronikov, A. S. (1973). *Dependability and Durability of Engineering Products*, Butterworth, London.

Ranis, G. (1975). Some observations on the economic framework for optimum LDC utilization of technology, in L. J. White (ed.), *Technology, Employment and Development*, Committee for Asian Manpower Studies, Manila.

Rosenberg, N. (1976). *Perspectives on Technology*, Cambridge University Press, London, especially Chapter 4.

Singer, H. W. (1970). Dualism revisited: a new approach to the problems of the dual society in developing countries', *Journal of Development Studies*, **7**.

Salter, W. E. G. (1966). *Productivity and Technical Change*, Cambridge University Press, London.

Sneed, M. C. and Maynard, J. L. (1942). *General Organic Chemistry*, Chapman & Hall, London, p. 352.

Solomon, Robert F. and Forsyth, David J. C. (1977). Substitution of labour for capital in the foreign sector: some further evidence, *Economic Journal*, **87**, 346.

Stewart, F. (1972). Choice of technique in developing countries, *Journal of Development Studies*, **9**.

Sutcliffe, R. B. (1971). *Industry and Underdevelopment*, Addison-Wesley, London, pp. 159–160.

Walker, J. W. (1958). *Applied Mechanics*, English University Press, London, p. 112.

Walshaw, A. C. and Jobson, D. A. (1972). *Mechanics of Fluids*, 2nd edn, Longman, London.

Wells, L. T. (1973). Economic man and engineering man: choice of technology in a low-wage country, *Public Policy*, **21**.

White, L. J. (1976). Appropriate technology and X-efficiency, *Quarterly Journal of Economics*.

White, L. J. (ed.) (1975). *Technology, Employment and Development*, Committee for Asian Manpower Studies, Manila.

APPENDIX 1 KEY CHARACTERISTICS AFFECTING THE 'FLEXIBILITY' OF MANUFACTURING TECHNOLOGY

In all, *eight* different characteristics of the physical aspect of production methods were identified as being potentially critical to the rigidity/ flexibility of these methods. They were:

1. *Process temperature*: Many processes can be carried out only at very

high or low temperatures, and this may make them wholly unsuitable for manual operation.

In particular, a wide range of chemical reactions simply will not take place in the absence of high temperatures. Furthermore, many processes which could be operated at lower temperatures are such — though there is no general statement relating the conditions under which a chemical reaction occurs to the nature of the reagents — that temperature has overwhelming consequences for the efficiency of the process. Thus, in accordance with van't Hoff's law of mobile equilibrium,[1] which applies to a wide span of reactions, a rise of 10 °C can double the velocity of some reactions.

Again, operations involving heat transmission are frequently very much more efficiently performed at high temperature: convection (within fluids) is greatly accelerated by raising the temperature of the fluid (as well as by inducing turbulent flow by means of pumps or compressors); radiation increases as the fourth power of temperature difference;[2] and conduction (and insulation) can be much improved by the use of sophisticated materials and techniques. In many industries special plant and equipment is essential to make possible the application and control of high or low temperatures, and manual methods cannot readily be employed.

2. *The presence of fluids*: All fluids (liquid or gases) used in manufacturing processes require containers. In some cases, depending on the physical or chemical properties of the substance, these may have to be of very special (and expensive) design, and the handling of the material by manual methods will certainly not be advisable where toxic or corrosive substances are involved. Here again capital-using methods may be necessary. It should also be noted that where containers are used there are often economies of scale to be reaped. The well-known 'six-tenths rule' states that the capital cost of new equipment increases in proportion to capacity$^{0 \cdot 6}$, so that considerable economies (not available where labour in some way replaces containers) are to be had by increasing scale.[3] By and large the opportunity to reap such economies will arise most often through the use of capital intensive technology, so that taking full advantage of them will tend to increase the capital–labour ratio. (This scale factor is not included in the ITR — but is treated as a separate influence on factor proportions.)

3. *Fluid pressure on materials in process*: Use is made of fluid pressure on the materials being processed in a very wide range of manufacturing industry.

Increasing fluid pressure can, for instance, greatly increase yields in certain chemical reactions,[4] and as such pressures may well be in excess of 500 atm it is clear that they cannot be replaced by manual means alone (especially in view of the heat generated through compression). In other cases, reduced pressures are useful, e.g. in permitting the controlled crystallisation which is often necessary in producing very pure substances, and these again cannot be applied using manual techniques.

A second important use for fluid pressure in manufacturing processes is the transmission of pressure itself. Mechanical pressure of the sort that labour-intensive methods might be used to apply is satisfactory where pressures are relatively low and/or the area over which the pressure is exerted is small. But where adjustable high pressures are required over large areas for sustained periods, gases or liquids are often the only feasible medium for achieving this, and there is no 'low-technology' means of applying them.

4. *Process speed*: Very high speeds are often required in manufacturing and these may not be feasible using labour-intensive methods.

Certain functions (for instance that of centrifugal separation) may only be performed using high-speed equipment, and the application of centrifugal force extends over a wide range of processes — ranging from sugar-processing to rock-crushing. The advantage of centrifugal techniques may be inferred from the standard formula:

$$F = \frac{Ww^2}{gR}$$

where F = centrifugal force, W = weight of the revolving body, w = velocity at radius R and g = the acceleration due to gravity. The value of F, the centrifugal force, depends on the square of velocity, and at high velocities this makes the use of centrifugal methods a particularly efficient converter of energy.[5]

Where the work that is to be done is of an intermittent nature, such as metal-punching and shearing, the incorporation of fly-wheels as a means of storing energy can result in very considerable savings.[6]

Once again, no satisfactory labour-intensive methods have been developed in this area.

5. *Manufacturing tolerances*: Close tolerances may be necessary in certain products because of the performance required or because of the need to reduce assembly costs. It is very often difficult for labour to produce output to close tolerance without the aid of fairly sophisticated equipment, especially where throughput is high. More generally,

where standardised items are required it is most unlikely that labour-intensive methods can be used successfully.[7]

6. *The use of electrical power — and of high-electrical-load factors*: In some processes there are no feasible alternatives to the use of electrical power, e.g. electrolysis of aluminium, and where a large electricity input is required the process equipment tends to be highly capital-intensive. Furthermore, where it is necessary to control speed within narrow limits — especially under varying loads — electrically powered machinery will normally be preferred to straightforward more erratic, manual motive power.

7. *The use of indivisible heavy materials*: Where large and /or heavy objects have to be manoeuvred in the course of manufacturing, machines will generally be preferred to manpower either simply to make the operation feasible or in the interests of avoiding damage and ensuring a smooth flow of production.

8. *Special hazards*: In the many processes where toxic, highly inflammable or otherwise dangerous materials must be used extensively, or where pollution risks are great, the possibility of substituting labour for capital will be substantially reduced.

NOTES TO APPENDIX 1

1 See Sneed and Maynard (1942), and Durrant (1952).
2 According to the Stefan–Boltzmann equation:

$$Q = K(T_1^4 - T_2^4),$$

where Q = heat transmitted per unit area of surface per unit time, K = constant, T_1 = absolute temperature of the heat source, and T_2 = absolute temperature of the heating surface. A detailed discussion is given in Oziak (1965).
3 See Walshaw and Jobson (1972); and Brockhurst and Harker (1973).
4 Static pressure in fluids is discussed in Lewitt (1958). See also the discussion of Le Chatelier's 'principle of least constraint' in Henghein (1969).
5 Hume (1951).
6 Beyan (1956).
7 Walker (1958).

APPENDIX 2

In the list below 181 manufacturing industries are classified into eight categories according to the inherent rigidity of their respective technologies — as measured by the number of 'technical barriers' scored. The ITR runs from 0 to 8, higher values of the index indicating greater rigidity. (In fact, no technology in the present sample scored 8.)

ITR = 7
Refined motor spirit and fuel oil
Smelted aluminium

ITR = 6
Paper board
Fibre building paper
Nitrogenous fertilizers
PVC
Pig iron made from ore
Electrical conduit, other steel and
    pipe fittings
Paper
Fibre board
Detergents
Plastic moulded under pressure
Cement

ITR = 5
Condensed milk
Refined and hydrogenated oils
    and fats
Particle board
Soap
Hardboard
Cast aluminium
Powdered and evaporated milk
Linoleum
Dehydrated/quick frozen vegetables
Cast iron
Steel rods and sheets
Paints, varnishes,stains, shellacs,
    lacquers and enamels

ITR = 4
Instant coffee granules
Beer
Pesticides
Sanitary pottery
Frozen fish
Refined vegetable oil

Sugar from cane
New tyres
Canned fish

ITR = 3
Mineral oil and gas prepared
    for refining
Canned citrus juices
Distilled ethyl alcohol
Domestic pottery
Razor blades
Synthetic fibres
Plywood
Canned citrus fruit
Fish meal
Scoured wool
Wood veneers
Bricks
Salt
Semi-conductors (transistors)
Other canned fruit and vegetable
    juices
Printed and finished cloth
Glass
Pharmaceuticals
Small rubber products
Ball and roller bearings
Other canned fruit and vegetables
Vegetable oil cake and meal
Rebuilt and retreaded tyres
Threaded fasteners other than
    wood screws
Plated, polished and finished
    metal products
Clocks and watches

ITR = 2
Roasted coffee
Animal glues
Margarine

Pulp made from wood, rags and
  other fibres
Matches
Pencils and pens
Office supplies
Tanned leather
Unrefined vegetable oil
Soft drinks
Tobacco prepared for cigarette
  manufacture, and cigarettes
Printed paper
Hollow metal ware
Scraped, tanned, bleached and
  dyed furs and other pelts
New and repaired ships
Switchgear and starters
Railroad locomotives and waggons
Jewellery made from precious
  stones
Optical equipment
Ventilation equipment, cooked
  and packed meats
Rendered inedible animal oils
  and fats
Rope, cordage and twine
Nails
Electrical insulators and in-
  sulating materials
Woven synthetic fibre
Hosiery
Bleached and dyed textiles
Quick, hydrated and dolomitic
  lime
Aluminium ware
Heavy structural fabrications
Concrete blocks

ITR = 1
Husked rice
Milled coffee
Carded wool

Wool yarn
Carded cotton
Cotton cloth
Carded jute
Jute cloth
Bed sheets and table covers
Aero-engines
Airframes
Internal combustion engines (for
  other than transport equipment)
Electrical sockets and switches
  (domestic)
Milled flour
Milled meal and stock feeds
Cleaned and polished rice
Cocoa butter
Woollen cloth
Cotton yarn
Retted jute
Jute yarn
Wood screws
Sawn and planed wood
Insulated wires and cables
Tufted carpets
Manufactured motor cars
Dried fish
Bread and other bakery products
Woven carpets
Assembled motor cars
Perfume
Assembled tractors
Enamelled metal goods
Electrical welding apparatus
Electric lamps, bulbs and tubes
Electric motors
Factory and other industrial
  buildings
Wooden barrels, drums, boxes
  and crates
Office-blocks and other multi-
  storey buildings

Costume jewellery

Dams, drainage, irrigation, flood control

Woodworking machine tools

Engineering jigs and fixtures

Chemical industry machinery

Domestic electrical appliances

Agricultural machinery

Wet and dry batteries

Electrical transmission pylons etc.

Pumps and gas compressors

Transformers

Radios, televisions, recorders etc.

Jobbing engineering products (pressed, machined and assembled goods)

Metalworking machine tools

Textile machinery

Office machinery

Materials handling equipment

ITR = 0

Underwear

Jackets and coats

Wooden sashes, doors, door frames and windows

Coachbuilt motor-car bodies

Metal door and window frames

Handbags and travel bags

Water storage tanks

Cutlery

Barrels (metal), metal drums, kegs, fire sprinklers

Dressed meat from abattoirs

Stationery

Containers and boxes, paper

Sports equipment

Ginned cotton

Leather footwear

Shirts

Trousers

Leather and fur apparel

Wooden furniture and fixtures

Houses

Hand-tools

School laboratory equipment

Mattresses and pillows

Boats and moulded plastic goods

Umbrellas

Wigs

Agricultural hand implements

Toys

Bicycles

Cocoa and chocolate powder

APPENDIX 3 SOURCES OF DATA

Data for the UK were taken from the *UK Census of Production for 1968* (HMSO, London). The 1968 census was used in all four country studies because the fine industry detail was not published in the later census. Thus, the UK data relate to 1968 whereas the LDC data cover the period 1967–1970.

The LDC data sources are as follows:

Ghana: *Industrial Statistics* 1966–68, (Central Bureau of Statistics, Accra 1970). The data used relate to 1968.

West Malaysia: *Census of Manufacturing and Construction in W. Malaysia 1971, Preliminary Release* (Department of Statistics, Kuala Lumpur).

The data used relate to 1970.

Philippines: *Economic Census of the Philippines* 1967, *Manufacturing*, Vol. II (Department of Commerce, Manila, Republic of Philippines). The data used relate to 1967.

Turkey: *Census of Industry and Business Establishments* 1970: *Manufacturing Industry, Large Scale Manufacturing Industry*, (State Institute of Statistics, Ankara, Republic of Turkey, 1976). The data used relate to 1970.

There is some variation in the coverage of these sources. The UK data relate to establishments employing twenty-five or more persons. The Ghana data relate to establishments employing thirty or more. The Turkish data relate to establishments employing at least ten persons or with installed power equipment with a capacity of at least 50 hp. The data from the Philippines relate to establishments employing at least ten persons. The exact coverage of the Malaysian data is not specified but may be assumed to be comparable in broad terms with the 'large' manufacturing sector of Turkey and the Philippines.

4 The choice of technique *vs* the choice of beneficiary: What the Third World chooses

J. L. ENOS

INTRODUCTION

To the extent that economists have succeeded in creating a social science it has been by abstracting from the complexity of the economic environment, abstracting in such a ruthless fashion that only a few variables and relationships survive. Most phenomena are excluded from consideration, while those that 'live' in the theory take on a prominence that they do not necessarily merit in the real world.

Such a relationship is the economic production function defined as the rule which associates any combination of inputs with the highest possible output that they could produce. Given knowledge of the production function the economist can, in principle, determine the various quantities of inputs that would be needed to produce any quantity of output; given additional knowledge of the cost of each of the inputs, he or she can, again in principle, determine the possibly unique combination of input quantities that would produce the output at minimum cost.

Of course, no economist has the vast knowledge encapsulated in a single production function, but that is not the issue here. What is the issue is that the existence of the concept of the economic production function limits the vision of the development economist, encouraging him to focus on a less important matter to the neglect of more important matters. It encourages him to look for changes in the production function, to the exclusion of other economic changes, and to the exclusion of economic constancies. Theory, and the production function is surely one of the integral constituents of contemporary economic theory, is a guide to enquiry, but it may not lead in the right direction. If one's destination is an understanding of the effects on the economies of the developing countries, of the borrowing of methods of production employed in the developed countries, a different guide should be sought.

To illustrate this proposition is the purpose of the following exposition. The first, short part will be devoted to the concept of the production function, pointing out its limitations as a guide to learning what methods of production are adopted and how and why. The second part will consist of a resumé of the recent experience of one rapidly developing country; and the third part of a comparison with experiences in some other countries. Finally two morals will be drawn — that what is sought in the developing country is not so much a production of goods as an assignment of benefits; and that what is employed in the seeking is not so much a technology as a political process.

THE CONCEPT OF THE PRODUCTION FUNCTION AS A DETERRENT TO ENQUIRY

The thrust of the argument in this section is that the concept of the economic production function limits understanding of what technique is chosen and by whom and why: in particular that what means of production are imported into a developing country, upon whose decision, and with what consequences cannot be seen by looking at merely the spectrum of alternative techniques.

One way of developing this argument is to examine the economic production function: what it reveals and what it hides. First of all, the production function is based upon the presumption that resources are combined efficiently, in the sense that the same output could not be obtained with less of any single input, all other input held constant. To presume is to limit consideration. If one presumes that efficient production prevails, one tends not to observe inefficiencies, not to enquire into their causes.

Secondly, the production function is a statement of the potential for combining inputs to yield outputs. What specific quantities of inputs actually are combined and what specific quantities of outputs actually are produced is largely irrelevant; the concern is with the *proportions* in which inputs may be combined and in which outputs may be produced. Yet casual comparison of different developing countries suggests that what varies is not the proportions in which inputs are combined to produce output but the total of inputs that will be employed and the total of outputs that will be obtained. Development is chiefly a matter of employing more inputs and producing more output, not of combining inputs in the correct proportions.

Thirdly, the economic production function is a relation between the physical quantities of inputs and the physical quantities of output — for inputs, this means so many units of a particular raw material, so many man hours of a particular skill, so many machine hours of a particular piece of equipment, so many bureaucratic hours of various types of administration. It is irrelevant to the production function how these raw materials are acquired, how the providers of the labour are organised, how the ownership of the capital goods is distributed, whose interests the bureaucracy has at heart and, in consequence, how each factor of production is rewarded. Guided by the concept of the production function one does not ask these 'hows?'.

Fourthly, in employing the concept of the production function one scrutinises only the technical aspect of choice. If, for example, in two different countries two identical pieces of equipment are operated with identical inputs in an identical manner to produce identical output they are operating under the same production function. If one's enquiry is guided by the concept of the production function one concludes that, in this matter at least, there is no difference between the two countries. One will miss entirely such phenomena as, (a) in one country all the profits go abroad, whereas in the other they are retained, (b) in one country all the skills are provided by its own nationals, whereas in the other they are provided by expatriates, (c) in one country the decisions are made by government, whereas in the other they are made by private businessmen, and (d) in one country the experience gained in production is exploited so as to increase productivity whereas in the other it is not.

Finally, and most important by relying upon the concept of the production function one may not be alert to the possibility that the seemingly separate phenomena identified in the previous paragraph – technical efficiency, capacity utilisation, distribution of rewards and locus of decision – are interrelated. Yet this is just what the results of the author's investigation suggest.

CHOICE OF TECHNIQUE AND OF FOREIGN SUPPLIER IN SOUTH KOREA

The occasion for the enquiry was a study of the absorption and dissemination throughout the South Korean economy of several advanced industrial techniques imported from abroad.[1] The techniques examined are those utilised in the contemporary manufacture of iron and steel, textiles, diesel engines, paper-making machinery, and petrochemicals, the selection being based on the ready availability of information. It is the last of these industries, petrochemicals, that will provide most of the data in support of the statements in this section and the next.[2]

Early in the enquiry it became apparent that in South Korea the choice of technique had been pre-empted. Many years before the manufacturing techniques were imported, the South Korean Government had decided to industrialise, which it interpreted as producing in large volumes a wide range of modern, sophisticated goods in large-scale plants employing the most advanced technology.

Following this strategy, the government had arranged for the construction, among other plants, of a complete, up-to-date petroleum refinery, moderate in scale by the standards of developing countries. During the country's Second Five Year Plan 1967–1971 a naphtha cracker was added to the refinery, thereby making available the chief raw materials, ethylene, propylene, and butylene, for a petrochemical industry. The establishment of this industry was to form the core of the chemical industry's contribution to the Third Five Year Plan 1972–1976.

At this point we will focus on the two petrochemicals, polyethylene (low density) and polyvinyl chloride (supplied to users as vinylchloride monomer, abbreviated as VCM) for which there is the greatest information. Scrutinising the lists of process design and petrochemical firms which had recently begun or completed the construction of polyethylene and VCM plants in the developed countries, the Korean Government discovered that there were thirteen which had patented processes for the manufacture of polyethelene and six for the manufacture of VCM. The government also discovered from its engineers that although the processes differed somewhat in their design and operating characteristics they were almost identical in their input requirements. In the language not of the engineer but of the economist all thirteen suppliers of a polyethylene process would employ the same production function for polyethelene and all six suppliers of a VCM process would employ the same production function for VCM. Across suppliers, a given quantity of output would require identical quantities of inputs. In these narrow terms, there was no choice of technique, only of technician.

But this did not mean that there was no choice, merely that technology was irrelevant to the choice. Choice there was, and although in choosing the Korean Government may not have devoted much attention to adapting the manufacturing technique to local conditions it none the less did devote attention to influencing the structure of the emerging petrochemical industry and the behaviour of its firms. Reconstructing the past, it appears that once access to a modern technique was assured foremost among the government's preferences were two items, one on the input side and one on the output side. Unsurprising was the desire to economise on a scarce input, foreign exchange. Given the ambitious programme of capital investment envisaged in the Third Five Year Plan and the necessity of expending most of the money on foreign equipment, it was natural that the Korean Government should try to raise as much as possible of the capital abroad. Surprising, in a capitalist country, was the determination to secure, from the equipment installed, output at the maximum rate, regardless of profitability.

Lower priority was apparently assigned to four other desirable attributes of an undertaking — government control over the prices of inputs and outputs, uniform treatment of foreign participants, full acquisition of technical knowledge by Korean engineers and automatic access to subsequent process and product improvements. Desirable, but conceded if necessary, seemed to be access to later innovations, government control over internal administration, acquisition of financial and marketing knowledge, localisation of capital goods purchasing, and majority ownership by Koreans. Still thought desirable, but assigned lowest priority in the Korean Government's ranking were a keen competitive spirit in the newly established industry, ready access to export markets for outputs of intermediate goods, and an inconspicuous and purely temporary presence of expatriates in positions of technical and financial control.

With this apparent preference order the Korean Government entered into negotiation with all possible foreign suppliers. A few foreign firms had previously approached the government. For the rest the Korean Government took the initiative. As negotiations proceeded and the government's terms became stiffer the candidates dropped out one by one, until finally only an American firm, the Dow Chemical Company remained. After a few weeks final bargaining both parties reached agreement and contracts were signed.

The terms according to which Dow Chemical entered into its joint venture with the Korean Government were as follows: Dow would supply polyethylene and VCM manufacturing processes in the latest versions, identical to those operated in its own plants in the United States; the equipment would be operated at the maximum rates technically possible; Dow would quickly train Korean engineers so they could design, utilise and improve equipment, and Korean managers so they could administer operations; the capacity of the facilities would be set approximately equal to the total domestic demand forecast for the first year after the plant came into operation;[3] Dow would provide half the equity capital (15 per cent of the total needed to finance the plant) and the Korean Government the other half (15 per cent); Dow would facilitate the floating of the foreign loans needed for the balance (70 per cent of the total, ultimately provided by a consortium of banks led by the Bank of America and the British merchant bankers, Hambros); Dow would permit the Korean Government to set the domestic prices for polyethylene and VCM, and to allocate supplies among domestic users, but would be able to distribute any excess through its own international sales network, receiving prices no less than it received for its own exports from the US; Dow would accept a Korean nominee for president of the firm, and would begin training Korean engineers immediately; and Dow would share with the Korean firm all process improvements secured in any of its world-wide plants. In exchange Dow was granted the rights of sole supply of raw materials other than ethylene (chiefly alkylchloride for VCM manufacture), of a fairly generous royalty (roughly 4 per cent of the value of output), of initial appointment of supervisory staff within the plant, and of restriction of the spread of technical knowledge of the process within the firm. Dow, as receiver of half the firm's profits, could hope to benefit also from the undertaking to produce at the highest possible rate. Chemical processing plants exhibit substantial reductions in average cost, with increases in output up to full-capacity; when the product is sold at a constant price the profit margin is highest at maximum output. Finally if it fulfilled the terms of its agreement, Dow might be permitted to expand its operations in step with the growth of the Korean petrochemical industry.[4]

Summarising the conditions of the agreement the Korean Government secured with the foreign owner of the technology, the former gained access to the most modern technique and assurance that it would be applied fully up to the limit imposed by the capacity of the equipment. Assurance was also given that its own citizens would become fully conversant with the technique and skilled in its operation and improvement. Finally, through its taking up of half the shares of the joint venture, the Korean Government could share equally in the profits of operation, initially for itself and subsequently for those of its private citizens who purchased the government's holding. The foreign owner of the technology secured for a limited period (which turned out to be seven years), a monopoly in the practice of the art; half of the operating profits (which, with output exceeding design capacity and attractive prices, have been substantial); and preferential treatment in the competition at the next stage of development of Korea's petrochemical industry.

The outcome in the case of polyethylene and VCM is typical. With one exception — caprolactam, the raw material for nylon — the agreements throughout the petrochemical industry were almost identical. The exception arose when the Korean Government found itself unable to secure equally satisfactory terms for a joint venture with any of three foreign manufacturers of caprolactam — du Pont, ICI and Union Carbide. Rather than concede to what it felt to be excessive demands, the Korean Government chose to license the technology from a Dutch process-design firm and supply all the other scarce outputs — capital, management, etc. — from its own resources. The enterprise, named the Hankook Caprolactam Corporation has also been successful both in its operations and as a model for two subsequent, domestic caprolactam ventures.

In other industries the choice exhibited by the Korean Government has generally been along the lines of the polyethylene and VCM ventures. Two exceptions have been massive undertakings financed by foreign governments or the World Bank (such as the iron and steel works, POSCO, for example) and small undertakings expanding the operation of existing private firms (such as new machinery purchased by Korean textile firms, for example). In the former case Korea receives both the technology and capital on favourable terms, without having to relinquish any of its other preferences. In the latter case, the terms are almost identical to those attained in caprolactam, although the government's role in the negotiations and control over subsequent operations are much diminished. Nevertheless, it is probably not inaccurate to state that the Korean Government deliberately and consistently imports industrial technology of the most modern type under terms which assure that equipment will be operated by its own citizens to the fullest extent, and that the goods which are produced will be made available, at reasonable prices and steady rates, to domestic manufacturers and distributers. That such matters do not stand at the top of the list of priorities of other developing countries is the theme of the next section.

CHOICES IN OTHER COUNTRIES

In Korea there is evidence documenting the choices of technology and technical agents, extending from, at the most general, national plans and programmes which are available to all; through industry schemes and company reports, available to those familiar with the language; to, finally, company and ministry records, available to scholars engaged in research. Such a wealth of material is not available in most other developing countries. The Korean experience can be described confidently, in the knowledge that that evidence can be checked, where the experience in other developing countries cannot. National plans and programmes are available, to be sure, but they are not national commitments; industry schemes and company reports are, in the former case often and in the latter case usually, fiction; and company and ministry records are secret. In generalising about the experience of most developing countries, economists can only fall back upon subjective evaluations, supported by little more than their own recollections that 'This was the way it was in — when I was there.' That they may be right, and by this author's observation almost always are, does not give these recollections the status of scientific evidence.

Yet it is such recollections that will chiefly be drawn upon in describing how choices are made in other developing countries. The author's are derived from work in certain countries of South and South-east Asia, the Middle East and Latin America, and extend across somewhat the same industries as he studied in Korea; in one case, they even cover the production of an identical product by identical means. Nevertheless they are only recollections, and one person's at that.

The only objective data that can be drawn upon are those observed in some other developing countries producing petrochemicals. In addition to Korea and four developed countries, three developing countries — Chile, Hong Kong and Spain — have permitted the manufacture of low-density polyethylene by companies affiliated with Dow Chemical, and from these there is some comparable evidence.

Looking at the experience of the other developing countries the two sets of observtions, subjective and objective, seem quite consistent: conforming closely to the Korean pattern were two choices, one technological and one procedural; diverging substantially from it was one choice, contractual. Similar to the choice in Korea was that of the most modern technique for the manufacture of industrial goods of standard design.[5] The desires on the part of other governments to license more than one firm or to continue to accommodate importers of the good to be manufactured domestically led usually to a concurrent choice of plants of relatively small scale, and consequently high unit costs; they had a greater incentive to adapt the advanced technology to local factor proportions, but exhibited no greater desire to do so.

In procedure, the other developing countries had in mind the same course of action as Korea; compiling a list of foreign suppliers of the technology, entering into negotiations with them all, and accepting the one which offered the best terms. In practice, however, they tended to respond to, rather than initiate, inquiries from potential suppliers. Negotiations were still intense and protracted but secured the best terms from only a subset of applicants, often restricted to just one firm. Foreign suppliers that did not initiate contact were not considered.

Moving on from technology and procedure the differences between the experience in Korea and in most other developing countries become more pronounced. From the outcomes of negotiations,both in terms of what was secured and what was not secured, it may be possible to construct a ranking of desirable conditions. As argued already, an 'appropriate' technology is not among the first rank, nor apparently are sustained operation at full capacity, availability of process and product improvements, mastery of the technology by nationals of the developing country, or access to markets abroad.

If these conditions, so important to the Korean government, have not been keenly sought by other countries, what have? From their outcomes it would seem that the most desirable conditions generally had to do with immediate emolument and subsequent financial control. These have been called contractual because they are settled during the course of the negotiations and are almost always independent of what transpires after those participating in the negotiations have come to agreement: immediate contractual items are the sums to be received by politicians and civil servants in the developing countries (so much for President X, so much for General Y, so much for Madame Z) who can supply scarce institutional inputs such as legislative enactments, planning consents, import licences, foreign exchange allotments, market shares, etc.; subsequent contractual items are the systems of accounts, pricing and invoicing mechanisms and other administrative arrangements undertaken by the owners or managers of the enterprise.

Once contracts have been signed, concern over the absorption of the technology into the importing country seems often to lapse, at least on the part of those who made the decision to adopt it. Construction and initial operation of plants are not carried out on schedule, the accumulation of inputs and the delivery of outputs is not expedited, training is not conducted and improvements not secured, and the full capabilities of the equipment are seldom realised.

The experiences of Dow's polyethylene plants in developing countries corroborates these tendencies; compared with the plant in Korea the others utilised fewer local components, took more time to construct and bring into operation, produced at lower rates (relative to design capacity), required higher unit inputs of raw materials and energy, and remained longer under the direction of US engineers.

One suspects that the attention of the policy-makers in these other developing countries was not directed towards achieving efficient operation of technologies already imported, of plants already constructed. The energies of those who participate in the decision to import one technology shift towards the next possible import. What benefits might accrue from an emphasis on the contractual conditions underlying the import of technology and to whom, is the subject of the next and final section of this paper.

THE CHOICE OF BENEFICIARY

To say who benefits from the implementation of economic decisions is no easy matter. It is customary among economic theorists to assume that there is a perfect correspondence between what is intended and what is achieved: plans are adhered to, commitments are honoured, contracts are fulfilled, delivery dates are met, and debts are punctiliously paid. Convenient such an assumption is and will be adopted for a first identification of beneficiaries from the import of technology.

The assumption that results match intentions enables us to dispose of the question of whether or not benefits are received by the foreign firm which supplies technology under different terms: we can presume that the contracting firm benefits whatever the conditions, otherwise it would not have agreed to supply the technology in the first place or would subsequently have withdrawn from production.

Turning to the developing country, which imports the technology, the first, and occasionally the only, beneficiaries are those individuals who are rewarded upon the signing of the licensing agreement. Omnipresent are the government officials who command the administration; their rewards may be both pecuniary (the proverbial 10 per cent of the total capital value of the undertaking, collected in one lump sum and then distributed, according to custom, amongst the officials' supporters) and reputational (most political credit accrues upon the publication of the agreement, little upon the subsequent fulfilment of its terms). In developing countries characterised by private industry, over-valued exchange rates and controls on capital exports, the owners of the undertakings may also benefit upon, or shortly after, the signing of the agreement, through the acquisition of scarce foreign exchange whose expenditure all too frequently bears little association with the purpose for which it was authorised.

Continuing with the attempt to identify beneficiaries, the next in chronological sequence are the suppliers of the physical inputs necessary to construct and operate the plant and equipment incorporating the imported technology — the contractors, the producers of capital goods and raw materials, and the engineers and workers and administrators and staff who operate the plant. Presuming that it is the intent of the owners of the firm adopting the technology to acquire physical inputs as cheaply as possible, the distribution of benefits often depends upon the division of expenditure between foreign and national suppliers: if most of the physical inputs are provided by foreigners — firms and individuals — most of the benefits can be assumed to flow abroad; if provided by nationals, to be retained within the developing country. The actual division will depend not only upon the level of economic development in the importing country but also, as has been seen in the case of Korea, upon the extent of its government's determination to replace foreign with domestic suppliers: the greater the determination, the greater the proportion of total benefits from supply that are received domestically.

A continued flow of supply benefits depends upon the adopting firm's maintaining a reasonably high rate of production, the higher the rate of output, the greater is the demand for inputs and the larger the expenditure upon them. Moreover, the higher is the rate of output, the greater generally are the benefits that local consumers of the product receive, partly through availability and partly through lower price. Like supply benefits, demand benefits are external to the producing firm, and also like supply benefits are dependent for their generation chiefly on the maintenance of output by the producing firm. To the extent that the government of the developing country provides incentives for high outputs, rather than for high profits, or large accumulations of wealth, or keen political support, to that extent, it will assure a high social return to the import of technology.

It is impossible to quantify benefits received, initially by those who authorise projects, subsequently and directly by the producing firm and its employees, and subsequently but indirectly by suppliers, customers and the rest of the economy; but the author's experience in Korea and other developing countries leads him to conclude that subsequent benefits arising from steady production at a high rate can outweigh the initial benefits arising from the decision to undertake production. Moreover, the distribution of benefits will be the more nearly uniform the greater is the proportion of the total accounted for through the maintenance of high rates of output. Maintaining high rates of production makes the import of foreign technologies worth the while of the developing country, where worth is defined as benefits accruing over time to the population as a whole, rather than benefits accruing to a few individuals at the outset.

Having identified actual beneficiaries, it is finally necessary to try to match these with intended beneficiaries, for only if they are identical can we infer that the actual outcome of applying foreign technology could have been the result of deliberate choice, i.e. that the domain of choice was over beneficiaries and not over technologies. We can never be certain, of course, for the observed range of outcomes could also be consistent with other sets of choices; all we will be able to say is that the results of importing foreign technology do not disprove the thesis that the conditions governing its acquisition are determined by those who have the power of decision, with the potential beneficiaries uppermost in their minds.

In the case of South Korea there seems to be support for the thesis: in the industries studied the prime beneficiaries have been the producers and consumers of the outputs, as was intended. Benefiting also, in terms of enhanced reputation and satisfaction from having fulfilled their duties, were the civil servants who negotiated the conditions governing the import of the technology. In the case of two countries, one Latin American and one Mediterranean, which imported a petrochemical technique identical to the one in Korea, there also seems to be support for the thesis: the prime beneficiaries appear to have been the civil servants and politicians who received tribute, and the local owners of the physical assets who received scarce foreign exchange on generous terms; and there is little evidence to indicate that this outcome was different from what was intended. Since, during their lifetime the plants in these two countries have been operated at lower rates of output and with fewer improvements in performance, those who produce and consume the output cannot be expected to have benefited to the extent that their counterparts did in Korea; again, there is little evidence to indicate that the interests of either of these two broad groups, producers and consumers, entered into the calculations of those who chose. We cannot say that the thesis is disproved.

It finally remains to ask what are the implications of substituting for the thesis that developing countries choose techniques the opposing thesis that developing countries choose beneficiaries. The first implication would be that the importance of technological choice must be down-graded: techniques are simply instruments, through whose selection or rejection rewards are chanelled into the proper hands. A second implic-ation would be that, to the extent that techniques do differ, the dimension along which differences should be measured is not an economic one, such as, say, the capital–labour ratio, but a political one, such as, say, who receives payments upon the signing of a contract. A consequence of this would be that economists studying the transfer of technology should direct their attention to the initial stages of the process, when the conditions under which technologies are made available are negotiated. They should focus not so much on the available set of blueprints as on the agenda for negotiations; they should make comparisons not so much with choices in developed countries as with procedures in other develop-ing countries; and they should look not so much at abstract economic agents (like labour or capital or raw material) as at real actors (like the Minister of Industry or the chief stockholder).

A third implication of accepting the thesis that developing countries choose beneficiaries rather than techniques would be that the domain of choice would be greatly extended. The set of possible conditions under which a technology might be made available, i.e. the set of contractual alternatives, is much broader than the set of possible engineering combinations, i.e. the set of technical alternatives. The number of potential suppliers is much greater than the number of potential techniques. The domain of choice for the developing countries seeking access to modern technologies is much broader than has been realised.

NOTES

1   This research is described in a forthcoming monograph edited by W. H. Park and J. L. Enos, *The Absorption and Diffusion of Imported Technology: The Case of South Korea* (Croom Helm).

2   Ibid., Chapter 4, 'Absorption and Diffusion in the Petrochemical Industry', by H. K. Rhee and J. L. Enos. A survey of the literature and statistics for the industry appear in OECD, Directorate for Science, Technology and Industry Sectoral Study No. 1, *Transfer of Technology in the World Petrochemical Industry* (Paris: 1979).

3   There was a constraint, set up by the capacity of the naptha cracker (150 000 tonnes per year of ethylene), on the total amount of raw material available for manufacture of the six petrochemical products, polyethylene (low density), polyethylene (high density), VCM ethanol, acetaldehyde and styrene monomer: the capacities of the six facilities were juggled so as not to exceed this overall figure.

4   This permission was given at the time of the planning of Korea's second petrochemical complex, when the joint venture with Dow — now called Korea Pacific Chemicals Corporation — was assigned the polyethylene and VCM plants, and Dow independently was assigned the chlorine alkali plant.

5   That there may be a 'choice of technique' for *other* goods and services is argued in, for example, Frances Stewart (1978), *Technology and Underdevelopment*, 2nd edn, Macmillan, London. Evidence as to the existence of a variety of techniques exhibiting different factor mixes is summarised in D. Morawetz (1974), 'Employment implications of industrialization in developing countries: A survey', *Economic Journal*, 84, 335, pp. 491–542. This author has expressed his views, and provided one example, in J. L. Enos (1977), 'More (or less) on the Choice of Technique, with a contemporary example', Seoul National University *Economic Review*, XI, 1, pp. 177–199.

PART II   X-EFFICIENCY, LEARNING AND TECHNICAL MASTERY

5   Productivity during industrialisation: evidence from Latin America

HOWARD PACK

The emphasis of most recent research on the relation between technology and economic development has been on the existence and range of technical alternatives which permit the use of more labour and less capital in the production of a given product. Almost all of these studies have neglected the issue of the efficiency with which a given technical alternative is used in an LDC setting as compared with its use in developed countries. Yet differences in the level of productivity as well as any non-neutral (with respect to capital and labour) efficiency differences will affect the choice of technique within LDCs. Apart from the issue of the choice of technology, the efficiency with which industrial technology is employed is obviously of great intrinsic importance: if total factor productivity in LDC industrial sectors is one-half or one-third that of the developed countries, a considerably smaller output will be produced from a given set of resources, thus reducing the standard of living below its potential. Low productivity will also adversely affect industrial employment in so far as the marginal product as well as the average product of labour is reduced.

In this chapter I pursue two questions using the cotton textile industry as an example: (a) the relation between best practice and realised efficiency in LDCs, and (b) the source of these discrepancies and their implications for industrial policy.

This chapter is part of a larger study on the interaction of technology choice and industrial efficiency in a number of countries including Kenya and the Philippines. The analysis of industrial performance in Latin America provides a convenient introduction to many of the relevant issues. The outline of the chapter is the following. The first section discusses the concept of best practice input requirements; the second presents single- and total-factor productivity indices for a number of Latin American textile mills; the third provides a framework for measuring the sources of the difference between realised and best-practice productivity. The final section presents some policy implications.

THE TECHNICAL FRONTIER

The Technical Frontier and Best Practice

An isoquant represents an efficient set of techniques. For each stage of the production process in cotton textiles there is a range of machinery currently available from machinery manufacturers, each machine or set of machines being operated by a group of workers using specified amounts of raw materials. The amount of machines, materials, and labour per unit of output of textiles as envisaged by the machinery producers may be described as engineering standards or norms. Some of these anticipated input–output relations primarily reflect physical relations governing the process; others will reflect economic and social factors such as relative factor prices and labour relations. The anticipated ratio of machines to output is more frequently realised than the labour–output relation. For example, the quantity of output per carding machine per minute, as envisaged by a card manufacturer, is likely to be fairly close to its actual productivity on the factory floor assuming that the preceding operations (opening and cleaning) have generated the supply of raw materials of required quality: the wastage rate, required floor space, and kilowatt hours of electricity are also likely to be close to the manufacturer's specifications, though they may be altered by worker or managerial inefficiency.[1]

The 'manning' levels suggested by machinery manufacturers are derived from a variety of sources including their own experimental workshops and extrapolations of the experience of current users of earlier versions of their equipment. Labour–output relations generated by these methods are, however, not technical data reflecting underlying physical relations. Apart from the Hawthorne effect, labour productivity in their own experimental plant or in the high productivity plants of their purchasers may reflect the rigour of the hiring process, incentive pay systems, supervisory quality, the ability of management to provide high-quality raw materials, and so on.. Unlike the case of the well-known Chenery engineering production function for gas flow, derivable from the laws of chemistry, the production function in textiles will reflect these non-machine behavioural relations.

The concept of best practice rather than that of engineering norms thus seems appropriate, where best practice reflects the realised performance of the best (or better) firms in an industry; best-practice input coefficients will be inferior to those physical maxima achievable under 'ideal' conditions. The evolution of best practice over time will largely reflect the development of the more basic engineering production function: however, at any given moment the product per worker or machine in even the best managed operating plant will be inferior to the then known maximum engineering standard, the degree of inferiority being related to the extent to which the operating plant conforms to 'ideal' practice in activities ranging from blending to humidity control to personnel relations.

One of the most complete studies of productivity in the cotton textile industry was carried out by the United Nations Economic Commission for Latin America (ECLA) in 1950.[2] The analysts constructed best-practice specifications for two hypothetical plants, one using older machinery produced in the first quarter of the century and one using then new (1950) equipment. Optimal combinations of equipment and the implied labour and material requirements were calculated and constitute the norm against which actual productivity was measured. Although there is only limited discussion of the basis of the construction of best-practice co-efficients, these are consistent with the productivity of the better operating plants in Western Europe at the time.[3]

PRODUCTIVITY LEVELS

Spinning

Using the detailed ECLA plant profiles of labour and equipment at each stage of production I have calculated unit-labour and capital requirements. The unit-labour requirements (operative hours per kilogram of 20s cotton) measure the labour input for the entire spinning process from the opening of bales of cotton fibre to the removal from ring frames of bobbins of spun yarn; they do not reflect labour used in processes subsequent to spinning such as preparation of yarn for weaving. The (physical) capital–output measure, spindles per kilogram, describes only the spinning process proper, omitting opening, cleaning, carding, drawing, and roving. Although there are variations among these processes, productivity per machine in these activities in most plants is clearly related to that in spinning proper and ring spindles constitute the major capital cost in the spinning sequence. A focus on spinning itself (for capital–output measures) permits a focus on the essential features of productivity differences without the presentation of excessive technical detail which would not, in any case, alter the results much.

In Table 1 the operative hours per kilogram of yarn for the sector as a whole in Brazil, Chile, Ecuador, Mexico and Peru, along with the best practice standard for the entire sector are shown. The data were adjusted for output levels to eliminate the small effects of economies of scale.

The features of particular interest are the following:

Table 1 Realised and best practice labour coefficients, industry averages Latin American spinning plants: 1950

Location	Type of equipment	Operative hours per kilogram		
		(1) Realised	*(2)* Best practice adjusted for size of plant*	*(3)* (1) ÷ (2)
Brazil				
São Paolo	Old	0.394	0.187	2.11
Rio de Janiero	Old	0.595	0.182	3.27
São Paolo	1950	0.201	0.166	1.21
Chile	Old	0.565	0.196	2.88
	1950	0.267	0.158	1.69
Mexico	Old	0.546	0.241	2.27
	1950	0.327	0.170	1.39
Peru	1950	0.320	0.178	1.80

Source: United Nations, *Labor Productivity of the Cotton Textile Industry in Five Latin American Countries*, Volume I.

*Differences among the best practice coefficients for the same vintage (Column 2) reflect differences in plant size within and across countries. All coefficients are for 20s cotton.

1. The general low level of average labour efficiency relative to best-practice norms, unit-labour requirements ranging up to 227 per cent above the norm.
2. The better productivity performance of 1950 mills relative to their norms than is the case for older mills. The ECLA analysts suggest the second result reflects the fact that firms willing to modernise their equipment were more concerned with efficiency, and the age of equipment is a determined rather than determining variable.

The productivity figures of Table 1 are sectoral averages extrapolated from plant profiles. The ECLA report also provides data on the individual plants and these allow calculation of capital–output (spindle per kilogram) ratios as well as labour–output ratios. Table 2 shows actual relative to best-practice unit factor requirements and capital–labour ratios (spindles per operative). These will be analysed below within an analytic framework and our comments here are limited to simple descriptive observations. The most notable characteristic of these data is the relatively close conformity of the actual spindle–output ratio to that characterising best practice. Indeed, the mean spindle–output ratio for 1950 plants is lower than the best-practice standard and that for old plants is slightly higher. In contrast, the labour–output ratios are considerably above best-practice standards, performance being worse on older than on more modern equipment.[4] Finally, observed spindle–labour ratios relative to best practice are, in all but one plant, considerably less than unity. Assuming that labour is not hired as an altruistic measure by private firms, the lower–labour ratio in operating plants implies that factor proportions are variable after installation of equipment.

It is evident from the comparative single-factor productivities shown in Table 2 that part of the reason for observed lower Latin American labour productivity (and, conversely, except in Brazil, high spindle productivity) is the difference in relative factor proportions (spindles per operative hour) between best practice and operating plants, presumably attributable to the differences in relative factor prices they face. Some measure of total factor productivity is thus necessary to provide at least notional indicators of plantwide productivity. To obtain this, I use the single-factor unit input requirements of Table 2. Given the capital–input measure there is reason to have more confidence in the calculation with respect to the 1950 plants than for earlier ones. The results shown in the last column of Table 2 confirm that part of the lower productivity is indeed attributable to lower capital–labour ratios. The major feature of interest is the quite high TFP exhibited by the modern plants, with one exception the ratio is above 0.90. The older plants reveal considerably weaker performance.

Since the capital–input measure is physical units per unit of output rather than the value of equipment (which would, in perfect markets, reflect productivity differentials among various machines), the resulting index of total-factor productivity is best viewed as indicating rough orders of magnitude rather than providing a precise measure.[5]

Weaving

Unit labour and capital requirements in the Latin American plants in 1950 are shown in Table 3.[6] In addition, the table shows for each plant ECLA's estimate of the number of looms each weaver would attend in a best-practice plant as well as the looms per weaver in the corresponding operating plant. When the sample is divided, on the basis of best-practice looms per worker, into 'old' and 'modern' technology firms, the ratio of actual to

Table 2 Unit labour and capital requirements relative to best practice, and total factor productivity: selected Latin American spinning mills: 1950

| | Actual/Best-practice standards | | | | Actual spindles per operative hour relative to best practice | | Total factor productivity relative to best practice | |
| | Operative hours per kilogram | | Spindles per kilogram | | | | | |
	Old	Modern	Old	Modern	Old	Modern	Old	Modern
Brazil								
1 Plant A	2.28		1.22		0.54		0.64	
2 B	1.85		1.14		0.62		0.72	
3 C	2.97		1.62		0.55		0.48	
4 D	4.28		1.31		0.31		0.48	
5 E		1.59		0.82		0.52		0.94
6 F		1.34		0.93		0.69		0.93
Chile								
7 Plant A	2.15		0.92		0.43		0.77	
8 B		1.75		0.71		0.41		0.95
9 C		2.05		0.47		0.23		1.18

Ecuador								
10 Plant A	3.79		0.92		0.24		0.62	
Mexico								
11 Plant A	2.10		0.77		0.37		0.87	
12 B	1.76		0.69		0.39		1.00	
13 C		1.20		0.90		0.75		0.99
14 D		1.02		1.27		1.25		0.86
Peru								
15 Plant A	2.23		0.87		0.39		0.79	
16 B	2.14		1.01		0.47		0.73	
Mean	2.60	1.58	1.05	0.87	0.42	0.62	0.72	0.91
Standard deviation	0.89	0.42	0.30	0.25	0.12	0.33	0.18	0.16

Source: Labour Productivity of the Cotton Textile Industry in Five Latin American Countries.

Table 3 Unit labour and capital requirement relative to best practice and total factor productivity: Selected Latin American weaving mills: 1950

	Actual/Best-practice standards			Looms per weaver		Total factor productivity relative to best practice	
	Unit labour requirement	Unit capital requirement	Capital/labour ratio	Actual	Best practice	Old	Modern
Brazil							
1 Plant 1	2.55	1.03	0.40	13	56		0.68
2 2	1.75	1.47	0.84	16	25		0.63
3 3	1.44	1.28	0.89	2.5	3	0.74	
4 4	2.57	1.22	0.47	3	6	0.61	
5 5	1.80	0.99	0.55	3	6	0.80	
Chile							
6 Plant 1	1.79	1.10	0.61	20	72		0.35

Ecuador							
7 Plant 1	8.00	1.37	0.17	1	4	0.36	
Mexico							
8 Plant 1	2.27	0.97	0.43	2	5	0.73	
9 2	1.56	1.39	0.89	3.75	4	0.69	
10 3	1.73	1.59	0.92	21	72	0.61	
11 4	1.04	1.27	1.22	47	63	0.85	
Peru							
12 Plant 1	1.82	1.16	0.64	4	6	0.72	
13 2	3.35	1.59	0.47	12	58	0.47	
Mean	2.44	1.24	0.65			0.66	0.60
Standard deviation	1.77	0.21	0.28			0.15	0.17

Source: See Table 2.

best-practice weaver productivity is considerably greater in the former.[7] In the firms in which the best-practice norm is ten looms or less, the mean ratio of actual to best-practice looms per worker is 0.58, whereas in firms in which best practice is more than fifty looms per weaver, the mean of actual/best-practice looms per weaver is 0.35. The potential increase in weaver productivity as modern looms were introduced was not realised.[8] More generally, neither unit-labour requirements relative to best practice nor relative total-factor productivity are correlated with the potential productivity of looms as measured by best-practice looms per weaver. High relative TFP occurs with old machinery (firms 3, 5) and with modern equipment (11), and poor performance with both types (e.g. 6 and 7).

A DECOMPOSITION OF PRODUCTIVITY DIFFERENTIALS

Framework

The difference between LDC and DC productivity has been noted many times and a number of explanations have been offered for the phenomenon.[9] These efforts rely on descriptions of the background of current characteristics of industrial workers but almost never consider the nature of the manufacturing process nor economic factors such as the rationality of using greater labour–capital ratios when lower wage–rental ratios prevail; they emphasise one major obstacle, occasionally tautological (absence of 'modernity') and are largely incapable of testing or quantification.[10] A more fruitful approach is the identification and the most-likely major sources of deviation from best-practice productivity and the quantification, where possible, of each of these.

A descriptive schema that I have found useful in other industrial analyses can also be utilised here.[11] A firm's productivity may be affected by conditions determined at the national or economy-wide level, at the industry level, the managerial capacities of the firm, and finally, the task level efficiency of individual workers.

The National Economy

If productivity is evaluated for a given time period such as a month, some features of the national economy will impinge on the plant: breakdowns in the transportation system, failures in electricity supply, and other intermittent sources of production delays will lead to fluctuations in capacity utilisation. Even if transient disturbances are omitted and productivity per hour of actual production is calculated, the national economy will impinge on the firm: thus, the absence of an adequate educational system will increase the training costs of firms which may then decide to provide less training than would otherwise be the case. Operatives or managers may then exhibit lower productivity.[12]

The success of the economy in providing jobs may affect the willingness of workers to accept rationalisation of the production process both in terms of general plant reorganisation and individual work loads. And national labour legislation and limits on the ability to fire excess workers may affect productivity. Finally, the entire incentive structure, from those incentives affecting international trade to those determining the recipients of loans from the financial system, will exert an important influence on the desire (and necessity) of firms to achieve productivity growth.

The Industry

Industry-wide features that can affect plant- and task-level efficiency include the industrial organisation of the industry and the existence of institutions such as industry financed training centres and research organisations. If an industry has been encouraged by trade or financial policies to grow artificially, so that its productive capacity exceeds the requirements of the domestic market, yet it is incapable of producing at sufficiently low cost to export, it will operate at higher than necessary average cost. In the cotton-textile industry such excess costs are not attributable in a major way to economies of scale in the conventional sense of average costs declining with increasingly intensive used of fixed facilities. The more important source of scale effects is the length of individual production runs in weaving and the range of yarn counts in spinning. For any given percentage of capacity utilisation, unit costs can be reduced if the variety of yarns or fabrics produced is decreased.

With high rates of effective protection, entry may continue to proceed in an industry and both new and existing firms may find themselves with excess capacity. To increase utilisation levels, an expansion of the product range is undertaken by each firm until a monopolistically competitive equilibrium holds in each product market. In this case, even if total sales were not increased, a reorganisation of the industry to allow product specialisation would reduce unit costs. Since marginal costs would decline, if these savings were passed on to consumers in the form of lower prices, the quantity demanded would increase, perhaps further reducing unit costs.

The Firm

A large number of operational skills at the firm level affect productivity. Among the technical factors that are important are the following: adequate blending of raw fibre at the beginning of the production process in spinning, inadequate blending leading to yarn imperfections such as weaker strength and hence more breakage both in spinning proper and in weaving; good humidity control in both spinning and weaving; appropriate quality of sizing, the liquid used to add strength to yarn before it is used in weaving; the use of chemical and mechanical (e.g. strength of fibre) tests throughout the process and quick identification and correction of production errors accounting for defects. Inadequate knowledge or implementation ability with respect to these and other conditions may lower capital, labour, or material productivity. Thus, yarn that is less strong than necessary as a result of poor blending may result in more breaks in weaving. This will lead to an increase in the labour–output ratio if more operatives per machine are used to permit the achievement of best-practice machine efficiency.[13] If more operatives are used, neither the equipment nor raw-material to output ratio would be increased; the ensuing increase in the labour coefficient should not be attributed to task-level labour inefficiency but to firm-level operating inadequacies.

Knowledge of these and other technical requirements of production is unevenly diffused among firms. The most efficient firms are usually in command of almost all of the relevant skills. The less efficient are aware of the general issues and make some attempt to achieve technical mastery of the production process, but often do not understand the precise methods for achieving these standards. Others may be aware of the latter but have decided that their implementation is too expensive in light of their benefits.

Though most of the technical knowledge must be obtained by the volitional efforts of firms, it might plausibly be argued that operating practices are partly dependent on the industry: with a well developed sector (a 'large' number of competent firms) possessing substantial technical knowledge, informal contact as well as interfirm mobility of workers and managers will lead to the diffusion of technical information. Thus, excessive yarn breakage and the ensuing added labour requirements might well be thought of as attributable to the level of development of the industry as well as to the failure of individual firms to obtain greater knowledge.[14] Similarly, it may be argued that while the immediate locus of inadequate training is the firm, the latter's own cost would be decreased and its training improved if there were greater formal education at the national level.

Task-Level Productivity

Finally, task-level productivity will depend on worker skills and motivation. These in turn may be affected by both the incentive structure and the quality and intensity of supervision. Most theories purporting to explain low LDC industrial productivity rely (though often not explicitly) on task-level productivity.[15] However, as will be seen below, this may not be a major source of inefficiency in semi-industrialised countries.

The above are conceptual categories and are not mutually exclusive as the discussion has indicated. A decomposition of the sources of productive inefficiency using these categories can indicate only the proximate, not the ultimate sources of industrial inefficiency. Thus the adverse incentive effects of a protectionist trade system may be the underlying problem, manifesting itself at the industry and firm levels in the form of excessive product differentiation and inadequate technical knowledge. The small growth in total job opportunities may lead to a conscious effort by workers to withhold achievable productivity gains and may show up, as a residual, in task-level inefficiency. Nevertheless, the decomposition can be useful in policy discussions, for example, in indicating possible fruitful loci of intervention even if a protectionist regime were to continue, or conversely, to catalyse by specific technological or economic policies the benefits to be obtained from general liberalisation.

Finally, note that lower productivity does not imply that the 'excess' labour can or should be removed. The normative question for the private firm is whether such reduction would raise or lower cost, given that almost any change, for increased training to learning more about blending, will require expenditures. From a social viewpoint the guiding principle must also be a benefit/cost calculus, albeit a different one. Thus, public provision of better vocational education may increase labour productivity in textiles but the social rate of return on such expenditures may fall short of the rate of return available from other expenditures.

To implement the decomposition we utilise a production theoretic frame work that has been extensively used at the aggregate level. Assume that plant A is being compared with a best-practice developed country, plant B. Both possess the same types and quantities of machines. Post installation variations in the labour–machine ratio are possible in the best-practice plant according to the relation

$$1 = k^{\alpha} z^{1-\alpha} \tag{1}$$

and labour productivity is given by

$$(Q/L)_{BP} = P_{BP}(K/L)^{\alpha}_{EP} \tag{2}$$

where P is an index of neutral technological differences. In the LDC plant-factor substitution is possible along the isoquant given in (1) and labour productivity in plant A is

$$(Q/L)_A = P_A(K/L)_A^\alpha$$

The difference between best-practice and observed labour productivity depends on both differences in the productivity index and those in the capital intensity,[16] or

$$\frac{(Q/L)_A}{(Q/L)_B} = \frac{P_A}{P_{BP}}\left(\frac{(K/L)_A}{(K/L)_{BP}}\right)^\alpha$$

It is of course only differences in the productivity index that constitute X-inefficiency. If we denote the ratio of predicted to actual labour productivity after the adjustment for differences in capital intensity by q_A/q this ratio can then be explained by measuring the sources of difference in P_A/P_{BP}. Normalising P_{BP} to 1 and concentrating on P_A, the latter is viewed as being composed of several multiplicative elements, P_i, $i = 1$–4 where P_1 corresponds to the productivity effect of features of the national economy, P_2 to industry-level effects, P_3 those at the plant level and P_4 those at the task level. Denote the level of P after the first three corrections as $\bar{P}$. Predicted output will then be $(\bar{Q}/\bar{L}) = \bar{P}(K/L)_A^a$. Task level inefficiency will then be defined as a residual, namely, $\bar{Q}/\bar{L}/(Q/L)_A$, where the denominator is observed labour productivity and the numerator indicates predicted labour productivity given the impact of national, industry-wide, and firm-level effects.

Empirical Results

Tables 2 and 3 presented the data on single- and total-factor productivities for individual Latin American spinning and weaving plants. The ECLA study also attempted to account for the differences between realised and best-practice labour productivity for the entire sector rather than for individual's plants in each country. Their explanation does not, of course, follow the framework just suggested, but nevertheless contains some estimates of the effect of specific conditions on single-factor productivities.[17] In the following I consider only the modern-sector plants and proceed with the decomposition indicated above. The first adjustment of realised unit-labour inputs is attributed to the failure to realise scale economies.

Although the individual plants visited and reported upon by ECLA (Tables 2 and 3 above) were not suffering from inadequate scale, this was not true of the entire sector in the countries studied; it is the sector-wide data that are used in the decomposition since it is only for this aggregation level that ECLA presents estimates of operating features such as speed and humidity control. To stay within the framework presented above it is necessary to assume that the scale effects are neutral with respect to both primary factors, an assumption consistent with the results of technical engineering studies. However, there is a difficulty in determining the elasticity of output with respect to capital, a parameter required for the calculations.

In obtaining the earlier results (Tables 2 and 3) on total-factor productivity, observed-factor shares were utilised to obtain the required elasticities. However, when returns to scale are greater than unity, observed-output shares will not reflect the elasticities. If it is assumed that the factor-limiting scale was 'entrepreneurship', then with the inclusion of this factor the sum of elasticities equals unity. If the return to entrepreneurship is included equally in both labour and capital shares, each will be overstated by some unknown percentage. Therefore, the effect of different factor proportions was calculated assuming that the true elasticity of output with respect to capital was alternately 10 and 20 per cent below that observed.[18] Since the numerical results are not much altered by the particular figure used, only the unadjusted set of results is presented.

The calculations for Latin America for 1950 are shown in Table 4. No reduced productivity is shown at the national/industry level as ECLA's data indicate no impact on labour productivity from the absence of specialisation by plant, perhaps reflecting still nascent import substitution.[19] Secondly, task-level inefficiency constituted a relatively small problem in modern Latin American plants in 1950, workers exhibiting productivity ranging from roughly that of best practice (Mexico and Peru) in spinning to at most, 27 per cent more labour per unit of output in Chilean spinning. As would be expected, given the known differences in operative skills required, weaving exhibits lower task-level efficiency in every country.

If the entire deviation of labour (and given the neutrality assumption, total factor) productivity, other than that due to factor proportions differences from best practice standards, is regarded as X-inefficiency most is accounted for by scale in the modern Latin American spinning sector (but not in the 'old' sector) and by task-level inefficiency in weaving. The result that factor substitution is a major source of lower labour productivity is of particular interest. A knowledgeable textile engineer who visited one of the textile plants described in Tables 2 and 3 might have concluded that the large number of workers on the plant floor, compared to those in a DC factory with similar equipment, was attributable to the inefficiency of workers or management. While many LDC textile factories were (and are) inefficient in the sense of total-factor productivity, this cannot be inferred

Table 4 Sources of difference between actual and best-practice unit labour input. New plants: Latin America, 1950

Sector-wide Averages

	$\dfrac{(L/Q)_A}{(L/Q)_{BP}}$	Percentage increase in unit labour requirement attributable to				
		Difference in capital/ labour ratio	Scale	Humidity* control	Yarn* preparation	Task level inefficiency
Spinning						
Brazil	154	26	9	0	—	12
Chile	229	57	20	0	—	22
Mexico	131	16	16	0	—	−3
Peru	246	62	54	11	—	−11
Weaving						
Brazil	198	45	5	0	9	20
Chile	258	66	13	0	8	27
Mexico	142	20	11	0	0	6
Peru	224	56	7	5	8	18

Notes: − insignificant

*Defective yarn preparation and inadequate humidity control are major contributors to excessive broken yarns, a feature which reduces both labour and machine productivity.

from plant–floor observation alone. However, many of the earliest theories seem to have been formulated to explain 'excess manning' based on impressions obtained in factory visits, not realising that the phenomenon was inconsistent with cost-minimising factor substitution. While the insights of these economists and sociologists are interesting, they are relevant largely to the analysis of task-level and perhaps firm-level efficiency.

Perhaps the major lesson to be learned from Table 4 is that the difference between actual and best-practice productivity can be fruitfully decomposed into a number of components, each of which may imply the need for a different remedy. X-efficiency defined as the difference between actual and best-practice productivity is not a single phenomenon and cannot have one overarching explanation. Even at the firm and task level, the existing explanations of inefficiency are too general in the case of the older work and, in the recent work of Leibenstein,[20] lacking in attention to the detailed nature of production processes.

Thus, Leibenstein's work implies that such productivity reducing production characteristics as low yarn quality are the result of an equilibrium in which the psychological marginal benefits and cost of correcting defective quality are equal. An alternative view, more consistent with a considerable amount of recent work on the nature of production functions and the transfer of technology, posits that firm managers may not know precisely how to improve current operating efficiency or where to acquire the relevant information.[21] To obtain information requires a costly search procedure, expensive in both explicit outlays such as consultants fees and travel, and implicit costs such as the opportunities foregone while searching and spending time with consultants.

The search may yield advice that cannot readily be utilised unless the firm has already undergone a process of accumulating technically competent staff members with sufficient experience and technical background to adapt the advice to specific plant conditions. For example, the problems faced in producing high-quality yarn may originate at many points in the production process from inadequate blending of fibres to faulty draft rollers at the ring spindles. Only quite careful quality control procedures at each step and the use of this information by production managers will yield improved quality. Often consultants will offer such advice, yet firms may not have adequate staff nor testing equipment so that, even when the correct information is obtained, it cannot be acted upon.

Thus, firms may not have knowledge of how to correct current deficiencies or be unwilling to incur the costs to do so. The problems appear to me to be better formulated in terms of vague knowledge about the production process and the high marginal cost of correcting deficiencies where knowledge is obtained. Though it is not possible to establish directly the relevance of this view for Latin American firms in 1950, it is certainly salient for many firms I have visited in 1980 and the risk of extrapolation does not seem large. While it is certainly true that a more competitive atmosphere, resulting from the greater play of competitive forces following a liberalisation of trade regimes, would provide incentives for firms to begin a learning (and investment) process, the underlying assumption in Leibenstein's work that the route is low cost and relatively certain is not an accurate depiction of the problems facing most firms. Considerably more than a psychological equilibrium needs to be overcome.

CONCLUSIONS

The calculations presented above indicate that even in a relatively simple industrial process, LDC factories may be characterised by lower productivity than occurs in the advanced industrial countries. The potential increases in output to be obtained from moving towards best-practice productivity levels were quite significant even at the time of the beginning of the intensive import substitution phase in Latin America. Evidence I have analysed for other countries indicates that currently considerably larger benefits can be obtained. Improving productivity has the immediate benefit of increasing industrial output. In addition, to the extent that greater average productivity also results in an outward shift of the marginal product of labour curve it will have the effect of increasing industrial employment, though the magnitude will depend on the elasticity of the labour supply curve and the extent to which the curve itself shifts as a result of productivity based wage settlements. Given the difficulties encountered in both identifying labour intensive production methods and in changing the factor-price environment to induce their adoption, productivity improvements constitute a potentially useful means to increasing industrial employment as well as augmenting output. Whether it is possible to achieve such growth inexpensively is another question.

It is possible to obtain a more precise and illuminating view of the difference between actual and best-practice technology than has characterised many studies of industrial development. At least in the Latin American countries of 1950, worker inefficiency in spinning was a relatively small source of low total-factor productivity compared to features characterising the national economy and the industry (the failure to realise scale economies). In weaving, task-level inefficiency was of greater importance but other features were also quantitatively important. In both spinning and weaving, low levels of capital intensity constituted the major source of low labour productivity. Theories of motivation and incomplete labour contracts apply at best to a limited percentage of the difference between actual and best-practice productivity.

Differences in productivity were found between plants operating old and new spinning equipment and old (semi-automatic) and automatic looms, a finding corroborated in present day Kenya and the Philippines. Those spinning plants using older technology exhibited lower productivity, the opposite was true in weaving. While in spinning the better performance of new technology may have been due to better-managed firms systematically purchasing new equipment, this is only a hypothesis. The differences in efficiency associated with different technologies suggest that official evaluators and private purchasers of new equipment cannot assume simple uniform productivity differences between LDC and DC factories. Without knowledge of the probable differential productivities likely to be experienced in actual plant operation, the usefulness of much elegant social cost-benefit analysis of prospective industrial projects is considerably attenuated.

The conventional policy recommendation in the presence of productive inefficiency is the reduction or removal of protective measures including tariffs and quantitative restrictions. The decomposition approach provides some rough measure of the benefits to be derived from more narrowly focussed policies. Assuming that firms do not undertake productivity-enhancing actions because of the high private costs and uncertainty about the appropriability of the benefits (training workers), it follows that industry-wide training programmes as well as technical-trouble-shooting programmes financed by taxes on the industry may be appropriate. Simultaneously, lower marginal tax rates on increased levels of production achieved with existing numbers of workers and no new investment can provide incentives to take advantage of these programmes. Though such a policy package has to be analysed carefully, particularly to determine whether the incidence of taxes is such that the desired behaviour is likely to occur, it provides an alternative to politically difficult changes in trade regime.

ACKNOWLEDGEMENTS

The research for this paper was financed by RPO 671–77 of the World Bank. I have received helpful comments from Jeffrey James, J. R. Pack, Y. W. Rhee and Larry Westphal.

NOTES

1   For example, a choice by a textile producer (whether based on explicit cost calculus or ignorance) to engage in less-careful blending of fibres at the opening line may alter the quantity of output per card or the wastage rate.

2   UN (1951).

3   The basis for this statement is a comparison of the ECLA labour-output and machine-output ratios for standard products with those for 1950 for Lancashire contained in *Cotton and Allied Textiles*, The Textile Council (1969).

4   The differences are not statistically significant.

5   Calculation of total factor productivity utilising physical input measures for capital is best viewed as an approximate device to obtain general orders of magnitude. It provides the most useful comparisons when comparing plants using equipment of similar vintages whose technical characteristics are likely to be the same. Thus, comparisons among 1950 plants are meaningful whereas comparisons between 'old' and '1950' plants are not.

  To obtain a measure of total factor productivity it is assumed that, even after installation, the ratio in which workers and machines can be combined is described by a Cobb–Douglas production function, $1 = Az^{0.4} k^{0.6}$ where k is the spindle/output ratio and z is the operative hours/output ratio. That post-installation changes in factor proportions are possible is clear from the evidence though the precise parametric variation is unknown and is not solely a technical datum but reflects managerial ability as well. Using the preceding equation, the relative total factor productivity can be obtained as follows:

$$A_{BP} \, k_{BP}^{0.6} z_{BP}^{0.4} = A_A \, k_A^{0.6} z_A^{0.4}$$

  or

$$\frac{A_A}{A_{BP}} = \left(\frac{k_{BP}}{k_A}\right)^{0.6} \left(\frac{z_{BP}}{z_A}\right)^{0.4}$$

  where A denotes plant A and B denotes best practice. Different assumptions about the elasticity of output with respect to capital in the Cobb–Douglas or the use of a constant elasticity of substitution function with non-unitary elasticity would, of course, alter the results. The 0.6 figure is roughly the average non-wage share of output in textiles for 1950 or the closest available year for which data are available for the five countries shown in Table 2. A common value for the five was chosen, as the share of any one country in a single year may be affected by a number of special circumstances.

6   A measure of capital per unit of output was constructed from the capital/labour and labour/output ratios provided in the firm data. This was very highly correlated with an independent measure based on loom efficiency and loom speed (picks per minute) also presented.

7   There are many workers other than weavers involved in the weaving process, total hours being reflected in the unit labour requirements in Table 3, column 1.

8   This does not necessarily imply higher unit cost will be incurred when newer looms are utilised. Loom cost and other input productivity (raw materials, power) must also be considered.

9   For a summary see Hagen (1975), Chapter 6.

10   This is not to deny the potential insight provided by some of the theories, but simply to note the difficulty in choosing among alternative hypotheses. How, for example, does one test whether the absence of light switches in one's childhood home results in an absence of a mind 'set' predisposing workers to be efficient in tying simple knots on broken yarn.

11   Pack (1981).

12 Whether a firm provides such training will reflect its own profit calculus. Even though productivity may be improved by additional training, the firm will view this in terms of an investment decision and may find it more profitable not to undertake the required training costs.

13 Efficiency is used here to denote the percentage of time during which a machine is actually in production rather than stopped awaiting attention. Whether the increase in the labour/capital ratio is economically efficient will depend on relative factor costs and marginal productivities.

14 The dependence of the firm's productivity level on the size of the industry underlies the concept of irreversible dynamic scale economies developed by Marshall, as well as the great faith in the external effects of industrialisation in many early development plans.

15 See, for example, Hagen (1975) and Moore (1951). Leibenstein's work on X-efficiency applies to firm-level determinants of productivity as well as task level but does not consider the implications of the industry and national setting.

16 It is necessary to analyse the technology carefully to discriminate between shifts in production function and movements along it. Thus, low quality yarn that leads to high breakage rates will, *ceteris paribus*, decrease labour and machine productivity by roughly equal percentages. Though a firm may react to this phenomenon by increasing the labour machine ratio to restore the initial machine/output ratio, this substitution effect is separable from the initial neutral downward shift in the production function and constitutes a movement along the production function.

17 The ECLA study did not employ an explicit production theoretic framework and hence failed to realise that a higher-speed operation will necessitate, for a given quality of yarn, a greater labour input if the quantity of output per machine is to be maintained. Implicitly they have calculated the effect of greater machine speed on labour requirements as

$$\frac{(L/Q)_A}{(L/Q)_{BP}} = \frac{(K/Q)_A}{(K/Q)_{BP}}$$

so that running a machine in Latin America at 5 per cent greater speed than in the 'standard' plant is assumed to reduce labour input per unit of output by 5 per cent. This ignores the fact that an increase in speed, quality of fibre being unchanged, necessitates an increase in unit labour input if the capital/output ratio is to be reduced.

18 Although there were no plant economies still to be exploited, in calculating the results for Tables 2 and 3, the output elasticity for capital may have been too high given this discussion. Recalculation suggests that the effect of even a 20 per cent lower elasticity is small.

19 Older plants in Brazil and Mexico, not included in the table, were calculated to require an average increase in unit labour input of 10 and 6 per cent respectively in weaving due to inadequate specialisation.

20 Leibenstein (1978).

21 See Nelson and Winter (1974), and Dahlman and Westphal (1980).

REFERENCES

The Textile Council (1969) *Cotton and Allied Textiles*, Manchester.

Dahlman, Carl J. and Westphal, Larry E. (1982), Chapter Six of this book.

Hagen, E. E. (1975). *The Economics of Development*, Richard D. Irwin, Homewood, Illinois.

Leibenstein, Harvey (1978). *General X-Efficiency Theory and Economic Development*, Oxford University Press, New York.

Moore, Wilbert E. (1951). *Industrialization and Labor*, Cornell University Press, Ithaca.

Nelson, R. R. and Winter, S. (1974). Neoclassical vs. evolutionary theories of economic growth: Critique and prospectus, *Economic Journal*, 84, 336, pp. 886–905.

Pack, Howard (1981). Fostering the capital-goods sector in LDCs, *World Development*, 9, 3, pp. 227–50.

United National (1951). *Labour Productivity of the Cotton Textile Industry in Five Latin American Countries*, New York.

6 Technological effort in industrial development — an interpretative survey of recent research*

CARL DAHLMAN and LARRY WESTPHAL

INTRODUCTION

The exploitation of technological knowledge is central to the development process. Less-developed economies typically obtain this knowledge from more advanced ones rather than by creating it themselves. This is to be expected, given the vast pool of foreign technological knowledge available to them for exploitation. It does not follow, however, that technological effort has only a minor role to play in the process of industrial development. Such an inference would only be valid if technological effort were conceived narrowly, as the employment of resources solely for the purpose of creating new knowledge. In fact, however, resources are also needed for the task of learning to make effective use of existing knowledge. It is in this broader and more realistic sense that the term 'technological effort' is used in this chapter — i.e. as the employment of resources not just to create technological knowledge, but also to master it.

It is worth defining at the outset some items of terminology used in this chapter. We define *technological effort* as the use of technological knowledge together with other resources to assimilate or adapt existing technology and/or to create new technology. A *technology* may be defined as a collection of physical processes which transforms inputs into outputs, together with the social arrangements (i.e. organisational modes and procedural methods) which structure the activities involved in carrying out these transformations (see Brooks, 1980; Hannay and McGinn, 1980). Thus technology may be thought of as the translation into practice of *technological knowledge* (see Salter, 1960; pp. 13 ff), which we define as information about physical processes which underlies and is given operational expression in technology. Finally, *technological mastery*

* The authors are members of the Development Policy Staff of the World Bank. The views and interpretations expressed here are theirs and should not be attributed to the World Bank, to its affiliated organisations, or to any individual acting on behalf of these organisations. Peter Bocock edited the manuscript for publication.

is defined as operational command over technological knowledge. Mastery manifests itself in the ability to use knowledge effectively, and is achieved by the application of technological effort. In summary, all four terms may be dynamically linked as follows: *technological mastery* is the effective use of *technological knowledge*, through continuing *technological effort* to assimilate, adapt and/or create *technology*.

Industrial technology is sometimes misunderstood as being thoroughly documented in codified form — in 'blueprints', as one prevalent metaphor would have it. If this simplistic view were valid, technologies could be transferred and assimilated effortlessly, and a narrow conception of technological effort would be appropriate. Available evidence, however, belies this view, in that ostensibly identical technologies are employed with vastly unequal levels of technical efficiency (or productivity) in different economies, and even by different firms within a particular one (Leibenstein, 1966).

Thus, the shorthand expression 'transfer of technology' is misleading, to the extent that it suggests that technologies can in fact be transferred wholesale and in working order. Capital goods can be transferred, but capital goods alone do not constitute a technology; they represent only that part of the technology which is embodied in hardware. As noted above, the remainder is comprised of disembodied technological knowledge and related social arrangements — and although knowledge can be transferred, the ability to make effective use of it cannot be. This ability can only be acquired through indigenous technological effort, leading to technological mastery through human capital formation.

In this chapter we are primarily concerned with technological effort and mastery as they relate to physical processes.[1] It is important to bear in mind, however, that these physical processes are undertaken within a framework of social arrangements which condition their operation; it is sometimes necessary, therefore, to broaden the boundaries of the concept of mastery to encompass the development of appropriate social arrangements as well. This is particularly true when discussing choice of technology (see pp. 109–13).

The application of technological knowledge within industry can usefully be broken down into four broadly defined categories of activities. In the order in which mastery is typically thought to be achieved in the development of particular industrial processes, they are:

production engineering — which relates to the operation of existing plants;

project execution — which pertains to the establishment of new production capacity;

capital-goods manufacture — which consists of the embodiment of
technological knowledge in physical facilities and equipment;

research and development (R&D) — which consists of specialised
activity to generate new technological knowledge.

More will be said about the acquisition of mastery in these categories of
activity in later sections of this paper. Several general observations are
none the less in order at this point.

Engaging in any of the first three activities at a given level of mastery
does not involve technological effort. Those carrying out these activities
may, however, find themselves involved in the solution of technical
problems not previously encountered; such problem solving represents an
exercise of technological effort (i.e. the use of technological knowledge to
adapt technology), and may lead to a higher level of mastery. More generally,
technological effort is also used in the assimilation or generation of new
technological knowledge, and hence in the invention of new technologies,
which may either be adaptations of known technologies or radically new
ones. Seen in this light, R&D is merely an extreme case, with respect to its
degree of specialisation, of the acquisition of new technological knowledge.[2]

Technological mastery is a relative concept. Thus the extent of a firm's
or an economy's mastery can only be gauged in relation to that of other
entities. Moreover, mastery is not something which can be fully quantified.
For one thing, it is only possible to make unambiguous measurements of
comparative technical efficiency between entities which use ostensibly
identical technologies. But, as we hope to make clear, technological
mastery, even narrowly defined, involves far more than technical efficiency as conventionally understood. For example, an important aspect of
mastery is the ability to adapt technologies so as to make them better
suited to local circumstances — either by altering output characteristics to
reflect local needs and preferences, or by modifying input specifications
to permit the use of locally available materials and resources.

Moreover, even if an entity's overall level of mastery could be measured,
the separate contributions of the various types of mastery — corresponding
to the categories of activity listed above — cannot be, because it is difficult
to be precise about the interrelationships between them. This is particularly
unfortunate, because many of the questions about technological mastery
concern the relative importance of different types of mastery. For example:
Up to what point in a particular industry's development is mastery of
production engineering sufficient? What is the relationship between mastery

in production engineering and mastery in project execution? Is local capacity in capital goods manufacturing, or in R&D, necessary before socially warranted adaptations of technology can be made? These and similar questions can all be subsumed under a more general one: how should technological mastery in its various manifestations evolve in relation to industrial development? In addition to this question, the ensuing discussion deals with the question of how technological mastery is acquired.

The discussion is organised as follows. The rest of this section provides an introduction to the next four sections, which survey the main areas of past research on the relationship between technology and industrial development. The survey focusses on those findings which are of greatest relevance to understanding the acquisition of technological mastery, and is necessarily brief; thus it does not cover all the findings that might be relevant in different contexts. The sixth section reviews the evolution of technological mastery in relation to one country's industrial development. The case study is of the Republic of Korea, which has been chosen because of the authors' comparative ignorance of other economies and — more importantly — because of the interest that attaches to understanding the sources of its successful attainment of semi-industrial status. The concluding section highlights several important issues that have not yet been given adequate attention in empirical research.

Past research has been prompted less by interest in the acquisition of technological mastery than by uneasiness about problems associated with imports of technology — most notably about the failure of the industrial sector in most developing economies to generate expected levels of employment (see Eckaus, 1955). The question typically asked in this connection is whether methods of production developed in capital-abundant, labour-scarce industrial economies are appropriate for economies with the opposite relative factor endowments. In addition to addressing this question, research on choice of technology provides an empirically-grounded understanding of technology. For this reason, and because the ability to choose technology is a critically important aspect of technological mastery, we begin our survey with this research.

A central problem in choosing appropriate technologies is the lack of experience with which decision-takers typically approach the process of choice. If choice is to be informed, some prior experience would appear to be essential, but it is all too often absent; moreover, it appears that technological mastery in practice is more a function of indigenous problem solving at the plant level than of acquiring ready-made experience from abroad. The empirical evidence for local technological effort and experience as sources of mastery is discussed in the third section.

In addition to the problem of appropriate choice, reliance on imported technology also raises the problem of the ways in which technology is often transferred. The proposition that foreign technology may sometimes be acquired on terms that are highly unfavourable is well known. This problem, though important, is touched on only briefly in this paper. Less extensively studied but gaining increased attention is the near certainty that some forms of technology transfer have the effect of undesirably retarding the development of indigenous technological mastery.

This problem, which is examined in the fourth section, is generally perceived to be of secondary concern compared to the issue of the undue capital intensiveness of foreign technology, which is considered to have an immediate bearing on employment generation. But employment generation suffers from the capital intensiveness of foreign technologies only when they are inappropriately chosen.[3] The acquisition of increased technological mastery, on the other hand, is what ultimately underlies the movement of labour from lower to higher productivity employments. The effects of technology transfers on the development of local technological mastery are thus of central concern.

Issues of technological choice, the promotion of indigenous technological mastery and the need to guard against some of the more damaging effects of certain kinds of technological transfer lead naturally into consideration of the part which public policy in developing countries might appropriately play in this area. The fifth section reviews the available evidence on various policy approaches adopted by governments, discussing in particular the relative merits of explicitly interventionist instruments on the one hand, and the promotion of a general climate for industrial development conducive to purposive technological effort at the entity level on the other. Finally, the sixth section provides data on Korean experience and the last section offers some tentative conclusions and questions for further examination.

CHOICE OF TECHNOLOGY

Research on technology choice has first had to ascertain whether there are in reality any efficient alternatives to the 'best-practice' technologies of the industrial economies and, indeed, whether there is only one 'best-practice' technique for any individual activity.[4,5] It is now well established that there is scope for choosing between techniques with different levels of labour intensity and productivity, but that the scope for choice is by no means uniform. The conventionally accepted method for choosing between alternative techniques is to evaluate each in terms of its associated benefits and costs, using shadow prices which properly reflect the relative scarcities of different factors of production (Sen, 1962). The best (or appropriate) technique is that which has the highest net benefit.

Where the scope for choice is quite broad (e.g. in textile weaving), relatively labour-intensive techniques, rather than the current 'best-practice' techniques of the industrial economies, tend typically to be most appropriate for developing-country economies.[6] These techniques often represent an older vintage of technological best practice in the industrial economies. They can frequently be obtained by buying used equipment which no longer has profitable uses in the industrial economies because of changing relative factor scarcities.[7] In addition, capital-goods producers somewhere in the world may continue to embody these older vintages in new machinery and equipment. Sometimes, however, the best technique may be one which originated in a developing economy, usually as an adaption of a former 'best-practice' technique in the industrial economies. Much less frequently, it may be innovative and radically different from others currently in use.

For most activities in the majority of industries, no single technique is best for all circumstances. Local factor endowments and requirements vary widely — both among different developing economies and between them and the developed economies. As well as differing significantly in their relative use of capital and labour, techniques may also exhibit equally and sometimes more important differences in regard to intermediate input requirements and joint production possibilities. Thus it is important to ask whether the techniques actually chosen in particular circumstances are the appropriate ones. A number of studies have found that they often are not.

The choice of an appropriate technology depends on the availability of technological information and on the choice-maker's ability to utilise the information effectively in making evaluative judgements. Lack of technological mastery is sometimes wholly responsible for the selection of inappropriate techniques. The causes generally extend beyond poor technological mastery, however; institutional behaviour and relationships often also play a part. Lack of motivation to search for appropriate alternatives is occasionally to blame. For example, government policies, such as excessive protection from imports, can effectively destroy rational incentives for search. Such policies can also induce producers to search for the wrong kinds of techniques (e.g. when they create artificial distortions in factor prices). More generally, inappropriate techniques frequently result from the absence of incentives for producers to make choices which are consonant with social objectives. In addition, producers sometimes fail to respond to price signals, and base their choices on criteria that are independent of economic forces (Wells, 1973). Finally, it is often not possible to choose appropriate techniques for activities that produce related products without giving explicit recognition to the interdependence between these choices (see Rhee and Westphal, 1979). The way in which activities are organised among producers affects whether and how such interdependencies are taken into account and has a major influence on whether appropriate choices are made.

Past research also suggests that the implementation of appropriate technology choices often requires complementary investment to enhance local technological mastery, because technological parameters are highly sensitive to local circumstances and experience-related elements. Technological parameters for a specific plant should not be confused with 'engineering norms'. The latter, which serve as points of reference for various modes of engineering analysis, are values for the former which are valid under an assumed set of 'standard conditions' for plant establishment, maintenance, and operation. Depending on whether or not the technology is established and its use has been widely researched, they may be based on extensive experience with numerous plants or they may simply be engineering estimates, based only on theoretical analysis and experimentation within a controlled environment. In any event, they pertain to conditions, real or ideal, which generally differ in important respects from the conditions which confront a specific plant.

A variety of local circumstances can cause plant technological parameters to depart from engineering norms. For activities connected with plant establishment, these sources of variation may comprise the particular characteristics of the site and the stage of development of local construction and engineering services. For plant maintenance activities, they include the availability of skilled maintenance workers and the capabilities of local machine shops to produce replacement parts. For plant operation, they encompass such factors as the level of labour skills and the characteristics of the intermediate inputs to be used. Managerial ability affects virtually all technological parameters.

Many studies of technology choice have been based on engineering norms, but studies based on actual plant data suggest that factors of the kind listed above can affect the operational outcome of a particular choice in extremely important ways. An example taken from a study of the operation of Korean textile weaving firms (Rhee and Westphal, 1977) illustrates the point. Based on a careful survey of a number of establishments, the average number of semi-automatic looms tended by a single operator was found to be 5.1, with a standard deviation of 4.0 looms per operator. Statistical analysis which eliminated the influence of loom and fabric specific differences indicated that differences in firm-specific characteristics — that is, in management practices and labour quality — accounted for variations between establishments which averaged more than 1.5 looms per operator. The standard deviation of the output per loom in the same sample was more than 20 per cent of the average output per loom. Thus differences in firm-specific characteristics alone were estimated to produce variations which on average were roughly equal to the standard deviation. The high degree of unexplained variance in the underlying statistical analysis, which employed standard textile engineering relationships, is further evidence that the key technological parameters in textile weaving are far from being universal constants.

In sum, while the parameter values potentially achievable under the best possible conditions may be universally given, the extent to which these conditions are realised depends upon local circumstances and varies widely between plants (Leibenstein, 1966). Differences in management ability and labour quality are of special importance, but other factors such as differences in available infrastructure (e.g. machinery repair facilities or the physical properties of available intermediate inputs) may also significantly affect operational outcomes.

Variations in local circumstances typically affect alternative techniques in different ways, and may correspondingly affect the appropriateness of a particular choice. In textile weaving, for instance, the relevant choice is often between semi-automatic and automatic looms. The former embody a far more labour-intensive technique — suggesting that they might be an appropriate choice for a plant in a developing economy. The two techniques differ in other ways as well, however. For example, the probability of yarn breakage during weaving is higher with semi-automatic looms, and the skills of the weavers determine whether yarn breakages can be repaired without causing imperfections in the cloth. In this respect, the prevalence of low skill levels would suggest choice of the automatic technology; indeed, it is sometimes argued that automatic looms are the appropriate choice in all cases where weavers have not attained exceptionally high skill levels.[8] Similarly, the absence of local machinery repair and spare-part production facilities — or, more generally, low levels of technological mastery in these activities — discourages the selection of older-vintage, more labour-intensive techniques embodied in used equipment for which maintenance services and replacement parts can no longer be obtained from the original manufacturer.

Thus, mechanisation — that is, the substitution of capital for labour — often does permit the substitution of less-highly skilled for more-highly skilled labour, and smaller-scale and/or more labour-intensive production methods often do require a larger input of a different type of management and organisational skills. Nevertheless, to the extent that they can be changed or offset through investments to upgrade levels of technological mastery, local circumstances need not impose absolute constraints upon the adoption of what would otherwise be appropriate techniques. Labour and management skills can be augmented through investments in human capital formation; local machinery repair and spare-part production facilities can be developed. Alternative choices should thus be considered in conjunction with whatever complementary investments may be desirable or necessary for their successful implementation.

In short, social objectives are often best served by choosing techniques whose input requirements are most nearly in line with relative scarcities in the economy, supplemented as necessary by complementary investments to enhance local technological mastery in the relevant sector and the sectors which provide necessary inputs. This point is forcibly illustrated by research on the scope for capital–labour substitution in civil construction (Sud *et al.*, 1976). In the first phase of this research, labour-intensive methods were found to be technically feasible for a wide range of construction activities, achieving product standards equal to those of more capital-intensive methods. They were, however, found to be economically non-competitive, even at extremely low wage rates. In subsequent phases it was found that traditional methods could be made economically competitive, even at more reasonable wage rates, by adapting them through the use of improved tools, proper wage incentives, better project organisation and more careful work management. It thus proved possible to make the traditional methods competitive with more recent capital-intensive methods as a result of an injection of technological mastery from outside (in the form of the researchers' ability to design improved tools and to upgrade management practices in the use of the traditional technology).

EXPERIENCE AS A SOURCE OF TECHNOLOGICAL MASTERY

As the preceding discussion has indicated, technological mastery is not achieved by passively importing foreign technology. Research on the transfer of technology, which will be discussed in some detail in the next section, leads even more directly to the same conclusion. The extent of indigenous effort required for the successful assimilation of technology is most clearly demonstrated, however, by case studies of technological changes that have occurred over time in individual firms. Much of this research has been prompted by dissatisfaction with a simplistic view of technology, which excludes the possibility that indigenous effort directed towards technological change in less-developed economies is an important part of the industrialisation process.[9] Uneasiness about this view has led researchers to seek direct evidence of technological effort and change in the industrial sectors of developing economies, and to develop a more realistic conception of technological mastery.

The simplistic view holds that technology is something absolute and static: knowledge of a particular production technology either exists or it does not. A more realistic perception is that 'manuacturing technology is characterized by a considerable element of tacitness, difficulties in imitation and teaching, and uncertainty regarding what modifications will work and what will not' (Nelson 1979; p. 18). In other words, important elements of the technology appropriate to a particular situation can be acquired only through efforts to adapt existing technological knowledge. Any venture — for instance, the initiation of a new production activity — requires a great deal of iterative problem solving and experimentation as the original concept is refined and given practical expression. This sequential process lasts for as long as changes continue to be made in the operation of the venture. Research on technological change at the firm level has demonstrated that this process can continue indefinitely, that it can produce technological changes which greatly increase productivity, and that it can yield substantially increased technological mastery.

Dahlman and Fonseca (1978), for example, examined the technological history of an integrated Brazilian steel producer whose first plant was established with the help of Japanese steel makers. In order subsequently to increase the plant's annual production capacity, the firm gradually built up its technological mastery through a carefully managed process of selectivity importing technical assistance where needed to supplement of its own engineering efforts. As a result, the plant's capacity was more than doubled from its initial nominal rating by means of a sequence of capacity-stretching technological changes implemented over seven years. Because these changes required very little additional capital investment and no additions to the work force, they more than doubled the plant's total factor productivity. Moreover, as a result of the increased technological mastery which this process stimulated, the firm was subsequently able to design and execute further additions to its capacity and to sell technical assistance to other steel producers, principally in Brazil but elsewhere in Latin America as well.

More generally, firms in less-developed economies have been found to undertake substantial technological efforts in order to achieve a wide variety of technological changes.[10] These changes include, for example, stretching the capacity of existing plants through various adaptations (as in the case just cited), breaking bottlenecks in particular processes within existing plants, improving the use of by-products, extending the life of equipment, adjusting to change in raw material sources, and altering the product mix. Some of the firms studied appear to have followed explicit technological strategies aimed at specific long-term objectives. Others seem merely to have reacted defensively to changes in their circumstances, or to obvious needs to adapt imported technology. On the other hand, some firms have undertaken no appreciable technological effort and have consequently experienced no technological change.[11] As yet too few case studies exist for it to be possible to generalise about what determines the extent and direction of technological effort by individual firms. Nevertheless, it is apparent that economic forces have an impact, as do characteristics peculiar to individual firms and types of technology.

Some of the technological changes described in the case studies appear to be inconsistent with social objectives. For instance, when account is taken of the effort involved, some capacity-stretching technological changes may be socially more costly than the alternative of building additional plants. Teitel (1981) argues that this is true of some of the technological effort found in case studies of Latin American firms; he further speculates that this is the result of the inward-looking development strategies and protectionist policies that have been followed by the countries involved. Most of the available case studies do not include sufficiently detailed information to permit even a partial quantification of the costs and benefits of the technological changes they describe. It is clear, however, that most of the effort so far examined has had social benefits in excess of social costs, even though the extent of the excess is unknown.

Most of the technological changes uncovered in existing research can be characterised as minor, in the sense that they do not create radically new technologies but rather adapt existing ones. None the less, as shown by the example of the Brazilian steel plant, a sequence of minor technological changes can have a pronounced cumulative effect on productivity. In fact, the cumulative sequence of technological changes following the initiation of a new activity may have a greater impact on the productivity of employed resources than that produced by its initial establishment.[12] This possibility has not — to our knowledge — been explored, but it is consistent with what has been learned about the process of technological change in the industrialised countries.

Studies of major technological changes in developed countries have found it useful to distinguish between what Enos (1962) refers to as the alpha and beta stages. The former includes all efforts leading to and including the introduction of a radically new technology. The latter covers all of the subsequent minor technological changes undertaken to modify and adapt it. In his own analysis of the development and diffusion of six new petrochemical processes between 1913 and 1943, Enos found that the cumulative reduction achieved in production cost per unit during the beta stage was greater than the initial reduction obtained in the alpha state. Studies show that other major technological changes have followed the same pattern — the economic impact of replacing the old technology by the new is generally less than the cumulative impact of gradual improvements made afterwards.

From the standpoint of a developing economy, the assimilation of a technology newly imported from abroad is a major technological change. The initial transfer is parallel to Enos' alpha stage. The comparable beta stage is the subsequent, gradual improvement in the productivity with which the technology is used. The relative significance of the beta stage for a developing economy's assimilation of a new technology appears to be much greater than the analogy suggests, however. To introduce a radically new technology into the world (as in Enos' alpha stage) requires mastery of that technology; by contrast, to import a technology (as in the technology transfer analogy) does not require mastery of it, at least not at the outset. Rather, the case study research suggests that it is in the beta stage that most of the increase in developing economies' technological mastery is achieved.

Only part of the impact of this increase is reflected in higher productivity using the particular technology; much of the impact spills over into related activities. For example, the mastery gained in assimilating one technology enables greater indigenous participation in subsequent transfers of related technologies, thereby increasing the effectiveness with which they are assimilated. A number of semi-industrial economies have even exploited their mastery to export technologies on a continually expanding scale to other developing economies (Lall, chapter 8, this volume). In more general terms, the increased mastery which results from experience with previously established technologies contributes to an economy's capacity to undertake independent technological efforts, including replication or adaptation of foreign technologies as well as creation of new technologies.

Most of the technological changes so far uncovered can also be characterised as having been derived from plant-operating experience. Even within the confines of an existing plant, production processes do not remain static, certainly not if the firm is able to prosper within a relatively competitive environment. Production experience provides insight into how the operation of a plant can be altered to improve its peformance. In addition, circumstances vary constantly over the life of a plant: input prices change, demand patterns shift, new competitors emerge and so on. (The many possibilities for improving performance and reacting to changing circumstances can be appreciated by recalling that inputs and outputs alike are highly differentiated in most industries.)

This process of capitalising on experience and reacting to varying circumstances requires continued technological effort to modify existing processes, which in turn represents an important source of increased mastery in production engineering — the first category of technology activity distinguished in the first section. Moreover this form of technological effort often extends to changing the basic design of a plant when capacity is stretched or particular bottlenecks are broken. Thus it can also be a source of mastery in project execution — the second category in the typology provided above. Nevertheless, although the type of technological mastery acquired through plant operating experience may overlap somewhat with that exemplified in project execution, the overlap can never be complete.

To understand this point, it is worth listing the tasks involved in project execution and considering the types of experience which are required to perform them effectively. Project execution includes: [13]

preinvestment technical and economic feasibility studies, using readily available information to ascertain the viability of the project by examining alternative product mixes, input sources and specifications, plant scales and locations, and choices of production technology;

if viability is established, more *detailed studies*, using more specific engineering norms obtained from prospective sources of technology, leading to tentative choices among the alternatives considered previously and to refined estimates of capital requirements, personnel needs, cost and mode of financing, construction timetable, and the like;

if viability is confirmed, *basic engineering* to supply the core process technology, by establishing the process flow through the plant and the associated material and energy balances (as well as designing specifications and layouts for major items of equipment and machinery);

detailed engineering, to supply the peripheral technology, by providing complete specifications of equipment and materials, detailed architectural and civil engineering plans, construction specifications, installation specifications for all equipment, and so on;

procurement, which includes the choice of equipment suppliers and firms to construct and assemble the plant, coordination and control of the various subcontractor's activities, and inspection of work in progress;

training of the plant's prospective personnel at all levels in various aspects of the plant's operation and maintenance, often through experience working temporarily in a similar plant elsewhere;

construction and assembly of the plant;

startup of operation, to attain predetermined project-specific norms and to complete the provision of training in the plant's operation; and

trouble-shooting, to overcome the various design problems encountered during the early part of the plant's life.

Mastery of almost all these tasks involves extensive 'learning by doing'. Only for pre-investment feasibility studies does formal education alone suffice to import the skills required. For the other tasks, the attainment of technological mastery requires previous experience in the same or closely related activities. Basic engineering, for example, calls for highly specialised knowledge of the core processes, which can frequently be acquired only through applied R&D, including pilot-plant experimentation. Startup of operation often demands less familiarity with the principles underlying the core processes, but entails knowledge that can come only from previous production engineering experience in operating similar plants. Post-startup trouble shooting calls for somewhat more knowledge of the principles, but not necessarily as much as is involved in basic engineering. Detailed studies (the second task in the sequence) do not demand precise knowledge of the industry. By contrast, many of the individual detailed engineering tasks — for example, providing architectural and civil engineering plans that conform to requirements determined in the basic engineering stage — require no specialised knowledge whatsoever of the particular industry, but instead require other forms of specialised knowledge such as ability to design structures and civil works.

Production engineering and project execution are not the only broadly defined uses of technological knowledge. Although they are not well incorporated into the existing research on technological change in developing countries, the two other categories of activity distinguished in the first section should not be overlooked. One is capital goods manufacture, which consists of embodying technology in machines. The other is specialised R&D to develop new products or processes.[14] These activities have strong links to production engineering and project execution, because to some degree they are prompted and given direction by the problems and opportunities that arise in connection with production and investment. Indeed, the kinds of technological effort associated with production engineering and project execution are frequently indistinguishable in concept from those involved in R&D.[15] Likewise, these efforts often involve changes in the design of capital goods. Relatively little is known, however, about capital goods producers and specialised R&D performers as initiators of technological change, or about their roles in successful industrialisation.[16] The rest of this paper therefore focuses on the achievement of mastery in production engineering and project execution; the discussion concentrates on how the development of this mastery is affected by the ways in which foreign technology is obtained, and by government policies regarding technology transfers and industrial development.

RELIANCE UPON TRANSFERS OF TECHNOLOGY

There are many means whereby less-developed economies can have access to foreign technological knowledge. Among them are various activities in which foreigners play a passive role, with the subsequent translation of this knowledge into technology being done indigenously. These activities include sending nationals abroad for education, training, and work experience; consulting technical and other journals; copying foreign products etc. As Korean experience indicates (see later dicussion), these kinds of activities are tremendously important channels of information; almost invariably, some of the technological knowledge underlying new industrial initiatives in developing countries comes via one or other of them. By contrast, transfers of technology constitute a crucially different class of activities, in that the translation of technological knowledge into operational form is made by foreigners.

Whether technology should be obtained locally or from abroad ought to depend upon the relative costs and benefits to the recipient of acquiring it from different sources. In this connection, the degree of local mastery in the various uses of the underlying technological knowledge is of critical importance. If little previous effort has been made to acquire mastery of the specific technology, reliance upon domestic sources will entail either the replication (and perhaps also the adaptation) of foreign technology or the creation of new technology through indigenous effort. Local development, however, is rarely the most effective way of initially obtaining all of the necessary elements of a technology. More generally, an economy's capacity to provide the various elements depends upon the stage of development of the relevant sector and those closely related to it. Firms starting up or already engaged in traditional or well-established activities may often be able to acquire additional elements of technology relatively easily — either through their own developmental efforts or through the diffusion of expertise from other domestic firms. The hiring of personnel with previous work experience elsewhere plays an extremely important part in the diffusion of expertise among firms, as does the interchange of information among suppliers and users of individual products, especially in the case of intermediate products and capital goods. Firms engaged in newly or recently initiated activities typically have much less opportunity to take advantage of previous experience (if any), or of diffusion or explicit transfers from other domestic firms.[17] Firms in such a position are likely to find it more cost-effective to rely heavily on foreign suppliers of technology. Even in relatively highly developed sectors, selective transfers from abroad may be equally cost effective aids to the process of increasing productivity.

Transfers of technology take place in a large number of ways and often incorporate not only the translation of technological knowledge into information about operational processes but other elements as well. Imports of machinery — an extremely important mode of technology transfer — represent a case in point, in which the additional element is the embodiment of the technology in hardware. Another example is direct foreign investment when used as a means to acquire technology, with the additional elements typically being financial capital, management, and marketing.

Many modes of transfer do not involve explicit and separate payment for transfer. This is frequently the case in the kinds of transactions instanced above which incorporate additional elements, as it is with indirect technology transfers. As an example of the latter, exporting firms often receive valuable free technical assistance as a result of their dealings with foreign buyers; in the conduct of their normal business operations, these buyers frequently provide various forms of assistance in such areas as the upgrading of product specifications and the achievement of improved quality control (see the later description of Korea's experience).

Significant though they may be, indirect transfers have not received much attention in past research. There has likewise been very little research into the acquisition of foreign technological knowledge through activities in which foreigners play a passive part. Information about these sources of knowledge is hard to obtain while the problems associated with direct transfers in which foreigners play an active part are more easily inferred. Thus past research has concentrated on transfers made through transactions for which a primary motivation is clearly to purchase technology.

Explicit transactions to transfer technology without any other elements take many forms. Among the simplest forms of transaction are contracts for the services of individuals or consulting companies to provide individual elements of technology (for example, to undertake specific design or process engineering tasks, to give technical assistance during various phases of the establishment and operation of a plant, or to provide technical information services). Other transactions include licensing and trademark agreements which transfer particular proprietary product and process designs.

The most all-inclusive form of transaction is a turnkey contract under which a general contractor is hired to assume complete responsibility for project execution, with the obligation to deliver an operating plant. Transfers of technology embedded in direct foreign investment are sometimes accomplished through turnkey contracts given to independent general contractors, but more often it is the foreign investor who acts as the general contractor. Either way, with respect to the division of labour between local and foreign technological effort, direct foreign investment is usually indistinguishable from a turnkey contract. Turnkey contracts, together with their counterpart in the form of direct foreign investment, are perhaps the most frequent mode of transferring technology for activities which are entirely new to an economy. Even if turnkey contracts are not used, the scope and scale of technology transfers involving the creation of a new industry are almost always greatest in the case of the establishment of the first, or the first few, plants.

For policy-making purposes, there are two critical distinctions to be made among the various forms of transactions to transfer technology. The first is between transactions which simply transfer technological knowledge and ones which incorporate other components as well. As we have indicated, these other components sometimes include proprietary elements, such as trademarks and brandnames; they may also involve transfers of capital, management, and marketing. The significance of this distinction will be indicated further below. The second distinction relates to whether the transaction involves multiple elements of technology transfer.

The problem confronted in the more all-inclusive forms of technology transfer is that tasks which could be performed locally are carried out by foreigners. This can increase project costs, because the services could have been provided more cheaply by local suppliers, and because intimate knowledge of local conditions may be required to optimise plant design. Moreover, failure to use qualified local suppliers precludes the possibility of local accumulation of human capital through experience-based learning. The economy is thereby deprived of experience that is directly relevant to the industry's subsequent development. (It is also worth noting that developing countries' inability to make effective use of such human capital as they have acquired is a contributing factor to the loss of highly trained local personnel through the 'brain drain'.)

In addition, turnkey contracts often deliver a plant together with instructions for operating it under the conditions assumed in its design, but fail to provide the recipient with an understanding of the full details of how the plant operates or of why it operates as it does. This hampers the recipient entity's ability to improve plant operating productivity or to adapt to changes which may occur over time in the circumstances that affect how the plant is best operated. As a result, the plant is likely to operate at lower productivity than could optimally have been achieved (with the entity probably also continuing to depend excessively upon foreign mastery for technical assistance in troubleshooting); alternatively, the entity will need to make greater efforts to achieve internal mastery than would have been needed if more complete information had initially been provided. These outcomes can be avoided by having the entity's personnel participate in every phase of project execution, even if only as intelligent observers who merely follow the work in progress and learn which are the relevant questions in gaining mastery of the 'hows' and 'whys'. Some foreign technology suppliers may be unwilling to permit such participation, however, for fear that it will transfer too much of their technological mastery.

The crucial role of experience in acquiring technological mastery has already been emphasised. Experience produces not only increased technological mastery but also greater productivity in supplying given elements of technology. Unless carried out with the explicit objective of doing so, technology transfers associated with project execution do not necessarily provide the experience which is critical to the development of indigenous technical and engineering services. For example, it has already been suggested that conventional turnkey contracts are not intended to provide mastery in any of the phases of project execution, and that they may fail even to transfer an adequate understanding of production engineering. In short, imports of technology need not transfer any of the technological mastery needed for the subsequent replacement of foreign by local expertise.

Given this state of affairs, it may be asked whether domestic firms have adequate incentives to take appropriate advantage of opportunities to increase domestic mastery through experience in supplying technology from local resources. Domestic firms may prefer to import technology when social objectives would dictate using local suppliers because of the increased experience which the latter would gain. In turn, where imports are consistent with social objectives, domestic firms may prefer methods of technology transfer which do not adequately provide for the kinds of local participation that would increase domestic technological mastery. Even the simplest form of participation — intelligent observation — entails a cost.

A rational firm seeking to acquire technology seeks to pay the lowest possible price consistent with having the greatest possible assurance of obtaining a technology which is reliable and well-suited to its circumstances. It is unlikely to use inexperienced local resources or to provide for their participation unless it expects to gain a long-run benefit that more than compensates for greater risks and/or higher costs in the short-run. The social benefit of increased technological mastery, however, generally exceeds the benefit which an individual firm can expect to capture; there are many avenues by which technological mastery can diffuse to other firms, and not all of these avenues are under the control of the firm that finances the initial acquisition. In addition, the firm may value the benefits that it does capture at less than their true social worth; likewise, the cost of acquiring technological mastery as seen from the firm's perspective may exceed the true social costs. Unless influenced by some form of public intervention, a firm acting alone may therefore not find it in its individual interest to take advantage of opportunities to increase domestic technological mastery as much as social objectives would dictate.[18]

The motives that underlie the packaging of multiple technological elements and of various non-technological components within a single transaction are different but no less powerful. Participants on both sides of the transaction benefit from packaging in so far as it increases their respective net returns. Thus, to the extent that packaging lowers the total cost of the undertaking,[19] and to the extent that the supplier and the recipient share in the savings, each has an incentive to accept a compound transaction. More than simply cost reduction may be involved, however, particularly as regards the inclusion of non-technological components.

What ultimately enables certain suppliers to impose packaging is their possession of some form of monopoly power, such as that conferred by a well-known brandname. In such cases, the price paid for the package necessarily includes a monopoly profit and can in that sense be considered 'excessive'. The principal motive behind the recipient's acceptance of the package is typically the desire to acquire the same monopoly power, at least within the domestic market. There is a convergence of interests between the domestic firm and the foreign supplier to agree on a compound transaction, since the domestic firm can offset the promise of monopoly profits against the excessive price paid.

Thus some compound transactions which transfer more than just technology are not socially desirable even though they are clearly in the interests of the domestic firms involved. That is, the motives which give rise to technology imports can sometimes be at variance with social objectives, because of the characteristics of the production which they make possible and the monopoly power which they confer.[20] Moreover, as indicated above, these motives can also be at variance with social objectives concerning the development of indigenous technical and engineering services.

GOVERNMENT POLICIES

Research on transfer of technology has shown that government intervention can serve several important purposes, including the following: to foster the choice of the most appropriate among alternative foreign techniques; to obtain imports of technology on the best possible terms; to avoid compound transactions which include components that are socially undesirable; to promote, where appropriate, the use of local suppliers rather than foreign sources; and to ensure, where technology is imported, that the method of transfer provides for adequate local participation designed to increase domestic technological mastery.[21] Some of these aims can be achieved through defensive measures, such as protecting local suppliers from import competition. Others can only be attained by taking positive steps, such as requiring local participation so as to ensure adequate absorption of imported technology.

Governments of many developing countries have intervened in transfers of technology, generally by imposing defensive measures to control the terms on which transfers are made and to protect local suppliers. These measures discriminate strongly against compound transactions and in favour of single-element technology transfers. They also prohibit foreign suppliers from imposing undesirable conditions — such as restrictions on exports produced using the technology, or obligations to make available to the supplier any improvements made in the technology. These measures often have the explicit aim of offsetting the asymmetry that exists in the relative bargaining strengths of foreign technology suppliers and domestic recipients; they may also be complemented by various forms of positive assistance in the negotiation process. The asymmetry results in large measure from the very differences in technological knowledge and access to information that the transfer is meant — at least in part — to remove. As a way of offsetting these differences, various governments also provide assistance to increase the knowledge available to technology-seeking firms. To promote the use of local suppliers, some governments maintain registries which give information about suppliers' capabilities. In a number of countries, local suppliers are protected by requirements that the prospective importer provide evidence that the desired technology cannot be obtained domestically.

It is difficult to evaluate the impact of these measures. Their proponents assert that they have reduced expenditures on imported technology and have helped to eliminate undesirable conditions without reducing the inflow of desirable technology imports (see Stewart, 1981), It is unclear, however, whether changes in the formal terms of transfer have been counterbalanced by the addition of informal terms, or whether the imposition of controls over formal terms has reduced the willingness of foreigners to supply technology. Positive assistance to increase the technological knowledge available to domestic firms, and to enhance their bargaining strength and negotiating ability, has undoubtedly had beneficial results, but their extent is unknown. In turn, no systematic body of evidence currently exists which could be used to assess the effects of promoting the development of local technology suppliers, whether by protection or by other means. Indeed, there is very little basis for judging what role the government should appropriately play in the development of local technological capacity.

To address this question, cross-country comparative evidence is needed which shows how government policies have affected the achievement of technological mastery, and how mastery of the various uses of technological knowledge is related to the attainment of social objectives through industrialisation. The research that comes closest to providing such evidence is the Science and Technology Policy Instruments (STPI) project, the results of which are summarised in Sagasti (1978).[22] This project sought to establish the comparative efficacy of different government policies aimed at creating technological mastery. It focused on what were termed 'explicit' policy instruments. These included the creation of technological infrastructure through institution building; the establishment of science and technology plans; promotion of the use of local technology suppliers; the provision of fiscal incentives and direct subsidies to various kinds of technological effort; the regulation of technology imports through measures of the kind discussed above; and other public actions directly in support of indigenous technological effort.

The central conclusion of the research was that explicit instruments had far less impact on technological change and the acquisition of technological mastery than did other policies (for example, related to trade, credit allocation, investment licensing, and the like) which affected industrial development more generally.[23] Explicit instruments did, however, appear to assume increasing importance as industrial development progressed.

It is unclear why the explicit instruments were found to have relatively little effect. It is possible that their ineffectiveness was a consequence of another finding of the research, which was that these instruments tended to be poorly implemented and often to work at cross-purposes. Thus, if properly applied, explicit instruments might have a much greater impact. It may equally be true, however, at least up to a certain stage of industrial development, that what is most important is to gain mastery in production engineering and project execution, that such mastery derives principally from technological efforts related to the experience of industrial firms, and that what matters most in this regard is the general climate for industrial development. These possibilities were not explicitly considered at the outset of the STPI project; consequently, they cannot be assessed on the basis of the information gathered by it, though the project did include a number of somewhat sketchy case studies that showed considerable technological effort at the firm level.

Other research, described in earlier sections of this paper, has found that firms in developing countries acquire increased technological mastery by engaging in purposive technological effort to assimilate and adapt technology, an effort which typically takes place in relation to experience gained in production engineering and project execution. These findings, cannot, however, be taken to show that experience *necessarily* leads to greater technological mastery and thereby to beneficial technological changes. Whether experience produces such results depends crucially on the extent and character of purposive effort to capitalise upon it, and this effort is by no means automatically forthcoming. Whether and in what directions the effort takes place depends – at least in part – on the combined impact of a wide variety of incentive policies which condition the climate for industrial development. Moreover, it is by no means certain that the technological changes which follow from such effort are always consistent with social objectives, or that sufficient effort will be forthcoming in all appropriate directions. Discussion of this last point is deferred to the concluding section.

KOREAN TECHNOLOGICAL MASTERY

Historical evidence forms the principal basis for considering how technological mastery might appropriately evolve in relation to industrial development. The Republic of Korea – often referred to as South Korea and in this Chapter simply as Korea – provides an instructive example. The broad outlines of Korea's remarkably successful achievement of semi-industrial status are well known and need not be repeated here. Less well known are what Korea's technological mastery consists of and how it was acquired. Available evidence on these points is summarised below for the period from the end of the Korean War until approximately 1978.[24]

The fundamental elements of Korea's industrialisation have been directed and controlled by nationals. Foreign resources have made substantial contributions, but the transactions involved have typically been at arm's length. Thus, although Korea has relied quite heavily on capital inflows, these have overwhelmingly been in the form of debt, not equity, and technology has been acquired from abroad largely through means other than direct foreign investment. The purchase of technology through licensing agreements has been of modest importance as the initial source of process technology. Machinery imports and turnkey contracts have been of much greater consequence in the transfer of technology, and a tremendous amount of expertise has been obtained as a result of the return of Koreans from study or work abroad. Moreover, in only a few sectors, such as electronics, have Korean exports depended critically upon transactions between related affiliates of multinational corporations or upon international subcontracting.[25]

Korea's success in assimilating technologies acquired through arm's-length transactions is in part explained by the nature of technology and product differentiation in the industries on which its growth has crucially depended. Many of these industries — such as plywood or textiles and apparel — use relatively mature technologies; in such cases, mastery of well-established and conventional methods, embodied in equipment readily available from foreign suppliers, is sufficient to permit efficient production.[26] The products of many of these industries are either quite highly standardised (plywood, for example) or differentiated in technologically minor respects and not greatly dependent on brand recognition for purchaser acceptance (textiles and apparel, for example). Thus, in most of the industries that have been intensively developed, few advantages are to be gained from licensing or direct foreign investment as far as technology acquisition and overseas marketing are concerned.

None the less, exceptions exist, of which electronics is perhaps the most notable. This is an industry in which technology is changing rapidly worldwide, product differentiation is based on sophisticated technological expertise, and purchasers' brand preferences are evident. Given these characteristics, it is not surprising to find that in this case Korea has relied extensively on direct foreign investment to establish production, particularly for export, and has so far failed to gain local mastery of many key aspects of production engineering. It should be noted, however, that the electronics and certain chemicals industries are unique in Korea in their almost exclusive reliance on direct foreign investment for acquiring the very latest technology and market access.

In other industries, where technology is similarly proprietary, a number of examples attest to the fact that Korean industry has managed to initiate, and in most cases to operate successfully, a variety of 'high-technology' industrial activities by means of licensing and turnkey arrangements. To cite two cases: Korea used arrangements of this kind to acquire the most modern shipbuilding technology in the world, and to incorporate the most recent technological advances in its integrated steel mill.

More generally, Korea's recent experience in promoting technologically sophisticated industries indicates that their development may involve greater reliance on licensing as a way of acquiring technology. This is not a matter of absolutes, however; it remains possible to substitute for licensing by replicating foreign technology through local effort. The difference is simply that the cost of doing so is higher in the industries which have been promoted in more recent years. It is unclear, however, whether overseas firms will be willing to license technology without restricting its use. They may impose restrictions on the sales of licensed products, prefer to give access to technology only through direct foreign investment, or even deny access. It is equally unclear whether the shift also implies greater dependence on licensing and direct foreign investment for access to overseas markets, if only to gain rapid consumer acceptance through the use of familiar brand names.

Nevertheless, there can be no doubt that Korea's past strategy for gaining technological mastery has relied heavily on indigenous effort through capitalising on experience and emphasising the selective use of foreign resources. In industries for which process technology is not product-specific, the initial achievement of mastery has frequently permitted the copying of foreign products as a means of enlarging technological capacity. The mechanical engineering industries, among others, afford many examples; such processes as machining and casting, once learned by producing one item, can readily be applied in the production of others. One case which has been closely studied is textile machinery, in particular semi-automatic looms for weaving fabric (Rhee and Westphal, 1977). In this as in some other cases, Korean manufacturers have not only been able to produce a capital good that meets world standards, albeit of an older vintage; they have, in addition, adapted the product design to make it more appropriate to Korean circumstances. (The adapted semi-automatic looms fall between ordinary semi-automatic and fully automatic looms in terms of the labour intensity of the weaving technology they embody.) In other industries in which technology is more product-specific, such as chemicals, mastery of the underlying principles has permitted greater local participation in the subsequent establishment of closely allied lines of production.

Export activity has proved to be a very important means of acquiring technological mastery. As a result of exporting, Korean firms have enjoyed virtually costless access to a tremendous range of information, diffused to them in various ways by the buyers of their exports. The resulting minor technological changes have significantly increased production efficiency, changed product designs, upgraded quality, and improved management practices. Exporting thus appears to have offered a direct means of improving productivity, in addition to the indirect stimulus derived from trying to maintain and increase penetration in overseas markets. This beneficial externality of export activity has gone largely unnoticed in the literature on trade and development. The Korean experience indicates that it is very real, and further suggests that it may in part explain why countries following an export-led strategy have experienced such remarkable success in their industrialisation efforts.

Furthermore, the fast pace of Korea's industrial growth has permitted rapid rates of technological learning because of the short intervals between the construction of successive plants in many industries. In some industries, including synthetic resins and fibres, the first plants were often built on a turnkey basis and on a scale which was much smaller either than that warranted by the size of the market or that which would exhaust scale economies. Construction of the second and subsequent plants — at scales much closer or equal to world scale[27] — followed quickly, with Korean engineers and technicians assuming a gradually increasing role in project execution. To this extent, Korea's technological mastery in these industries can be said to extend beyond production engineering to project execution.

Korea's experience demonstrates that indigenous entrepreneurs can be relied upon to identify profitable ventures, to exercise selectivity in the use of foreign resources, including technology transfers, and to manage industrial undertakings. But Korea's entrepreneurial talent has not been deployed in industry alone; government also has benefited. Indeed, Korea's remarkably successful industrialisation would not have occurred if the government had not designed and implemented effective policies to foster industrial dynamism.

Korea's experience further demonstrates that a high level of technological mastery in all aspects of the uses of technological knowledge

is not required for sustained industrial development. This is evident from
the fact that its mastery has progressed much further in production
engineering than in project execution. In addition, Korea has relied on
foreign suppliers for necessary capital equipment and has only recently
embarked on a concerted programme of import substitution in the capital-
goods sector. None the less, Korean industry has acquired and exercised
the capacity to choose the technologies to be imported, and Koreans have
become increasingly involved in other phases of project execution. Fundamentally, however, Korea has become a significant industrial power mainly
as a result of its proficiency in production. It thus appears that mastery of
production engineering alone is nearly sufficient for the attainment of an
advanced stage of industrial development.

Contemporary pronouncements about the nature of, and the constraints
imposed by, the existing international economic order are contradicted by
Korea's experience. In the context of calls for a 'new international
economic order', it is frequently alleged that existing international markets
are non-competitive, and that developing countries are either denied
access to technology and overseas markets or are granted it only on highly
unfavourable terms. It is further asserted that foreigners exercise the
initiative in transfers of technology and in the organisation of export
activity. If true, these assertions would imply a severe constraint on
industrial development. Far from supporting them, Korea's experience
shows them to be false for many important industries.

To summarise, in the process of its industrialisation, Korea has effectively
assimilated various elements of foreign technology, but without much
direct foreign participation in its industrial sector. Assimilation was
achieved through a succession of technological efforts over time, largely
undertaken by domestic firms to extend their technological mastery and
to accomplish minor technological changes. Korea's experience supports
the argument that indigenous effort is of overriding importance in the
achievement of technological mastery, but the causal forces that contribute both to the presence and to the effectiveness of indigenous effort
have yet to be uncovered.

CONCLUSION

This chapter has stressed the role of technological effort in relation to
production engineering and project execution as a source of technological
mastery. Such effort involves not only assimilation but also adaptation of
technology. Foreign and indigenous technologies alike can be adapted in
numerous ways to make them better suited to local circumstances. This

fact gives rise to an important question: is the technological effort which takes place sufficient to ensure that all socially warranted adaptations are made? [28]

As indicated in the earlier dicussion, it is clear that individual firms sometimes undertake technological efforts which are inconsistent with social objectives and conversely that they often do not have sufficient incentives to undertake socially warranted technological efforts. Though it is only one of many determinants, market structure exerts a strong influence on the extent and direction of technological effort. Socially wasteful effort tends to be associated with either the exercise or the pursuit of monopoly power. By contrast, producers in highly competitive industries are unlikely to engage in enough technological effort; uncertainty, indivisibilities in the effort required, and inability to appropriate the full benefits all contribute to the latter result (Arrow, 1962).

Government intervention designed to promote socially warranted adaptations can take many forms. Producing firms can be encouraged by subsidies or other means either to undertake technological efforts directly or to contract for them. In addition, the development of specialised agents of technological change can be promoted. In following the latter approach, the governments of a number of less-developed economies have concentrated on establishing publicly-supported R&D institutes to undertake scientific and technological research. Underlying the creation of many of these institutions was the belief that technological change is a linear process which starts with R&D and proceeds by stages automatically to commercial application, with at least the initial stages being quite distinct and easily separable from production activity. R&D institutes were expected to be able readily to identify where their services would have the greatest payoff and to generate the requisite technological changes. Subsequent empirical evidence has shown that the initial faith in the efficacy of creating specialised R&D agents was misplaced, as the newly established R&D institutes almost universally had virtually no contact with or impact upon producing firms. [29]

The adaptation (and creation) of technology cannot be separated from its use. Warranted adaptations must first be identified before they can be implemented. To identify them requires experience-based familiarity with both the technology and local circumstances. Moreover, warranted adaptations emerge in sequential fashion over time, as more is learned and as local circumstances change. Foreign entities are not well placed either to gain the necessary degree of familiarity with changing local circumstances or to make continued use of such familiarity as they may possess. Hence indigenous entities which are able to adapt technologies can be expected to play an important role in the process of industrialisation.

To what extent should or must this role be played by specialised agents of technological change? The past failings of R&D institutes notwithstanding, particular circumstances can provide a strong rationale for their establishment, as long as their activities are properly linked with those of producing firms. For example, centralised publicly-supported R&D may be warranted to adapt traditional indigenous technologies employed in highly competitive industries characterised by small-scale production. Such technologies may not continue to be viable unless adapted, and properly adapted they may be better suited to local circumstances than are competing foreign technologies. A general case can also be made for publicly-supported promotion of the local production of capital goods, since there appear to be many socially warranted adaptations which cannot be accomplished without some degree of local mastery in the embodiment of technology in capital goods.[30]

Among the manufacturing sectors of the industrially advanced economies, R&D activity is concentrated not only in the industries that produce capital goods but also in those that produce the major intermediate inputs (chemicals, fabricated materials) used elsewhere. Underlying this pattern of specialisation are close relationships involving frequent information interchanges between the suppliers and users of producers' goods. This suggests that it may not be enough for developing economies' governments to rely solely on explicitly targeted policies to correct for differences between private and social returns to the development of different types of technological mastery. Government action may also be required to promote and maintain an environment conducive to decentralised technological effort, together with a market structure in which technological changes are rapidly diffused. Furthermore, it must not be forgotten that the acquisition of technological mastery is an element of a country's human capital development – although the implications of this fact for government involvement in formal education and experience-based skill acquisition lie beyond the scope of this paper.

Finally, the dependence of an economy's fund of technological expertise on the mastery of previously introduced technologies has important implications. It means that initial decisions about choices of technology and degrees of local involvement in investments to implement them are critical determinants of the directions in which an economy's technological mastery will develop. Although the empirical evidence derived from research is not yet comprehensive enough to provide a clear basis on which to make prescriptions about how an economy's technological mastery ought to evolve in relation to its industrial development, it seems clear that a synergistic relationship can develop between them, with advances in each prompting new gains in the other. As Korean experience demonstrates, however, high indigenous levels of all types of technological mastery are not necessary for the initial stages of industrial development; in the Korean case, a mastery which has been mainly confined to production engineering has been sufficient. The Korean example also suggests that by relying on foreign sources of technology, it is possible to choose a technology without having first mastered its use. In the same way, it is also possible to use a technology without having the mastery required to replicate it through project execution, or to manufacture the capital goods involved.

Nevertheless, it should be remembered that, just as the initial choice of production method may greatly constrain the direction of technical change, so the kinds of technological effort in which an economy acquires experience may constrain the type of technological mastery which it can develop. Furthermore, there is an important difference between attaining mastery in relation to given circumstances and in attaining the capacity to adapt to changing circumstances. The objective of acquiring technological mastery is not simply to produce in the present; it is equally to be able to adapt technology and to anticipate changes in world and domestic markets. Thus it is also necessary to develop the capacity to innovate in various respects. It is unclear how far this capacity can be developed solely on the basis of production engineering or project execution experience.

The effects of different policies on the development of indigenous technological mastery have yet to be ascertained. Further research to uncover historical evidence from different country cases is necessary to reach any soundly-based generalisations about the determinants of the extent and appropriateness of technological effort in different directions. Such generalisations are needed to formulate policies that will direct the attainment of increased technological mastery in ways which are in line with social objectives.

NOTES

1   Under this narrow definition, a firm or an economy could have a great deal of technological mastery and yet not deploy it effectively, owing to inappropriate organisational or procedural factors.
2   Nelson (1980) provides an illuminating discussion that relates the possibility of specialisation in the acquisition of new technological knowledge to the feasibility of codifying technology.
3   Up-to-date foreign technology is frequently the appropriate choice in activities

that are inherently capital-intensive, such as the core processes of chemical fertiliser production. Assuming that the products involved should be produced rather than imported, employment generation can be said to suffer from the use of foreign technology in these activities only in the sense that it would be preferable if efficient and more highly labour-intensive alternatives existed.

4   'Efficient' has a very definite meaning in this context. An efficient technique, or combination of inputs, is one that uses less of at least one input than is used by any alternative technique to produce a given level of output. A technique may be efficient at some, but not at other, levels of output.

5   The principal centres for this research have been the World Employment Program of the International Labor Organization, the David Livingston Institute of Overseas Development at the University of Strathclyde in Great Britain, and the Economic Growth Center at Yale University in the United States, though important research has also been carried out by numerous individuals having various institutional affiliations. See Westphal (1978) for a policy-focussed survey and list of references.

6   See Pack (1980) for a succinct compilation of the evidence from a number of industry studies.

7   For a discussion of the difficulties associated with the employment of used equipment, see Cooper and Kaplinsky (1974), where means of circumventing these difficulties are also discussed.

8   The argument is not necessarily valid, since the frequency of breakage can be reduced by using more expensive yarn having greater uniformity and strength. Alternatively, depending upon relative input costs, it may be economical to employ the labour intensive technique and to suffer higher rejection rates, thus using more yarn to produce the same amount of acceptable product in order to save on capital costs.

9   See Stewart (1982). As she indicates, a realistic conception of technological mastery has yet to be incorporated in a theory of dynamic comparative advantage.

10 The largest block of case-study research has been carried out under the auspices of the Regional Program of Studies on Scientific and Technical Development in Latin America, jointly sponsored by the Inter-American Development Bank, the United Nations Economic Commission for Latin America, the United Nations Development Program, and the International Development Research Center in Canada, and under the direction of Jorge Katz. See Katz (1978) for a summary of the research so far.

11 For an in-depth case study, and a highly illuminating discussion of why technological effort is not automatically or necessarily forthcoming, see Bell, *et al.* chapter 7, this volume. For evidence across firms in the same sector in one country, and an equally illuminating discussion, see Pearson (1977).

12 The reference here is to technological changes that occur after the achievement of predetermined project-specific norms (e.g. the nominal capacity rating). Baloff (1966) discusses what is entailed in achieving these norms.

13 Note that several of these tasks pertain to choice of technology, which is a fundamental element of project execution.

14 Several cases of the development of new products or processes through R&D have been observed in research in progress at the World Bank to investigate the technological mastery which underlies exports of technology by Brazil and Mexico. It is important to note, however, that in most of these cases, the R&D was undertaken within producing enterprises, and not by independent institutions.

15 These efforts have typically been found to take place in various production-

oriented departments within firms and engineering companies. Only occasionally have they occurred in separate R&D departments.

16 References to surveys of what is known appear on pp. 130–3.

17 The opportunity is least when new process technologies must be mastered. It is much greater if the new activity simply involves applying known process technologies to the production of a new product.

18 See Cooper (1981) for a survey of the various issues involved here.

19 Packaging can reduce costs in numerous ways. Here only a few examples are given. Combining long-term contracts to supply key intermediate inputs together with the supply of core process technology lowers the cost of supplying the latter in cases where the supplier's technological mastery is related very specifically to the use of particular inputs. In turn, the motive for including multiple technological elements, as in a turnkey contract, is sometimes to give the supplier greater control over the transfer in order to minimise the risk of cost overruns. Alternatively, the motive may be to avoid the costs of coordinating with other suppliers. These costs can be quite high, especially when the other suppliers are local companies which may be unfamiliar with standard procedures. There may also be other barriers to communication to overcome when local companies are involved.

20 Product differentiation is frequently the origin of the monopoly power that is packaged with technology transfer. Differentiation may reflect very substantial differences in important dimensions of technological mastery or very trivial ones. Whether particular forms of foreign-induced product differentiation are at variance with social objectives is a matter for public authorities to determine and to act upon through appropriate incentive and control measures. But acceptance of some forms of product differentiation is undoubtedly desirable, since no one specification of a product's characteristics is equally suited to all of its uses.

21 The principal centres for research on technology transfer have been — from the outset — the Science Policy Research Unit at the University of Sussex in Great Britain — and subsequently — the secretariat of the Andean Pact, the Organization of American States, the United Nations Commission on Trade and Development, and the United Nations Industrial Development Organization. Research on the behaviour of multinational corporations also often focuses on technology transfer issues. Such research has been conducted by the United Nations Center on Transnational Corporations and by various faculty members of the Harvard Business School, among others. See Stewart (1981) for a comprehensive policy-focussed survey and list of references.

22 Ten developing economies were included in the project, which was sponsored by the International Development Research Center in Canada.

23 Sagasti (1978) is quite vague about how these other policies affect technological change and the acquisition of technological mastery. Moreover, the project did not attempt to determine whether different development strategies (e.g. inward-versus outward-looking) have distinct, identifiable effects. The case studies of Latin American firms (see pp. 113–19) and Korean experience (see pp.126–30) suggest that they might.

24 The following discussion is based on detailed evidence given in Westphal, *et al.* (1979).

25 International subcontracting refers to export activity that is wholly organised by an overseas firm; the domestic, exporting firm is responsible only for overseeing production.

26 This does not imply the absence of rapid technological change in the industry in developed countries. It simply means that developing countries can — at least for a while — maintain a comparative advantage, once established, based on

mastery of conventional methods more appropriate to their factor endowments.

27   The observed pattern of time-phased plant construction in these industries might be an optimal strategy, with small scales chosen for the first plants to minimise the costs and risks entailed in learning the technology. It is not known, however, whether these or other considerations were the controlling ones at the time the first plants were constructed.

28   A particular adaptation is warranted only if the benefits to be achieved can reasonably be expected to repay the costs of the technological effort involved in undertaking it, with benefits and costs being measured in relation to social objectives.

29   See Crane (1977) for a comprehensive review of the evidence.

30   See Pack (1981) for a survey of what is known about the role of the capital goods sector both as an agent of technological change and in relation to industrialisation more generally.

REFERENCES

Arrow, Kenneth (1962). Economic welfare and the allocation of resources for invention, in *The Rate and Direction of Inventive Activity: Economic and Social Factors* (Ed. Richard R. Nelson), Princeton University Press for the National Bureau of Economic Research, Princeton, New Jersey.

Baloff, Nicholas (1966). Start-ups in machine-intensive production systems, *Journal of Industrial Engineering*, **17**.

Brooks, Harvey (1980). Technology, evolution, and purpose. *Daedalus*, **109**, 1, pp. 65–81.

Cooper, Charles (1981). Policy interventions for technological innovation in developing countries, World Bank Staff Working Papers, Washington, DC.

Cooper, Charles, and Kaplinsky, Raphael (1974). *Second-hand Equipment in a Developing Country: A Study of Jute-Processing in Kenya*, International Labor Office, Geneva.

Crane, Diana (1977). Technological innovation in developing countries: A review of the literature, *Research Policy*, **6**, pp. 374–395.

Dahlman, Carl J., and Fonseca, Fernando Valadares (1978). From technological dependence to technological development: The case of the Usiminas Steel Plant in Brazil, IDB/ECLA/UNDP/IDRC Regional Program of Studies on Scientific and Technical Development in Latin America Working Paper, no. 21, Economic Commission for Latin America, Buenos Aires.

Eckaus, R. S. (1955). The factor-proportions problem in underdeveloped areas, *American Economic Review*, **45**, pp. 539–565.

Enos, John L. (1962). Invention and innovation in the petroleum refining industry, in *The Rate and Direction of Inventive Activity: Economic and Social Factors*, Princeton University Press for the National Bureau of Economic Research, Princeton, New Jersey.

Hannay, N. Bruce, and McGinn, Robert E. (1980). The anatomy of modern technology: Prolegomenon to an improved public policy for the social management of technology, *Daedalus*, **109**, 1, pp. 25–53.

Katz, Jorge (1978). Technological change, economic development and intra and extra regional relations in Latin America, IDB/ECLA/UNDP/IDRC Regional Program of Studies on Scientific and Technical Development in Latin America Working Paper, no. 30. Economic Commission for Latin America, Buenos Aires.

Leibenstein, Harvey (1966). Allocative efficiency vs. 'X-Efficiency', *American Economic Review*, **56**, pp. 392–415.

Nelson, Richard R. (1979). Innovation and economic development: Theoretical retrospect and prospect. IDB/ECLA/UNDP/IDRC Regional Program of Studies on Scientific and Technical Development in Latin America Working Paper, no. 31. Economic Commission for Latin America, Buenos Aires.

Nelson, Richard R. (1980). Production sets, technological knowledge, and R&D: Fragile and overworked constructs for analysis of productivity growth? *American Economic Review*, **70**, no. 2, pp. 62–67.

Pack, Howard (1980). Macroeconomic implications of factor substitution in industrial processes, World Bank Staff Working Paper, no. 377. World Bank, Washington, DC.

Pack, Howard (1981). Fostering the capital goods sector in LDCs, *World Development*, **9**, 3, pp. 227–50.

Pearson, Ruth (1977). The Mexican cement industry: Technology, market structure and growth, IDB/ECLA/UNDP/IDRC Regional Program of Studies on Scientific and Technical Development in Latin America Working Paper, no. 11. Economic Commission for Latin America, Buenos Aires.

Rhee, Yung W. and Westphal, Larry E. (1977). A micro, econometric investigation of choice of technology. *Journal of Development Economics*, **4**, pp. 205–238.

Rhee, Yung W. and Westphal, Larry E. (1979). Choice of technology: Criteria, search, and interdependence, in *International Economic Development and Resource Transfer: Workshop 1978* (Ed. Herbert Giersch) (Institute fur Weltwirtshaft an der Universitat Kiel), J. C. B. Mohr (Paul Siebeck), Tubingen.

Sagasti, Francisco (1978). *Science and Technology for Development: Main Comparative Report on the STPI Project*, International Development Research Center, Ottawa, Canada.

Salter, W. E. G. (1960). *Productivity and Technical Change*, Cambridge University Press, Cambridge.

Sen, Amartya Kumar (1962). *Choice of Techniques: An Aspect of the Theory of Planned Economic Development*, Basil Blackwell, Oxford.

Stewart, Frances (1981). International technology transfer: Issues and policy options in *Recent Issues in World Development* (Eds. P. Streeten and R. Jolly), Pergamon, Oxford and New York.

Stewart, Frances (1982). Industrialization, technical change and the international division of labor, *For Good or Evil: Economic Theory and North-South Negotiations* (Ed. G. K. Helleiner), Croom Helm, London.

Sud, I. K., Harral, C. G. and Coukis, B. P. (1976). Scope for the substitution of labor and equipment in civil construction — A progress report, Papers for Panel Discussion: Indian Road Congress, 37th Annual Session, Bhopal, pp. 1–34.

Teitel, Simon (1981). Towards an understanding of technical change in semi-industrial countries, *Research Policy*, **10**, pp. 127–47.

Wells, Louis T., Jr. (1973). Economic man and engineering man: Choice in a low-wage country, *Public Policy*, **21**, pp. 319–342.

Westphal, Larry F. (1978). Research on Appropriate Technology, *Industry and Development*, **2**, pp. 28–46.

Westphal, Larry E., Rhee, Yung W. and Pursell, Garry (1979). Foreign influences on Korean industrial development, *Oxford Bulletin of Economics and Statistics*, **41**, pp. 359–88.

7 Limited learning in infant industry:
A case study*

MARTIN BELL, DON SCOTT-KEMMIS
and WIT SATYARAKWIT

INTRODUCTION

In this section we outline the main issues to which the case study relates, and then clarify what we mean by 'learning' and by 'technical change'. We briefly describe the growth of the industry and the context of government policy within which this took place. Finally we outline the technology involved in the case study. The second section presents the results of the analysis of technical change in the plant and describes aspects of the extent of 'learning' which took place over a thirteen-year period. The possible influence of the prevailing policy regime on the behaviour of the firm is discussed in the third section.

This case study relates to three sets of issues:

1. The substantial literature about those forms of technical change in manufacturing industry which have been described as 'learning' is largely based on DC industrial experience — little is known about these phenomena in LDCs — and contributes little to our understanding of the underlying processes by which technical change is generated.
2. The process by which industrialising economies acquire and accumulate the complex of capabilities necessary to control and manipulate the technical basis of their industrial development.
3. A central feature of policy regimes for industrialisation in most developing countries has been some form or other of protection for local industry against the competition of established foreign manufacturers. These

---

* This is a shortened version of the paper originally presented at the DSA Workshop, March 1980. The full original paper ('Learning and technical change in the development of manufacturing industry: A case study of a permanently infant enterprise') is available from the Science Policy Research Unit, University of Sussex. A paper similar to this shortened version was first presented at the 'First International Conference on Technology for Development 1980', Canberra 24–28 November 1979; The Institution of Engineers, Australia.

policy measures are usually justified by reference to some version of the infant industry argument for protection.

These arguments rest on assertions about the nature of technical change within manufacturing industry — basically on the assertion that, with protection, technical change *will* take place in infant industries such that the gap between the initially inefficient level of production and 'best practice' levels of efficiency will be narrowed to the extent that internationally competitive production will take place. The long-run benefits of protection will therefore, as a result of technical change, offset the short-run costs.

Interest in these three issues has been stimulated recently by the appearance of two related sets of studies which have examined technical capability within Third World industry. Both of these represent reactions against the wilder generalisations about the technological sterility of industry in the 'dependent' peripheral economies of the Third World.

The first set consists of a number of firm-level case studies of technical change (e.g. Katz *et al.*, 1978; Maxwell, 1977; and Dahlman, 1978). These studies demonstrate that some of the generalisations about LDC 'technological dependency' are ill-founded. Significant technical change can and does occur, at least within some firms in some of the more industrialised of such economies. They also add significantly to understanding about *how* such technical change occurs; it is a deliberate response by firms to specific stimuli in their environment, and it is a response which is effected by quite distinct and identifiable resources within the firms involved.

The second set of recent studies has been concerned more with the process of accumulating technological capability. These have focussed on the evidence of exports of capital goods and technological services from developing countries. Such studies (e.g. Katz and Ablin, 1979; Lall, 1980, and Chapter 8) have suggested that these exports reflect a degree of autonomous technological development within economies which are supposedly 'technologically dependent'. A process of accumulation of technological capability, which must be more substantial than hitherto presumed to be likely, lies behind the appearance of these developing countries as sellers in the international market for technology.

Katz and Ablin make the important point that the process of effecting technical change is part of the process of capability accumulation, and that this *interaction* shifts the comparative advantage of developing countries. They suggest technical change contributes to the shift in comparative advantage in three ways:

1. It raises the efficiency of techniques of production.
2. It incorporates an 'adaptive' dimension by which techniques are produced

which are better suited to use in Third World situations than the techniques available from the industrialised economies. The product of (a) and (b) is 'a "new" technology able to earn profits by itself in third markets' (Katz and Ablin, 1979; p. 31).

3. The process of effecting technical change also generates *increments* to the local endowment of technical knowledge, skill and capability. The very process of 'doing' the tasks involved in effecting technical change gives rise to various forms of 'learning' about how to do those tasks better.

These recent studies are also creating renewed interest in the relationship between industrial protection policies and the rate of technical change in 'infant industries'. The necessity of protection to ensure an adequate rate of technical change and the inevitability of technical change under protection have both been questioned. Balassa (1971), for example, has stressed two points. The domestic market focus of import-substituting protectionist regimes will tend to limit markets and hence limit the possibilities of using larger-scale, more efficient techniques. He suggests that with the limited competition and high profits behind protective barriers, firms will 'have little incentive for product improvement and technical change' (Balassa, 1971; p. 79). Rather than facilitating the process of technical change, protection may result in a cost in the form of opportunities foregone for improvements in productivity.

The recent studies of technical change in developing countries, and of technology exports from them, have given rise to a more optimistic view about the effects of protectionist policy on the rate of technical change. It has been noted that technical change and technological maturation have taken place within economies which have pursued protectionist import-substituting regimes. As a result, it has been suggested (e.g. by Lall, 1979) that the longer-term benefits of technical change may offset the short-term costs.

'Learning' and 'technical change': Some conceptual clarifications

The term 'learning' has been used in at least two ways.

1. The popular usage of the term usually refers to the process by which, through education, training or experience, an individual accumulates particular sets of skills. However, in the economics literature two slightly different derivatives of this meaning are encountered.
   (a) 'Learning' is used in an aggregated sense to refer to the processes by which an enterprise (or even an economy) accumulates the technological and managerial skills to carry on the business of production.

We shall use terms like 'the accumulation of technological capability' to refer to this kind of process, which may arise from any combination of education, training or experience – or even simply from hiring skills and capabilities which have been created elsewhere.

(b) 'Learning' has also been used to refer much more specifically to that process of capability accumulation that results from experience. 'Learning-by-doing' leads to enhanced skills and capabilities for carrying out a particular task as a result of the experience derived from actually carrying out the task concerned.

Thus learning, in the sense of learning-by-doing, came to be seen as a kind of costless by-product of production activity. It is usually suggested that ongoing improvements in the efficiency with which a particular task is carried out will, unless there has been some other input like better equipment, reflect the value of such experience-derived increments in capability.

In this paper, we shall use the term 'learning' in this rather narrow sense. We shall use it with recognition of the existence of the division of labour (Jacobsson, 1978). We do not assume that the increased experience of direct production workers will necessarily generate any significant improvement in the efficiency of, for example, designing machinery.

2. The term 'learning' has also been used in a quite different way in the economics literature. Rather than referring to some process of skill and knowledge accumulation, it has been used to describe some of the *effects* that are presumed to result from those processes. In particular, various forms of 'technical change' have been described *as* 'learning'. As we shall discuss later, learning may *contribute* to technical change, but other inputs may also be involved. In this chapter, when we wish to refer to technical change, we shall use the term 'technical change'.

The term 'technical change' will be used in this chapter more in the manner of engineers and managers than in the rather specialised sense with which economists use it. By 'technical change' we mean those concrete changes in the physical (or organisational) parameters of a production system, by which its physical efficiency may be altered. Such changes in physical performance will give rise to changes in the various economic parameters by which economists tend to measure production efficiency, such as labour or capital productivity (Maxwell, 1977; Eilon *et al.* 1976).

This study focuses on technical change in the process of production. It is not concerned with technical changes in input or product specification except to the extent that these affect production performance. The study is, therefore, concerned with change in the efficiency of using inputs to produce a given product. This concept of technical change is very similar to Hollander's ' "technical change" in the narrow sense' (Hollander, 1965). This narrow concept of technical change closely relates to that used in studies of 'learning' in the process of production and in discussions of technical change in debates about protection.

However, this study focusses on two kinds of process-related technical change: (a) evolutionary change which might be effected over time in an exiting production system (intra-vintage technical change), and (b) technical change which might arise from the introduction of incrementally novel, new production systems (incremental, inter-vintage technical change).

Some further clarification is necessary. It is the first of these categories which is most often described as 'learning', but we are not concerned here with the initial 'startup learning' phase of this phenomenen. Numerous studies have shown ongoing improvements in the operation of 'fixed facilities' whereby 'minor' modifications and adaptations are carried out on physical plant and 'minor' increments of capital are built into the existing system (David, 1975; Hirsch, 1952; Conway and Schultz, 1959; Hirschman, 1964; Enos, 1962). This is the first form of technical change examined in this study. While it is difficult to draw a clear distinction between capital-embodied and disembodied forms of technical change it is less difficult to distinguish between changes which are incorporated within existing systems (intra-vintage) from the establishment of new production systems (inter-vintage). New vintages of capital which incorporate incrementally improved old vintages of basic technology — as in this case — have been considered as resulting from 'learning' in the activity of *producing*, rather than *using*, capital goods (Arrow, 1962). This type of incremental, inter-vintage technical change is the second form of technical change examined here, and it is assumed to originate at least in part from 'learning' in the *production* of capital goods.

It appears that increases in efficiency which arise with the cumulative experience of operating particular production systems is a widespread phenomenon which contributes in substantial ways to the overall growth of productivity in the dynamic industrialised economies (Andress, 1954; Conley, 1970; Bump, 1974).

The small number of case studies of these kinds of technical change in developing countries suggest that their economic significance may be similar to that observed in more industrialised economies (Katz *et al.*, 1978; Dahlman, 1978).

The industry and its context

The manufacturing plant which is the subject of this study was one of three which produced galvanised steel sheets in Thailand. By 1960 imports of this product had reached a level of about 50 000 tons per year. In that year, one firm was set up. The firm which is examined in this study was established in 1961, and a third was established in 1963. The second entrant started with a higher level of capacity (about 36 000 tons) and added capacity of about 24 000 tons per year, and also added to that in later years.

The result of this pattern of capacity expansion was that total annual capacity kept roughly in line with total annual production for the first few years, but thereafter rose above the level of output. Rapid capacity expansion in the 1963–66 period substantially exceeded the rate of growth of output, and, with growth levelling off sharply from 1968, a very wide margin of excess capacity opened up. However, investment in stocks and fixed capital was used to enable the industry to meet peak levels of demand which usually arose for only one month in the year.

The firms operated within a framework of government policy which had three main elements that impinged most immediately and directly on the industry. The infant industry was protected by a tariff which was equivalent to about 45 per cent of the price of imported galvanised sheets in 1961. The structure of the industry was controlled by a procedure for licensing the establishment of new enterprises. The licensing of three firms was, in part, a reflection of the usual general concern to ensure that there is a degree of domestic competition within industries which are established behind protective tariff barriers. Finally, all three of the firms were granted one of the standard packages of tax concessions designed to encourage (foreign) investment in industry.

The technology and the forms of technical change examined

The particular form of production technique was relatively simple. The starting material — rolled steel sheets — was imported. The opened stacks of sheets were placed on a loading platform at the start of the line, and were manually lifted and placed on the mechanised conveyor system which carried them through the various stages to the unloading point where they were stacked ready for transfer to the corrugating stage.

Each galvanising line was operated by a crew of eight and these had relatively indivisible tasks at specific points in the line. Labour costs were a very small component of total costs — about 3–5 per cent of the total variable costs. For one firm, the sum of reported depreciation, rent and interest charges amounted to a similar absolute amount. The cost of raw materials (steel and zinc mainly) dominated production costs, and since these were imported, domestic value-added probably constituted only around 15 per cent of the value of output.

A pattern of incremental expansion was followed by the firm involved in this study. Production started in 1961 on the basis of three lines which were imported from Japan. Two more lines were added in 1963–64. These two lines were built in the firm's own workshops, as were two more lines which were brought into operation in 1968.

This study is concerned with the production performance of three of these lines.

No. 3 — imported from Japan and operated from mid 1961
No. 4 — locally built, and operated from 1964
No. 5 — locally built, and operated from 1968.

This allows us to distinguish between the two forms of technical change outlined above:

1. The analysis of intra-vintage technical change will be based on observations of changes over time in the efficiency of each of the three different lines (from 1964 to 1973 for lines 3 and 4, and from 1968 to 1973 for line 5).
2. The analysis of incremental, inter-vintage technical change will be based on observations of differences in efficiency between the three lines.

THE ANALYSIS OF TECHNICAL CHANGE

The measurement of technical change

The data on production efficiency are derived from the records which the firm itself used to measure production performance on the galvanising lines. These records noted for each shift

1. Total output (tons) per shift. This is transformed in the analysis to a rate of production per line per hour. This provides an accurate indicator of trends in capital productivity and, also a reasonably accurate indicator of trends in labour productivity.
2. The percentage of shift output which was passed as 'grade one' quality.
3. The level of downtime during the shift. This indicator is inversely correlated with line productivity, but is far from being the sole explanation of productivity changes.
4. The weight of zinc used (kg) per ton of output. This may vary around the standard coating weight (for the product concerned) of 106 kg/tons.

Efficiency with respect to 'zinc productivity' was probably a matter of greater economic significance than efficiency with respect to the use of labour and capital.

The data used in this study were derived from an irregular sample from the records for every second or third day throughout the periods covered. The sampling procedure yielded a total data-base for the three lines (approximately twenty-three line-operating years) which incorporates performance measures for 1100 days and about 2000 shifts. Since performance differs with different product types, only data relating to a standard product type is included. These three lines usually produced this product. However, periods when other products were run on the line were omitted from the analysis. In an attempt to limit the extent to which the analysis included performance variations due to 'external' and 'non-production' factors, data for any shift or day for which zero output was recorded were not included in the analysis.

The analysis of performance

Mean monthly estimates of productivity, quality and downtime were calculated from their respective daily estimates. Estimates of the mean monthly deviation from standard zinc use were calculated from the absolute value of the deviation in each shift.

Trends in performance over time on individual lines

First, bivariate regressions of performance against time were calculated for each performance indicator on each line. If a plot of performance against time suggested a possible non-linear relationship a second regression, using polynominal terms was calculated — such a second regression accounted for significantly more variance than a simple regression in only one case. Second, as Line 5 operated only from 1968, a further set of regressions was calculated for the performance of Lines 3 and 4 over this shorter period. The estimated regression equations are shown in Table 1.

Two general observations can be made from the results shown in Table 1. First the generally low levels of the coefficient of determination (r^2) reflect the high short-term variability of performance even when monthly averages are used for analysis. Secondly, only eight of the twenty regressions indicate a statistically significant trend, at the 5 per cent level, over time.

As measured by the rate of output (tons per hour) the productivity of all three lines declined over the 1968–73 period. Hence, while there is no evidence of an ability to sustain improvements in productivity there is evidence to suggest that the ability to maintain productivity levels declined from the late 1960s.

Table 1 Trends in performance over time

Performance indicator	Line Number 3	Line Number 5	Line Number5
Productivity 1965–73 (tons per hour)	$P = 1.54 + 0.0002t$ $(F = 0.06)$ $n = 69 \quad r^2 = 0.001$	$P = 1.39 + 0.007t - 0.0001t^2$ $(F = 5.76)**$ $n = 5.4 \quad r^2 = 0.18$	
Productivity 1968–73 (tons per hour)	$P = 1.75 - 0.003t$ $(F = 7.74)**$ $n = 47 \quad r^2 = 0.15$	$P = 1.67 - 0.003t$ $(F = 6.97)**$ $n = 43 \quad r^2 = 0.15$	$P = 1.62 - 0.003t$ $(F = 6.08)*$ $n = 48 \quad r^2 = 0.12$
Quality, 1965–73 (percentage of output passed as Grade I)	$Q = 96.49 - 0.024t$ $(F = 3.13)$ $n = 63 \quad r^2 = 0.05$	$Q = 96.45 - 0.009t$ $(F = 1.83)$ $n = 52 \quad r^2 = 0.04$	
Quality, 1968–73 (percentage of output	$Q = 96.49 - 0.024t$ $(F = 0.88)$	$Q = 96.87 - 0.015t$ $(F = 2.33)$	$Q = 95.63 + 0.016t$ $(F = 1.81)$

Downtime 1965–73 (percentage of shift time)	$TL = 17.59 - 0.039t$ $(F = 6.09)*$ $n = 68$ $r^2 = 0.08$	$TL = 17.16 - 0.013t$ $(F = 0.64)$ $n = 54$ $r^2 = 0.01$	$TL = 18.34 - 0.062t$ $(F = 5.31)*$ $n = 48$ $r^2 = 0.10$
Downtime 1968–73 (percentage of shift time)	$TL = 20.22 - 0.077t$ $(F = 15.49)**$ $n = 47$ $r^2 = 0.26$	$TL = 14.66 + 0.022t$ $(F = 1.06)$ $n = 43$ $r^2 = 0.03$	
Deviation from zinc use standard, 1965–73	$D = 7.33 + 0.023t$ $(F = 2.33)$ $n = 69$ $r^2 = 0.03$	$D = 7.46 + 0.050t$ $(F = 1.76)$ $n = 54$ $r^2 = 0.03$	
Deviation from zinc use standard 1968–73	$D = 4.78 + 0.061t$ $(F = 5.15)*$ $n = 47$ $r^2 = 0.10$	$D = 3.49 + 0.108t$ $(F = 3.47)$ $n = 43$ $r^2 = 0.08$	$D = 8.44 + 0.036t$ $(F = 0.90)$ $n = 48$ $r^2 = 0.02$

* = significant at 5% level; ** = significant at 1% level; t = months from start of period.

The trends in quality of output are less ambiguous. The temporal variation in output quality is lower than that of other performance indicators, and no significant trends in quality performance over time are evident.

Downtime performance shows a significant improvement over time on both Lines 3 and 5 but there is no significant trend on Line 4. This is the only performance indicator which suggests some improvement over time, although the magnitude of this improvement is not substantial.

On all three lines there is an apparent trend towards increasing deviations from the standard zinc use rate. However, only for Line 3 over the 1968–73 period, is this trend statistically significant.

Considered overall the performance of these three lines generally did not improve, and in some cases declined, over time.

Comparative performance of the three lines

Three sets of comparisons were made to assess the comparative performance of the three lines. First, the estimated overall mean performance of each line on each indicator was calculated using monthly averages from all periods during which each machine was operating.

These means were then compared by analysis of variance or, if group variances were significantly different, by the non-parametric Kruskal–Wallis test. If significant differences were indicated — at the 5 per cent level by either the F of the ANOVA or the χ^2 of the Kruskal–Wallis test — t tests were employed to test pairs of means. Pooled or separate variance estimate models of the t test were used depending on the similarity of the variance of the two comparison groups.

Secondly, this process was repeated but mean performance was based only on the years 1968 to 1973 when all three machines were operating. Thirdly, the mean performance of machines was compared for periods when they were of similar ages. As a comparison between machines 3 and 5 would have been based on a very short period, comparisons only between 3 and 4, and 4 and 5 were carried out — t tests as described above were used to test significance of the differences between means. The results of these three sets of comparisons are shown in Table 2.

With respect to all four indicators the mean performances of these three lines are markedly similar. Only three comparisons result in statistically significant differences at the 5 per cent level; none is significant at the 1 per cent level (see Table 2). Furthermore, the magnitude of the observed differences in mean performance among these three lines is of little practical significance.

These analyses of comparative performance, including those comparisons which take into account the different ages of the lines, provide little evidence

Table 2 Comparative performance of lines

	All production years	1968–73	Similar age comparisons
Productivity (tons per hour)	$\bar{P}_3 = \bar{P}_4 = \bar{P}_5$ (1.55) (1.50) (1.52)[a] ($F_{2,168} = 198$)	$\bar{P}_3 = \bar{P}_4 = \bar{P}_5$ (1.57) (1.50) (1.52) ($F_{2,136} = 2.95$)	$\bar{P}_3 > \bar{P}_4$ (1.56) (1.50) ($t = 2.08$)* $\bar{P}_4 = \bar{P}_5$ (1.15) (1.51) ($t = -0.15$)
Quality (percentage Grade 1)	($\chi^2 = 6.55$)* $\bar{Q}_3 = \bar{Q}_4$ (95.3) (96.0)[a] ($t = -1.72$) $\bar{Q}_3 < \bar{Q}_5$ (96.2) ($t = -2.08$)*	($\chi^2 = 11.27$)** $\bar{Q}_3 = \bar{Q}_4$ (95.0) (95.9) ($t = -1.98$) $\bar{Q}_3 < \bar{Q}_5$ (96.2) ($t = -2.39$)*	$\bar{Q}_3 = \bar{Q}_4$ (95.8) (96.0) ($t = -0.70$) $\bar{Q}_4 = \bar{Q}_5$ (96.2) (96.3) ($t = -0.45$)
Downtime (percentage of total)	$\overline{DT}_3 = \overline{DT}_4 = \overline{DT}_5$ (15.7) (16.5) (16.3)[a] ($F_{2,167} = 0.99$)	$\overline{DT}_3 = \overline{DT}_4 = \overline{DT}_5$ (15.4) (16.1) (16.3) ($\alpha^2 = 0.96$)	$\overline{DT}_3 = \overline{DT}_4$ (16.3) (16.1) ($t = 0.43$) $\overline{DT}_4 = \overline{DT}_5$ (16.9) (16.2) ($t = 0.88$)
Zinc use (deviation from standard)	$\bar{D}_3 = \bar{D}_4 = \bar{D}_5$ (8.5) (10.1) (9.6)[a] ($\alpha^2 = 1.21$)	$\bar{D}_3 = \bar{D}_4 = \bar{D}_5$ (8.6) (10.2) (9.7) ($\alpha^2 = 0.89$)	$\bar{D}_3 = \bar{D}_4$ (7.9) (10.2) ($t = -1.91$) $\bar{D}_4 = \bar{D}_5$ (8.1) (9.9) ($t = 1.49$)

a = group means; * = significant at 5% level; ** = significant at 1% level.

that the three lines differed significantly in *mean* performance. They
certainly suggest that (in terms of these indicators) the lines built in the
plant — Line 4 and 5 — did not show a significant improvement in performance over the fully imported Line 3. Nor did Line 5 show any significant
improvement over the earlier locally built vintage of equipment.

One simple conclusion emerges from this analysis. Over a period of at
least about nine years this infant industrial firm did not improve any of four
important aspects of the production efficiency of three lines which produced its basic standard product. Nor did operating efficiency improve
following the introduction of the two new vintages of capital equipment.
In terms of production efficiency, the firm seems to have remained technically stagnant during this period. There were no technically fixed limits
which prevented minor modifications and improvements of these lines.

These observations are in marked contrast to those reported in almost
all the micro studies of technical change in the industrialised economies.
There were no signs of 'short-term learning curves', or even of capital
embodied technical change, the fact that firms learn by 'doing' the ongoing
business of production has almost come to be taken as a basic 'law' of
industrial economics in the more industrialised countries. This firm does
not seem to have conformed to that 'law'.

As noted above, Katz and Ablin (1979) have suggested that 'doing'
technical change contributes increments to the stock of technological
capability as the result of a learning process.

This kind of learning process might be seen as one half of an inter-active
process of technological maturation. The other half consists of the process
of capability accumulation which provides both the other resources to
effect technical change and the capacity to absorb the knowledge derived
from 'doing' production or 'doing' technical change. In the case of this
firm, the absence of technical change eliminated one important opportunity
for learning — one half of the interactive process of technological maturation could not occur. It is possible to indicate in outline what happened in
this firm with respect to the other half — the process of capability accumulation. First, however it may be useful to elaborate a little on the nature of
the two components of this interactive process.

The learning process

The underlying notion about learning-by-doing is that the experience of
production yields information and stimuli which prompt the making of
improvements. Indeed many production engineers see industrial plants as
producing two outputs: products and information. However, it is quite
possible for a plant to be operated without any very significant information

about the operation being captured in any useful way. Recording and analysis of basic performance data is a pre-requisite for any but the most simple and random learning about performance to take place. This requires an allocation of resources which may not be made, or which may be made inadequately.

However, although such learning may be *one* input to the process of technical change, on its own it is probably inadequate. The information emerging from the experience of production needs to be related to *another* set of information — technical knowledge about the underlying process, about possible changes which might be made, and about the likely effects of such changes and adaptations.

Thus, if the experience of production is to contribute to technical change, *two* sets of knowledge and information are required. One set arises from the specific experience of production. The other (perhaps more general) must be acquired from elsewhere and brought into intimate contact with the more immediate and more specific production experience.

It is likely that the relative importance of these two kinds of knowledge and expertise will vary with differences in the type of technical change that is needed and carried out. Technical change which involves raising efficiency towards consistent achievement of the initially specified levels for a particular system will probably draw relatively heavily on knowledge relating to and derived from that system itself. A particular kind of specialised change-effecting resource will be needed for those kinds of change which must be embodied, at least in part, in physical modifications and adaptations to the facility.

In order to *reproduce* an item of equipment, knowledge and information derived from the immediate experience may be particular important, but on its own will be inadequate. To redesign equipment and improve it will require a stock of skills and knowledge that is probably different from that required to copy what is already there. The relative importance of learning from the immediately available experience will be less, and that of other experience and other knowledge will be greater.

Existing studies of the technical change process tell us very little about the kinds of knowledge that are generated from the experience of production and technical change, or about how such knowledge contributes to effecting technical change. They tell us little about the resources which are involved in acquiring this knowledge and in relating it productively to the other kinds of knowledge that are needed to make technical change happen.

Thus, the learning process requires resources, and effecting technical change requires resources. In the firm examined in this case study there appears to have been a very limited effort to accumulate the resources which might constitute a technological capability for activities other than the most basic and rudimentary process operation.

The firm employed about 540 people. It had no kind of R&D section and had never carried out any kind of R&D work. The quality-control section included only three people. The maintenance section included about twenty-five people, of whom only three had any kind of formal technical education. The 'engineering department' seemed to consist of only one person — a Japanese employee of the company who had started work as a labourer in a galvanised steel plant in Japan, and had accumulated fifty years' experience in this area, rising to be 'chief engineer' at that plant.

Little effort seems to have been made over the thirteen-year history of the plant to accumulate a stock of technical resources beyond those needed for basic *operation* of the plant. All training seems to have been undertaken with only that as an objective. At the same time, even the knowledge about process operation that was acquired seems to have been largely confined to knowledge about the specific process used in the plant. Most of the training was provided 'on the job' in the Thai plant, and was carried on in any systematic way for only eighteen months. Three 'technicians' were trained in plant operation for only six months in Japan, and this probably constituted the only *possible* access of the organisation to technical knowledge other than that derivable from the specific experience of the plant operated, and other than that imported already embodied in the Japanese self-made 'engineer'. It was this imported component of the firm's technological capability which provided the blueprints for the machinery which the firm produced. For this reason, one has to be rather precise about defining what the enterprise learned about machinery production. It may have learned a little about how to *manufacture* the equipment. However, it imported but did not produce, copies of the equipment specifications and seems to have learned nothing beyond how to replicate the physical embodiments of those.

With the exception of the one imported 'engineer', the enterprise seems to have been stripped down to the bare minimum of technological capability that was required for basic operation. With the firm having failed to invest in the resources needed to effect technical change and to capture the experience of production, it is perhaps not too surprising that it also failed to improve its production efficiency over the nine-year period.

These observations emphasise the need to question the often presumed efficacy of protectionist measures for encouraging the maturation of infant enterprises. This particular enterprise gives the appearance of permanent, or at least very protracted, infancy. Indeed, the efficiency gap between this firm and established producers in the industrialised economies probably *widened* during this thirteen-year period.

THE FIRM'S ENVIRONMENT AND ITS IMPLICATIONS
FOR TECHNICAL CHANGE AND LEARNING

A firm's technological behaviour can be seen as a set of responses to stimuli
in its environment. However, it is important to recognise that this may
involve a two-step process. The environment may generate demands for
technical change within firms. However, the firm must first invest (or have
invested) in the resources needed to effect technical change (response step 1)
before it can define and implement technical change (response step 2). This
draws attention to two points:

1. The influence of environmental factors may impinge on the technological
   behaviour of firms in one or both of two ways. These factors may affect
   the demand on the firm for technical change. They may also affect the
   firm's investment in the resources needed to supply technical change.
2. The same kinds of stimuli may, in different situations, evoke different
   kinds of responses. For example, in situations where the cost of investing
   in the resources for producing technical change involves only the cost
   of hiring them, or the opportunity cost of reallocating resources already
   employed by the firm, then a given type of stimulus for technical change
   may evoke a response. In other situations where the investment cost also
   includes the cost (and time-lags) involved in first creating the resources,
   then the same type of stimulus may evoke no response at all.

Our examination of the way in which government policy may have influenced the technological behaviour of the firm in this case will reflect the
first of these two points. Apart from the reduction in the demand for technical change, due to the prevailing tariff-induced uncompetitive environment, and the over-capacity which was encouraged by the fragmentation
of the industry, the policy regime possibly had a major influence on the
availability of technological expertise.

Thailand launched into the development of this industry without any
expertise in the technology relating to this line of production. This seems
to have applied as much to the government agencies which determined
the policy framework for the industry's development as to the industrialists
who were involved in establishing the firms.

In the case of this particular firm, the background of the Thai personnel
who were involved in its initiation and management was confined to the
areas of commerce and finance. The initiating entrepreneur had previously
been engaged in importing and marketing galvanised sheets and, for all technical aspects of setting up the plant, he turned to the technological resources
of his previous supplier. Discussion with the senior Thai management

suggested that 'technology' seemed to be regarded as something fixed and given which one acquired. It was not something which one changed, let alone produced. It was something which one either had or had not, and in the latter case one simply bought it in the form of the particular, imported product/process system that was needed to carry on a business.

This type of background and associated perspectives probably generates two kinds of influence on a firm's responses to its environment:

1. Technical change is seen as being effected by intermittently importing the necessary goods and services, while investment in the resources for effecting technical change within the enterprise has a low priority.
2. The competitive response to the firm's economic environment is predominantly focussed on product differentiation and marketing effort rather than on responses which centred on production efficiency, and on cost and price reduction.

An initial lack of relevant technological expertise took on a self perpetuating character. The initial imports of the capital goods and technical services which were needed to start production pulled in a degree of control over decision-making by those who had an interest in continuing to provide such goods and services. This reinforced the inbuilt preference of the firm's management to seek modes of response to stimuli for change which were responses other than those involving investment in the resources which would have been necessary for the firm itself to effect its own technical change.

No aspect of government policy was designed to break this situation. There were no arrangements to provide either the government administrative machinery or the industry itself with independent sources of relevant technological expertise *before* launching into the rapid development of the industry. Nor were there any policy elements designed to stimulate subsequent investment in such expertise. Indeed, aspects of government policy were more likely to have had a quite contary effect. Tariffs and sales taxes on imported equipment were remitted for five years for 'promoted' firms, while any local purchases would have attracted sales taxes. Expatriation of all profits on foreign capital and of management and royalty fees was guaranteed. In effect imported products of foreign technological and managerial expertise were subsidised relative to those which might have been locally supplied.

Similarly, the fragmentation of the industry may have constrained the firm's technolgical behaviour — both by limiting the demand for technical change and by constraining the accumulation of technological resources.

Two points about this situation seem to be important. First, these kinds of external conditions interact with each other. Changing any one aspect of the firm's environment might, on its own, make little difference. Second, discussion of the effect of government policy on the dynamic performance of infant industries should not be confined to the effect of tariff protection *per se*. At least in this case, this was only one element in an interrelated structure of policy instruments which impinged on the firm.

In this case, the protectionist development strategy that was followed seems to have contributed to the long-term technical stagnation of the firm; and behind that to its failure to invest in those technological capabilities which are needed to effect technical change and, through learning, to link the accumulating experience of (changing) production to increases in production efficiency.

REFERENCES

Andress, F. J. (1954). The learning curve as a production tool, *Harvard Business Review*, **32**, January/February.

Arrow, K. J. (1962). The economic implications of learning by doing, *Review of Economic Studies*, **XXIX**, June.

Balassa, B. and associates (1971). *The Structure of Protection in Developing Countries*, Johns Hopkins, Baltimore.

Bump, E. A. (1974). Effects of learning on cost projections, *Management Accounting (US)*, May, pp. 19–24.

Conley, P. (1970). Experience curves as a planning tool, *IEEE Spectrum*, June.

Conway, R. W. and Schultz, A. (1959). The manufacturing progress function, *Journal of Industrial Engineering*, **X**, 1, January–February.

Dahlman, C. J. (1978). From technological dependence to technological development: the case of the USIMINAS steel plant in Brazil. Buenos Aires, IDB/ECLA Research Programme in Science and Technology, Working Paper No. 21 (2 vols).

David, P. A. (1975). *Technical Choice, Innovation and Economic Growth*, Cambridge University Press, London.

Eilon, S., Gold, B. and Soeson, J. (1976), *Applied Productivity Analysis for Industry*, Pergamon Press, Oxford.

Enos, J. L. (1962). Invention and innovation in the petroleum refining industry, in National Bureau of Economic Research, *The Rate and Direction of Inventive Activity: Economic and Social Factors*. Princeton University Press, Chicago.

Hirsch, W. Z. (1952). Manufacturing progress function, *Review of Economics and Statistics*, **34**, May.

Hirschman, W. B. (1964). Profit from the learning curve, *Harvard Business Reveiw*, **42**, January/February.

Hollander, S. (1965). *The Sources of Increased Efficiency: A Study of Du Pont Rayon Plants*, The MIT Press, Cambridge, Massachusetts.

Jacobsson, S. (1978). Learning in technical progress, MA Thesis, University of Sussex.

Katz, J. and Ablin, E. (1979). From infant industry to technology exports: The Argentine experience in the international sale of industrial plants and engineering works, Buenos Aires, IDB/ECLA Research Programme in Science and Technology, Working Paper No. 14.

Katz, J., Gutkowski, M., Rodrigues, M. and Goity, G. (1978). Productivity, technology and domestic efforts in research and development, Buenos Aires, IDB/ECLA Research Programme in Science and Technology, Working Paper No. 13.

Lall, S. (1980). Developing countries as exporters of industrial technology, *Research Policy*, 9, pp. 24–52.

Maxwell, P. (1977). Learning and technical change in the steel plant of Acindar SA in Rosario, Argentina, Buenos Aires, IDB/ECLA Research Programme in Science and Technology, Working Paper No. 4.

Maxwell, P. (1979). Implicit R&D ˑstrategy and investment-linked R&D, Buenos Aires, IDB/ECLA Research Programme in Science and Technology, Working Paper No. 23.

PART III   THE CREATION OF THIRD WORLD TECHNOLOGY

8   Technological learning in the Third World: Some implications of technology exports*

SANJAYA LALL

INTRODUCTION: THE SIGNIFICANCE OF THIRD WORLD EXPORTS OF TECHNOLOGY

A copious literature exists on the economics of technological innovation and diffusion and on technology transfers to, and its absorption by, developing countries. It has, however (with a few exceptions noted later), tended to ignore the generation of technology by indigenous industrial enterprises in poorer countries. There are several possible explanations for this neglect. First, as Rosenberg (1976) and others have noted, there has been a long-standing tendency for economists to be obsessed by major innovations as the main source of technological progress. This 'break-through syndrome', the blame for which is often laid at the feet of Schum-peter, has detracted from a proper appreciation of the contribution of technological changes made in the process of diffusion, imitation and adaptation.

Secondly, there seems to have been an implicit assumption on the part of the analysts in the field of innovation that developing countries must have little capacity for generating technology, even in a minor adaptive fashion. Economies with relatively poor scientific infrastructure, practical-ly no investment in research activities, underdeveloped entrepreneurial capabilities and very recent entry into modern manufacturing industry are hardly likely to be able to improve on complex technology. They are even less likely to be able to sell it internationally in competition with established technology sellers from industrialised countries. While there has been little explicit discussion of the process of technological change or creation in developing countries, there has been a sort of 'technological pessimism' implicit in the exclusive attention given to the problem of

* This chapter is updated from an article written in 1978, which was expanded and published as a book entitled *Developing Countries as Exporters of Technology*, Macmillan (1982). It draws upon research being conducted for the World Bank on exports of technology and technological development in selected countries. Only the author is responsible for the views expressed here.

absorbing technology by LDCs, the prime role of transnational companies (TNCs) in transmitting technology and to the terms and conditions under which technology transfer from rich to poor nations takes place.

Thirdly, development economists who deal with problems of employment, industrialisation and choice of technique, have shown considerable interest in problems of technological adaptation, but mainly from the viewpoint of finding 'appropriate' technologies for labour surplus, skill- and capital-scarce conditions. Much of the empirical research has therefore focussed on factor-substitution accomplished in the direction of using older techniques and machinery: experience with the use of advanced techniques has been relatively neglected, in extreme cases even to the extent that modern technology is rejected as economically, socially and politically pernicious.

Finally, economists who deal with international trade and investment have tended to identify the role of developing countries as exporters of labour-intensive and low-skill manufactures, and as recipients of skill and technology-intensive (the two are generally treated as interchangeable) and capital-intensive imports, and of technology and capital (by direct investment and/or licensing) from the industrialised countries.[1] There are signs that this conventional approach is changing, as we shall see below, but the basic model which dominates current analysis is one which assigns developing countries a place at the bottom of the technology and skill ladder, and sees them only as recipients of direct manufacturing investment.

There is, in sum, little in the different branches of the received wisdom on technology and the Third World which would lead us to expect significant technological advance there. There is even less to lead us to expect that indigenous enterprises from developing countries would enter international markets as competitive sellers of fairly broad ranges of technology. It must be admitted at the start that the technological advance which occurs in the Third World, and on which its exports of technology are based, is of a 'minor' kind. Technical improvements in developing countries do not constitute major Schumpeterian 'breakthroughs' and they are often not even on the world 'frontiers' of the relevant technology. Nevertheless, they constitute technical progress, in that they raise productivity, they utilise different techniques and materials and often produce somewhat different products.

From the viewpont of the individual firm, such minor innovation cannot be distinguished from the innovation of 'new' technology — in fact, it is highly questionable whether, at this level, it makes sense at all to distinguish between movements *along* a 'given' production function and movements *of* the function itself. Traditional neo-classical economic theory regards only the latter as technical progress. But there is a growing, and very persuasive, line of argument (best represented by the 'evolutionary' school of Nelson and Winter (1977)) that any conscious technical effort on the part of a firm, which leads to products and processes which are *new to the firm*, should be regarded as technical progress. There is, in other words, no basis on which to draw a distinction between movements along a production function and movements of the function itself. A firm essentially operates on a technological point rather than a function and is familiar only with the area immediately surrounding its operational technology.[2] Any shift of its technology, whether or not the resultant technology is known to other firms, requires conscious effort and involves risk for the firm. It should, therefore, be regarded as an 'innovation' for the firm, regardless of whether it adds to the existing global stock of technologies, or reproduces a technology already held by another firm, or even goes 'backwards' in simplifying existing technologies or reviving older technologies.

Once the theoretical blinkers which restrict our view of innovation (to a shift in the world 'frontiers' of knowledge) have been put aside, we may start to appreciate the possibility that innovation and technical progress can occur, to a significant extent, even in newly industrialising economies. It is, however, difficult to find hard evidence to assess the extent to which this possibility has been realised. With a few exceptions[3] the process of technical change in Third World manufacturing industry remains an area of ignorance, and the preconceptions (noted above) with which we approach the subject, tend to make us fairly pessimistic. This is why an examination of technology exports (TE) by developing countries can make a very useful contribution.

TE can in this context serve as an indicator of the *dynamic comparative advantage* of developing countries. The 'products' which comprise TE — turnkey industrial plant (or 'project exports'), consultancy services, direct overseas investment and licensing — are based on technological knowhow, experience and design skills, backed by the ability to organise, manage and finance large and complex activities. They are, in other words, at the newest and most advanced end of the spectrum of industrial activity. They show, not only the direction in which growing industrialisation leads the competitive advantages of developing countries, but also the underlying factors which enable them to build up such advantages. These underlying factors, 'minor' innovation broadly defined, are clearly of great significance to policy and to our understanding of the dynamics of industrial growth. And the existence of TE is *prima facie* evidence that technical progress has taken place and has reached international levels of competence.

To the extent that TE serves as a crude indicator of technological prowess, therefore, a comparison of TE by different developing countries can indicate their respective levels of internal technological development.

The study of TE can serve another purpose. To the extent that different developing countries have different areas of strength in TE, and to the extent that different forms of TE require different kinds or blends of technological skill and other expertise, a comparison of the 'revealed comparative advantage' of the different exporting countries in exporting technology can help us to draw inferences about the factors which have led to the observed patterns of TE. In part the differences may be accounted for by respective government policies on export promotion or TE. In part they must reflect different environments in the home countries where the 'minor innovations' occur. It is the latter which is of interest to the study of technological change.

The data on TE are at present extremely limited and patchy. The following discussion must, therefore, be treated with due caution. The conclusions which are drawn are of some value, but they should be treated as hypotheses, to be subjected to further empirical testing, rather than established propositions. It may be noted, however, that since some of the ideas in this chapter were put forward in 1978 subsequent research has tended to support the main findings on TE surprisingly well. We may, in consequence, be slightly more confident about the broad empirical picture, to which we now turn.

THE EVIDENCE ON TE

Technology exports are defined in this chapter as market based transactions of four types: the sale of complete industrial plant (turnkey projects); the provision of consultancy services; direct investments (including joint ventures between host country firms and those from the technology exporting country); and licensing (including the sale of patents and brand-names, the provision of components for assembly, and the sale of technological and management services of various kinds). This definition excludes purely inter-government technical assistance agreements which are conducted outside a market framework, as well as the transfer of knowhow and skills by means of migration or scientific interchange.

Turnkey projects

On a strict definition, an industrial turnkey project only comprises those cases where the developing country concerned takes the role of the prime contractor in setting up a complete industrial plant. It excludes cases where it assumes the role of a subcontractor or where it assumes responsibility for an extension to a plant. However, we use a wide definition where all sorts of industrial project work (i.e. provision of services of various kinds to accompany the supply of capital goods) are counted as 'turnkey' projects. It should be noted that purely *civil* construction work (which, in fact, constitutes the predominant element of overseas contracts by developing countries) is not included here. The 'technology' of civil construction is very different from that of manufacturing industry, and this chapter is only concerned with the latter.

The export of turnkey industrial projects is generally undertaken by capital goods manufacturers who 'package' their product with the provision of various skills, services and finance to provide a functioning plant to the client.[4] However, the ability to deliver a turnkey plant requires more than the capability to produce capital goods: while machinery can be manufactured in a developing country under licence, with relatively low local content and no local basic design skills, the setting up of a turnkey project involves several other capabilities. e.g. project design, plant engineering, procurement and manufacture of equipment, construction management, commissioning and training, and subsequent problem-solving. The sale of turnkey plant entails, in particular, the ability to tailor entire technologies to specific needs, since each plant is different from every other and has to be individually designed and engineered.

The demand for turnkey industrial plants has risen dramatically in recent years in many parts of the Third World. It is not only countries without an industrial base and the necessary engineering skills that have sought to buy turnkey 'packages' (though the oil-rich countries have certainly led the rest). Every country which has sought to import advanced technology, especially in process industries like chemicals, petrochemicals and metallurgy, has drawn upon the services of highly specialised contractors to transfer, quickly and effectively, the technology embodied in a functioning plant. (And within the developed countries themselves these contractors are widely employed by producing companies.)

A number of Third World countries have emerged as exporters of industrial turnkey projects. The field seems to be led by India, in terms both of the value of total projects won and the range, diversity and complexity of industrial technologies involved. Indian exports of relatively simple plant (like textiles, sugar or electrical transmission) have been taking place for many years, but the period since 1975 has witnessed the sale of over one hundred projects including some complex industries like power generating plant, cement and chemical mills, paper mills, machine tool factories and even automatic (not electronic) telephone exchanges. According to my collection of rather diverse data, Indian firms had won $1100 million worth of industrial turnkey contracts by end-1979, of which 54 per cent was destined for the Middle East, 14 per cent for Africa, 25 per cent for South and East Asia and 7 per cent elsewhere (including power plant for New Zealand).[5] A turnkey project for a rayon plant had even been won in China. Power generation (28.2 per cent) and distribution (27.1 per cent), followed by cement mills (10.9 per cent) and machine-tool plants and steel plant (12.1 per cent) accounted for much of the value.

Of other developing countries, the available (scattered) data show the following rough magnitudes: Argentina $211 million;[6] Brazil $111 million;[7] and Korea $387 million (until end-1977).[8] Mexico had undertaken relatively few industrial turnkey projects abroad and the value of such work appeared to be much less than that of Argentina or Brazil.[9] Taiwan appears to be very active in the export of industrial machinery, but the small average value of the transactions ($0.3 million in 1976) indicates that many of the 'turnkey' exports were in fact sales of equipment as such.[10] However, some genuine sales of complete plants were probably also made; the total value of such sales is not known, but circumstantial evidence suggests that it would not have exceeded that of South Korea.

By industrial specialisation, Brazilian turnkey exports were mainly in the fields of steel and alcohol distilling; Mexican ones were in food processing and oil exploration; Argentinian ones were in food processing, chemicals and glass; Korean mainly in cement, chemicals, paper, rubber and metal products; and Taiwanese in metal products, paper, plastic products and water purification.

Smaller industrialised countries like Hong Kong or Singapore did not seem to engage in this sort of TE activity. This is entirely expected since they lacked a domestic capital-goods base as well as previous experience at home of heavy industrial construction activity. As noted previously, most other turnkey exporters used their domestic capital-goods manufacturing base to sell complete plant, but Korea was something of an exception. Its firms generally moved into industrial construction from overseas operations in civil construction, relying on their organisational and financial strengths (backed strongly by the Korean Government) to execute contracts on the basis of technology and equipment produced elsewhere.

By now Third World enterprises have won some 500–1000 industrial turnkey contracts, almost entirely in other developing countries. The total value of such contracts (not exceeding $3 billion) is miniscule in relation to the volume of similar contracts currently being executed by developed country firms.[11] The entry of developing country enterprises should not, therefore, be seen as a major challenge to the existing technological order. Much of the large-scale, high-technology work is confined to developed country firms, and the dent which developing countries are making is a very small one. Having acknowledged this, we must also note that it marks only the beginning of the process and even a small dent is significant as a valuable indicator of a capability acquired in an area till now presumed out of their reach.

Consultancy

The part played by consultancy organisations in the transfer, adaptation and development of technology has been largely ignored in the economic literature, though its real significance can hardly be underestimated. The growth of the size, complexity and specificity of a large number of industrial processes has made them heavily consultancy-dependent: steel, non-ferrous metals, power generation, mining and all the continuous-process industries (oil, petrochemicals, chemicals, paper etc.). 'Engineering consultancy . . . is the *organic link between machine building – the supply of investment goods – and real capital formation by industrial enterprises*' (Roberts, 1973; p. 42, emphasis added). Consultants are essential to the design, commissioning and construction of a large number of industries: in a sense they embody the 'pure' technology of setting up modern industry. Nearly every manufacturing firm depends on them, since they possess a range of specialised skills which even large TNCs do not have (or do not find economical to retain in manufacturing operations, though several consultants are offshoots of manufacturing firms).

Consultants can provide a wide range of services encompassing areas of both 'high' and 'low' technology. Specialised engineering consultants can render extremely complex services in carrying out the basic and detailed engineering of chemical or metallurgical projects, while management and technical consultants can provide relatively routine services of personnel recruitment, accountancy, plant trouble shooting or construction supervision. The same consultants can sell a spectrum of different kinds of services, and a proper evaluation of the *content* of this form of TE requires that we know the details of what each country is exporting.

Unfortunately, such detail is not available for most developing countries. What we do know is that many of the newly industrialised countries named previously *are* active and growing exporters of all kinds of consultancy services. By 1979, some forty-odd enterprises from India had sold

$48 million worth of consultancy abroad, annual sales rising from $5 million in 1975–6 to $20 million in 1978–9. The main sectors in which Indian firms were active abroad were metallurgy (25 per cent of foreign earnings in 1978–79), power generation (14 per cent), civil construction (13 per cent), computer software (13 per cent) and chemicals (11 per cent).[12]

Brazil's accumulated earnings from consultancy exports totalled approximately $48.4 million by 1980[13] and Mexico's about $38.4 million:[14] both figures are very rough and should be treated with caution. No comparable data are available for other countries, though Argentinian and Taiwanese consultants are known to be active overseas.

In general, Indian consultancy exports appear to lead those of other developing countries. As with turnkey exports, they seem to reach a broader range of countries, and to span a more diverse and complex range of technologies. Mexico's consulting firms, in particular Bufète Industrial, the country's technology exporter, seem to come nearest to Indian ones in their range and sophistication. Both seem capable of undertaking basic design and engineering in fairly high-technology activities, and have undertaken independent R&D work to develop some of their own technologies.

As with turnkey exports, developing country consultants tend to work abroad in a distinctly 'lower' technological level than firms from industrialised countries. The incidence of subcontracting the more 'labour intensive' parts of engineering work (e.g. detailed engineering, supervision) from developed country firms is greater for Third World consultants than turnkey contractors. The difficulty of establishing their credentials abroad often leads Third World consultants to take on jobs much simpler (and less remunerative) than their work at home, but there are signs that this is changing as customers get to know their capabilities better.

Direct investment

Direct investment abroad in manufacturing by developing country enterprises generally takes the form of joint ventures with local firms. 'Third World MNCs' in manufacturing have aroused a great deal of interest recently,[15] but such ventures are only a part of a larger process of the internationalisation of banks, hotels, construction firms, consultants, insurance companies, trading houses and primary-product firms. Some early MNCs from the Third World (e.g. Bunge y Born and Alpargatas, both from Argentina) went abroad as early as before the First World War, while some 'expatriate' MNCs (e.g. Jardine Matheson in Hong Kong) have long used a Third World base to establish a wide network of international operations. However, the real growth of foreign activity by indigenous

Third World enterprises has come in the past decade, and shows all signs of a sustained 'take-off'.

The competitive edge of Third World manufacturing MNCs seems to lie in their mastery over specific manufacturing technologies, which are generally sufficiently adapted to the environments of less-developed countries to yield them a 'proprietary advantage' in world markets. Contrary to some earlier analyses, such MNCs are *not* confined to simple, small-scale technologies producing undifferentiated goods that sell on the basis of low prices. Such 'low technology' MNCs undoubtedly exist, but they are being rapidly overtaken by firms which utilise advanced, capital-intensive technologies, and/or produce differentiated goods which demand sophisticated marketing. There are, however, interesting and significant differences between MNCs from different developing countries, a point to which we return below.

Let us first review the existing data.[16] Hong Kong leads the Third World in direct foreign investments, with equity overseas of up to $2 billion (mostly in manufacturing). It is followed, at some distance, by Singapore with investments of up to $500 million (a lot of which is in manufacturing). These two highly industrialised island economies, with their liberal trading policies, long experience of entrepôt trade and rising wage and rental costs are in a class by themselves as far as international-isation of production is concerned.

In the rest of the Third World, the second group comprises India (foreign equity of around $100 million in some 200 foreign operations), Argentina ($65 million), Brazil ($65 million) and Mexico ($40–60 million). Of these, over 95 per cent of Indian investment is in manufacturing, with lower proportions for the other countries. Medium-sized countries with significant manufacturing investments abroad are South Korea ($15 million in manufacturing out of a total of $60 million), Taiwan ($60 million in total, no details available), Colombia and Venezuela ($55 million and $54 million, again without details).

To return to the industrial specialisation of Third World MNCs, let us start with Hong Kong firms (very little is known of Singapore firms). Hong Kong MNCs (see Chen, forthcoming) are concentrated in textiles and garments, plastics and simple consumer electronics, the products in which they have shown such impressive export performance. They invest abroad mainly to exploit lower wage and rental costs, and to gain access to protectionist OECD markets: they are generally not geared to host country markets. They provide mainly managerial, production and marketing expertise: there is little 'technology' (designs, local equipment) provided from Hong Kong. The most striking aspect of their growth is their export orientation and highly developed marketing acumen.

166   *Sanjaya Lall*

In contrast, MNCs from the larger industrialising countries are primarily engaged in serving local markets and are active over a much wider range of industries and provide much more technology from the home country. Indian MNCs, in particular, contribute nearly all their equity in terms of equipment and know-how, and range over such activities as truck assembly, diesel engine manufacture, machine tools, precision tools, rayon, paper, mini-computers, pharmaceuticals and soft drinks (besides the 'traditional' ones like textiles and simple metal products). The Latin American MNCs are more specialised in food products, paper, cement, simple metal products and some consumer durables, though some public sector enterprises are engaged in more sophisticated activities like petrochemicals and steel. Korean and Taiwanese investments are generally confined to simple technologies like textiles, plastics, cement and metal products, though some firms are buying into high-technology activities (sophisticated electronics, petrochemicals) by entering joint ventures in the US. In general, all these MNCs are weak in consumer marketing and are at their strongest in intermediate products and undifferentiated consumer goods.

In sum, India emerges, not as the largest foreign investor in the Third World, but again, as the one with the most diverse and complex range of activities and the highest embodiment of local technology. Indian MNCs are, like most Third World MNCs except for those from Hong Kong, deficient in marketing skills, but have sufficient technological strengths to be able to continue growing internationally. A recent liberalisation of Indian government policy has led to an acceleration of their investments overseas, and foreign ventures are being officially regarded as an increasingly important means of promoting the exports of Indian components and products for assembly overseas (by end-1979, equity of $38.1 million in projects already in operation had generated additional exports of $77.5 million and earnings of $12 million). Other countries, in particular Brazil and Korea, are also actively promoting overseas production by their firms as a means of export promotion, though in manufacturing *per se* they lag well behind Indian firms. Hong Kong firms, on the other hand, are pushing further afield on their own, and actively exploring investment possibilities in Europe and North America.

Licensing

'Licensing' is defined here to cover the sale of patents and brandnames as well as technical assistance, sale of knowhow and assembly under contract. The value of TE by licensing is probably very small for the Third World, but it is an extremely active area, in particular where the sale of technical assistance and unpatented knowhow is concerned. By its very nature, there is little hard data on this sort of TE, but sufficient anecdotal evidence exists from all the newly industrialising countries to argue that in terms of *numbers* of transactions it is the most important form of TE.

For Indian firms, a few instances have been recorded of local patents (for drugs, leather, chemical processes) and design (machine tools industries, boilers) being sold overseas, but most licensing has taken the form of overseas assembly and/or the supply of technical knowhow and management. Indian trucks, scooters and bicycles are assembled in several Third World countries, and several firms are selling managerial services to counterparts in Sri Lanka, Philippines, Indonesia, the Middle East and East Africa. Technical assistance based on experience of trouble shooting, production engineering and quality control is also very common. Several Indian enterprises have helped other developing countries to set up training centres, and to train their personnel at plants in India.

Such sales of production-experience technology also appear to be very common in the large Latin American countries.[17] In addition, some notable sales of licenses based on local innovations have been recorded: Hojalatas y Laminas (HYLSA) has pioneered a direct reduction process for producing sponge iron from iron ore using natural gas (which is cheap and abundant in Mexico). The HYLSA process has been licensed to six foreign countries, and is counted as one of the 'frontier' technologies in its field. Brazilian steel firms have licensed firms in developed countries in charcoal-based steel-mill technology. In the Mexican and Brazilian pulp-paper industry and the Mexican glass industries, new processes and designs have been developed which are in use overseas. A Mexican engineer has innovated a technology for non-woven textiles which is licensed to nine countries abroad. There is little doubt that similar examples could be found for Argentina, Korea and Taiwan. Unfortunately, the evidence is too scanty to permit inter-country comparisons.

ASSESSMENT

There is little doubt, even after a cursory survey of the evidence that TE by developing countries is a real and growing phenomenon. The total values involved are small in relation to total world trade in technology, but what we are witnessing is only the first hesitant steps of developing countries into this arena. Despite this, Third World TE already covers a broad array of high- and low-skill, large- and small-scale, and technologically simple and complex, activities. If TE is indeed a true indicator of developing countries' dynamic comparative advantage, then the growth of their industrial capabilities will reveal itself in increasingly sophisticated and widespread sales of technology. Moreover, such sales will spread mainly from other parts of the Third World to specialised areas of the industrialised world, a point to which we return later.

If we look at the range, diversity and complexity of indigenous technology and capital equipment contained in the TE of the main developing countries, India probably emerges as the overall leader. Hong Kong undoubtedly has larger direct investments overseas, Mexico has more advanced steel and petrochemical technology, while Brazil is particularly developed in charcoal and alcohol-based technologies, but, taking the industrial sector as a whole, India seems to have assimilated the greatest amount of technology and moved furthest in terms of the ability to design and reproduce it abroad. This is something of a paradox. Among the group of newly industrialising countries, India stands out as the one with the slowest rate of growth, the worst performance in terms of expansion of manufactured exports and the most inward-looking, highly interventionist government policies (which are supposed to have led to the creation of a heavily protected and inefficient industrial structure).

The paradox becomes more puzzling when we look at the different compositions of TE by the different developing countries. The small, open economies of Hong Kong and Singapore are strong in managerial and marketing knowhow, which they exploit overseas in the form of direct investments in relatively small-scale, technologically simple, consumer goods. They provide practically no capital goods from home, and reveal technological capabilities only for production knowhow and shop-floor engineering. The larger economies with some capital-goods base are active over the whole range of technological sales, but the variety of industries covered is quite narrow and the local 'embodiment' of capital goods and basic designs provided relatively limited. India, by comparison, covers a larger spectrum of industrial activity, from the very simple to the very sophisticated, and is able to provide locally designed equipment and knowhow for many activities in which no other developing country exports technology.

This statement is quite compatible with the fact that other developing countries, in particular Brazil, have much greater local production of technologically advanced industrial goods than India, and nearly all the others are larger exporters of engineering products. However, the ability to manufacture a product locally and export it is quite different from the ability to master its technology and to sell it internationally. The first requires the assimilation of a certain level of *production technology* ('knowhow') and marketing skills — in some cases, like the assembly of electronic components (a large part of engineering exports by several developing countries), the level of knowhow assimilated may be extremely low, and the marketing may be handled entirely by foreign enterprises; in others, like automobile production in Brazil, the level of knowhow in the country may be quite high, and encompass the engineering capability to modify the product and the marketing ability to export complete packages for overseas assembly. The second requires the assimilation of *basic design technology* and the ability to engineer all the components of a complete new plant ('know-why'), as well as the skills to put together and sell a complex combination of goods and services.

The distinction between 'knowhow' and 'know-why' is a very fruitful one, and essential to an understanding of the difference in the performance of India and the other newly industrialising countries. A country may reach high levels of industrial production and exports on the basis of a build-up of knowhow, remaining dependent on the more advanced countries for know-why or basic designs of new technologies and equipment. The most rapid method to achieve this sort of growth is probably by the direct entry of foreign multinational companies, but the Korean experience (where nearly three-quarters of exports are accounted for by local enterprises, and nearly half by a dozen leading trading/industrial houses) shows that a dynamic indigenous sector can also expand very rapidly on the basis of know-why imported at arm's length. In fact, it may be argued[18] that, for poor countries just embarking on industrial development, the acquisition of knowhow rather than investments in building up know-why is the most appropriate policy. India's slow industrial growth and poor export performance may (in part, at least) be attributed to its desire to become technologically 'self reliant', and the technological lags which many of its industries are now experiencing may be due very largely to this strategy. On the other hand, it may be argued that India's slow industrial growth was due to a number of other factors and policies which had little to do with the acquisition of technological know-why. After all, Japan managed to achieve miraculous industrial growth and diversification on the basis of a highly interventionist policy of 'know-why' development.

This is not, however, the place to debate the broader issues of the sources of economic growth or the proper place of technological development in industrialisation. Here we are concerned simply with accounting for differences in technology-export performance, without evaluating its overall costs and benefits to the exporting economies. Let us return, therefore, to the question of how the ability to export technology arises in a developing economy.

The export of technology is such a diverse phenomenon that it can arise from several different kinds of acquisition of both knowhow and know-why (technological 'learning' broadly defined). The agents of 'learning' can also be numerous: production engineers, skilled workers, design engineers, component suppliers, consultants, engineering constructors, independent R&D institutes, and the like — and this excludes all the agents of non-technical (managerial, marketing, financial) learning. As indicated earlier, different kinds of learning by different agents reveal themselves in different extent and form of technology exports. Let us consider a very simple six-fold classification of the learning process which I had advanced in my first paper (Lall, 1978) on this subject:

(1) Simple 'learning by doing', whereby an imported technology is unchanged, but its utilization is made more efficient simply through the experience of workers.

(2) 'Learning by adapting', whereby small changes are made in a plant by shop-floor technicians, managers and engineers, to raise productivity within a given technology or to adapt the product slightly to particular needs.

(3) 'Learning by design', whereby imported equipment and processes are replicated, and knowledge is gained by design engineers and capital-equipment manufacturers of industrial processes. This stage involves the setting up of a capital goods industry.

(4) 'Learning by improved design', the next step in the design of equipment or products, where productivity-raising changes are made, or the design is scaled down, adapted to local raw materials, conditions and skills. Here design engineers generally need a separate R&D department, and, at later stages, a basic science and technology infrastructure.

(5) 'Learning by setting up complete production systems', whereby the ability is acquired, not just to produce items of equipment, but to engineer and tailor entire factories or plants to specific needs. At this stage, the country gains the capacity to set up independent engineering consultancy and contracting enterprises.

(6) 'Learning by designing new processes', whereby R&D departments or separate research institutions extend into basic research and development, and are able to offer new processes and to make new products. This 'basic' R&D is still of a different order of magnitude from basic R&D done in advanced countries, and may not lead to major breakthroughs. However, it may still lead to processes (as has happened, say, for chemical products) or products which are completely different from those first imported into the country.

These stages do not necessarily follow each other in temporal sequence. The ability to undertake certain types of construction or consultancy may arise after stage 2, even without a local capital goods or R&D capability, or an R&D capability in a process industry may develop even when the requisite capital goods have to be imported. However, this classification, crude as it is, provides a workable approximation to the stages of technological development, and helps to explain the different performances we observe in the TE field.

Thus, countries which have little or no capital goods capability (the small island economies) have learnt to implement and adapt given production technologies, and so have only exported little embodied technology or know-why. Their TE has been generally confined to direct investment, with the main competitive advantage residing in managerial and marketing skills. Countries which have large enough markets to support capital goods industries have exported a correspondingly broader range of technologies.[19] However, those which have (like India) *adopted specific policies to protect and expand domestic know-why have gone much further than those which have relied on passive imports of technology from abroad*. Despite the fact that Brazil has an industrial sector twice the size of India's and produces a broader range of sophisticated 'modern' industrial products (including heavy capital goods), India is a larger exporter of technology because its indigenous enterprises have been forced to go further down the learning sequence and to assimilate more know-why than their Brazilian counterparts.

How can this be explained? There are two stages to the answer. First, as learning progresses further than the elementary stages of learning by 'doing' and 'adapting', it becomes more risky and uncertain. Elementary learning concerned with the implementation of a given technology progresses in every production unit, more or less automatically with the passage of time, regardless of where the basic technology and equipment originate. Further learning requires the production of capital goods and the acquisition of design skills, an understanding of the scientific and mechanical principles involved, and the ability to try out new processes and products commercially without going bankrupt. Even when the technology is well-known abroad, a developing country enterprise engaged in 'minor' innovation necessarily faces innovative and commercial risk. To permit and induce it to assume such risk, *the government must afford it protection* against competition from proven technologies from abroad. It must, in other words, give it 'infant industry' protection, not only to assimilate knowhow (the classic case of permitting new producers to achieve scale economies and the benefits of elementary learning by doing) but also to build up its know-why (to invest in R&D, design skills, project execution skills etc.)[20]

Secondly, the protection of know-why necessarily requires some protection of the final product against imports (i.e. classical infant industry protection). But this is not enough. It also requires the *protection of the technological development process, by impeding a free flow of technology from abroad*. It is always cheaper and easier to import well-tried designs and equipment from abroad than to invest in creating them in a developing country. Where the free inflow of technology is permitted, either by direct foreign investment or by a passive reliance on continuous licensing, the local capability to acquire know-why develops more slowly. That is why the large Latin American countries, which have relied heavily on foreign multinationals and licensing in the advanced sectors of their economy, have developed a smaller TE capability than India, which has severely limited foreign entry and restricted foreign licensing.

The argument is supported if we look at the sectors in which the Latin Americans do export technology. Their capabilities are strongest in precisely those industries where the governments have stepped in (by direct ownership or protection) to restrict foreign presence (petrochemicals and steel), where an abundance of a certain resource has given them an industrial edge over industrialised countries without such a resource (sugar-based alcohol distilling in Brazil or food processing in Argentina), or where the sector is so undifferentiated and the technology so simple that multinationals are not active in it, giving a 'natural' protection to learning (textiles, garments, simple metal products). In contrast, where MNC presence is strong (machine tools, heavy electrical equipment, automobiles), local enterprises do not have the capability to sell projects overseas, when Indian enterprises have been engaged in setting up machine-tool complexes, power stations and truck assembly operations, all based on their own design and equipment, abroad.[21]

It is important, in sum, to appreciate the difference between technological learning of knowhow and know-why, and to realise that both require protection of different kinds. The buildup of knowhow needs protection against imports, for the period in which scale economies are realised and operational techniques and skills assimilated. The buildup of know-why needs protection against imports of finished products and also a restriction of the free import of foreign technology into the economy. As with all protection, this must not be carried too far: once the enterprise concerned has assimilated a certain level of know-why it may need a further injection of foreign technology to take it to the next level. The Indian experience shows that while a great deal of know-why can be built up, a lot of it can stay well behind rapidly changing world frontiers. What is needed is a judicious mixture of imports and local assimilation: the

Japanese experience again provides the best case in point. It also shows that the protection of local learning need not inhibit an aggressive strategy of export promotion. Inward-looking technological policies do not necessarily imply inward-looking trade strategies — it is unfortunate for India that they have gone together.

LIMITATIONS ON TECHNOLOGICAL LEARNING IN THE THIRD WORLD

Even given all the right conditions for technology generation, however, the pace and limits of successful learning, even on a minor scale, will differ from industry to industry. Progress will be faster when innovation involves design of discrete items; when the processes involved are not subject to rapid change; when skills required are based on engineering-design activity rather than on science-based R&D; when the commercialisation of technology does not depend crucially on marketing and promotion abilities[22] (the acquisition of marketing knowhow seems to involve a longer learning process, and even more investment, than production technology); when commercialisation does not require very long production runs or very large orders; and when the technology can be subjected to adaptation, scaling-down, simplification etc., to suit the conditions of developing countries.

The export of technology by developing countries is, therefore, based on specific kinds of skill advantages. A simple categorisation by low-skill and high-skill, or low-technology and high-technology, is likely to be misleading. Countries whose size, level of industrialisation, education system and policy towards technology imports permits an independent assimilation of technology, should be able to gain a comparative advantage in various forms of high-skill activity where: (a) major innovations have been made abroad and are in the process of diffusion in advanced countries;[23] (b) the necessary skills are acquired through engineering expertise gained through design and implementation of production processes and capital goods, rather than through large-scale scientific activity on the frontiers of technology; (c) the activity is not aimed at meeting changing needs of high-income, brand-conscious consumers; and (d) the technology involves large inputs of detailed design and adaptation to suit each application.

These considerations point to an evolving division of technological work between nations whereby the more industrialised developing countries can, given their cost advantages and their experience of relatively primitive conditions, increasingly undertake transfers to developing countries of technologies which are intensive in their types of 'high' skills. They can also enter developed countries to perform costly skilled jobs where their cheap manpower can provide a massive advantage (e.g. engineering consultancy in certain industries, 'software' components of various technologies, project construction management, detailed design work). High technology firms in the industrialised countries can participate in one or both of two ways — subcontracting activity to Third World technology firms, or establishing affiliates in developing countries to directly exploit their low cost, experience and skills. There are signs that both these courses are being adopted, again with national differences depending on the protection given to local enterprises by their respective governments.

It is important to note that the dividing line *does not fall by industry but by particular technologies within each industry*. There will be complex, innovative technologies within the most traditional industries which are beyond the reach of developing countries; and there will be relatively standardised, diffused and easily assimilated technologies within the most sophisticated industries in which developing countries can become proficient.[24]

There are lessons for students of trade theory here. Most recent empirical examinations of comparative advantage in manufactured trade of developed and developing countries[25] have identified the competitive edge of the former as lying in high-technology and high-skill activities, and of the latter as lying in standardised technology, low-skill activities (physical capital intensity seems generally to have been discarded as a significant influence). In many studies, high skill and high technology are regarded as practically synonymous, and both are treated as being the preserve of high-income countries.

An examination of technology exports by developing countries suggests that, with the natural accumulation of skills in the process of industrialisation, the comparative advantage of developed *versus* developing countries will be determined, not so much by skill requirements *in general*, but by skill inputs based on *specific learning processes which cannot be replicated in developing countries*. The four conditions we have just mentioned, for instance, will determine, even for highly skill-intensive activities, which can most economically be performed in rich or poor countries.

This will lead to a change in the specialisations of developed and developing countries: rather than concentrating on different types of industries, as they have tended to do till now, they will specialise in different processes within the same industries. Developed–developing country trade will, in other words, come more and more to resemble inter-developed country trade, with the growing sway of the sorts of considerations that Grubel and Lloyd (1975) have advanced as determining 'intra-industry trade'. These include such factors as 'gaps' in technology, product differentiation and scale economies, all similar to the ones we have advanced as the limitants to learning in developing countries.

Some recent literature on manufactured exports by developing countries has remarked on the rapid diversification of these exports into high-skill activities. In part this has been traced to the activities of MNCs, which have transferred the simpler parts of high-skill, high-technology processes to some developing activities. In part, however, if the technology export scene is a reliable index, it is due to the efforts of indigenous enterprises. It may be argued, of course, that such diversification, which necessarily entails investments in capital goods production and probably involves heavy learning costs, is somehow unnatural. Developing countries which go in for a policy of technological development may be accused of distorting their 'natural' comparative advantage, which lies in labour-intensive, low-skill activities. This is a controversy which cannot be resolved without a much more detailed examination of the costs and benefits of 'learning' technology. Certainly a strong case can be made, on historical consider-ations, in favour of developing countries investing in the building up of their technological capability, of the diversification of their exports into dynamic, modern activities, and of the exploitation of their human re-sources and accumulated experience.

These considerations also point to the possibility that developing countries which have built up a strong technological capability will reveal different sorts of comparative advantage in their exports to other develop-ing countries as opposed to more developed ones. As far as pure tech-nology exports are concerned, we would expect developing country enter-prises to sell only certain complementary services to the advanced countries. As far as engineering exports are concerned, similarly, we would expect to find that in general they would sell simpler products (e.g. hand tools, simple machinery) to developed countries, which would need a higher degree of sophistication at the advanced end than developing countries can competitively provide, than to developing ones, which would prefer the sorts of older, simpler or smaller-scale equipment provided by them.[26] The 'sourcing' activity of MNCs, however, may impose a uniform tech-nological level on all their exports, regardless of their destination.

CONCLUSIONS

To conclude, the explanations advanced in this chapter for the observed patterns of technology exports are still very tentative. However, they call into question some of the simpler analysis of technical progress in developing countries which do not distinguish between the various stages and agents of the learning progress, and identify the transfer of technology within the multinational corporation with the development of technological capability within the host country. Findlay (1978) has argued, for instance, that multinationals can be the main agents of technical progress in backward countries. Since they possess the most advanced technology and since direct investment by them is the most powerful means of transferring it, it follows, in Findlay's reasoning, that a greater multinational presence will lead to a more rapid 'catching up' of the host country with the advanced countries.

This argument may be valid as far as the transfer of production technology at the elementary levels is concerned. If, however, we consider the ability of the host country to master the technology as a whole, and to engender its own technical progress, Findlay's argument no longer applies. Multinationals may contribute to local technological capabilities in certain specific circumstances, but in general a strong foreign presence (or a heavy dependence on licensed technology) may inhibit the local process of learning. Foreign enterprises still have two crucial roles to play, of providing the initial injection of new knowledge on which the host country can build, and of supplying the sorts of new technologies which cannot be mastered in the developing countries: whether this is best done in the form of wholly-owned foreign subsidiaries, joint ventures or licensees, depends on the nature of the technology and the state of development of the recipient. For the large area of technological work which lies beneath the difficult frontiers of advanced innovation, however, developing country enterprises can progress substantially on their own, and here a degree of protection may be a necessary condition for progress. The inter-relationship between domestic and imported technologies is thus both a complementary and a competitive one. Over time it fluctuates between them, and policies which veer too much either to protection or to free imports of technology can be harmful.

NOTES

1 See, for instance, Hirsch (1977) and Vernon (1966).
2 For a brief, succinct exposition of the relevant theory see Nelson (1980).
3 Mainly the detailed enterprise-level studies conducted in Latin America by the IDB/ECLA Research Program in Science and Technology, summarised in Katz (1978).
4 While this is generally the case, there are exceptions; for instance, the prime contractor can be a civil construction firm from a developing country which buys all the basic technology and equipment in industrialised countries and simply 'packages' it for the client. Of the Third World technology exporters,

only South Korean firms undertake this sort of turnkey project. The others (India, Brazil, Mexico and Argentina) all base turnkey exports on their own capital goods and engineering capabilities.

5   These data are taken from my study for the World Bank on TE by India, which will be published in due course. An earlier assessment, based on less-complete data but providing more firm-level detail, is available in Lall (1982a).

6   Derived from data presented by O'Brien (1981); civil construction projects have been excluded.

7   Sercovitch (1981). The Brazilian figure includes the value of technical services rendered abroad, so is a slight overstatement.

8   Rhee and Westphal (1978).

9   Dahlman (1981).

10 Rhee and Westphal (1978).

11 For instance, work in hand by three US engineering contractors by 1 September 1980 was: Fluor Corporation $13.6 billion, with one single contract in Saudi Arabia worth $5 billion; Parsons $6.6 billion; and Brown and Root $6.0 billion. See *Business Week*, 'The Construction Boom', 29 September 1980, p. 84. US firms are probably lagging well behind their Japanese rivals, especially in winning contracts in the Third World.

12 By destination, Indian consultancy exports in 1978–79 went to: Middle East 23.5 per cent; Africa 26.9 per cent; South East Asia 11.4 per cent; OECD 14.5 per cent and unallocated 23.7 per cent. The sales to the OECD countries consisted mainly of computer software.

13 Sercovitch (1981).

14 Dahlman (1981). This total is for TECNIMEXICO, a consortium of the leading consulting firms. It includes services which are classified under 'licensing' for India, and so overstates the Mexican figure in relation to the Indian.

15 See Wells (1977), Diaz-Alejandro (1977), Lecraw (1975), Lall (1982b) and various papers in Kumar and McLeod (1982).

16 For further details and sources see Lall (1982a and 1982b).

17 See Dahlman (1981), Sercovitch (1981). A large number of industries, from traditional to modern, are covered by this activity.

18 As Dahlman and Westphal have done in this volume.

19 On the crucial role of the capital goods sector in generating and diffusing technological progress see Pack (1981), Rosenberg (1976) and Stewart (1977).

20 For a review of the issues and a clear analysis see Westphal (1981).

21 It is possible that Brazilian affiliates of MNCs produce more advanced versions of these products than Indian enterprises can, but they import the know-why from centralised R&D facilities of the parent companies in the developed world. It is also likely that technological improvements which do take place in affiliates of foreign MNCs are transmitted abroad and commercialised by the parent company.

22 This is why most exports of high technology by developing countries have taken place on a tender basis, to 'informed' buyers who are not as swayed by brand names as the ordinary customer.

23 There is considerable literature on industrialised countries (e.g. Mansfield 1969), which shows that the size of investment required and the risk and returns associated with the change interact to produce an S-shaped curve of diffusion of innovations. Such considerations may also influence the course of diffusion in developing countries, but for the present such factors as basic design capabilities, a certain technological ability and confidence, a structure capable of absorbing innovation (which are taken for granted in advanced countries) need more emphasis and analysis. Once these factors exist, we may expect to find a narrowing gap between imitators in developing and industrialised countries.

24   In some industries this would involve learning different processes (e.g. in chemicals or assembly line techniques); in others it may involve learning to operate processes of a certain *scale* (e.g. in power generation technical progress takes the form of increasing the capabilities of machines without changing the basic engineering processes).
25   See Hirsch (1977).
26   See Amsden (1980).

REFERENCES

Amsden, A. (1980). The industry characteristics of intra-Third World trade in manufactures, *Economic Development and Cultural Change*, October, pp. 1–19.

Chen, E. K. Y (1982). Hong Kong multinationals in Asia, in K. Kumar and M. G. McLeod (Eds), *Multinationals from Third World Countries*, D. C. Heath, Lexington.

Dahlman, C. J. (1981). Technology exports by Mexico: Back to office report, World Bank (unpublished).

Diaz-Alejandro, C. F. (1977). Foreign direct investment by Latin Americans, in T. Agmon and C. P. Kindleberger (Eds) *Multinationals from Small Countries*, MIT Press, Cambridge, Mass.

Findlay, R. (1978). Relative backwardness, direct foreign investment and the transfer of technology: A simple dynamic model, *Quarterly Journal of Economics*, February, pp. 1–16.

Grubel, H. G. and Lloyd, P. J. (1975). *Intra-Industry Trade*, Macmillan, London.

Hirsch, S. (1977). *Rich Man's, Poor Man's and Everyman's Goods: Aspects of Industrialization*, J. C. B. Mohr, Tübingen.

Katz, J. (1978). Technological change, economic development and intra and extra regional relations in Latin America, Buenos Aires: IDB/ECLA Research Program in Science and Technology, Working Paper 30.

Kumar, K. and McLeod, M. G. (1982), *Multinationals from Third World Countries*, D. C. Heath, Lexington.

Lall, S. (1978). Developing countries as exporters of technology: A preliminary analysis, paper presented to conference in Institut fur Weltwirtschaft, Kiel and published in *Research Policy*, 1980.

Lall, S. (1982a), *Developing Countries as Exporters of Technology*, Macmillan, London.

Lall, S. (1982b). The emergence of Third World multinationals: Indian joint ventures overseas, *World Development*, **10**, 2.

Lecraw, D. T. (1977), Direct investment by firms from less developed countries, *Oxford Economic Papers*, pp. 445–57.

Mansfield, E. (1969). *The Economics of Technological Change*, Longman, London.

Nelson, R. R. (1980) Production sets, technological knowledge and R&D, *American Economic Review, Papers and Proceedings*, pp. 62–67.

Nelson, R. R. and Winter, S. (1977). In search of a useful theory of innovations, *Research Policy*, pp. 36–76.

O'Brien, P. (1981). The Argentinian experience in export of technology: Retrospect and prospect, UNIDO, Vienna, (mimeo).

Pack, H. (1981). Fostering the capital goods sector in LDCs, *World Development*, 9, 3, pp. 227–50.

Rhee, Y. W. and Westphal, L. E. (1978). A note on exports of technology from the Republics of China and Korea, World Bank (unpublished).

Roberts, J. (1973). Engineering Consultancy, industrialization and development, in C. Cooper (Ed.), *Science, Technology and Development*, Frank Cass, London.

Rosenberg, N. (1976). *Perspectives on Technology*, Cambridge University Press, London.

Sercovitch, F. (1981). Brazil as a technology exporter, Washington, Inter-American Development Bank (unpublished).

Stewart, F. (1977). *Technology and Underdevelopment*, Macmillan, London.

Vernon, R. (1966). International investment and international trade in the product cycle, *Quarterly Journal of Economics*, pp. 190–20.

Wells, L. T. (1977). The internationalization of firms from developing countries, in T. Agmon and C. P. Kindleberger (Eds) *Multinationals from Small Countries*, MIT Press, Cambridge, Mass.

Westphal, L. E. (1981). Empirical justification for infant industry protection, World Bank (unpublished).

9 Opening Pandora's Box: Technology and social performance in the Indian tractor industry*

WARD MOREHOUSE

CONVENTIONAL WISDOM ON INDIGENOUS AND FOREIGN TECHNOLOGY

Conventional wisdom in many circles holds that, while technological self-reliance is an attractive political slogan in developing countries, in the real world where investment decisions and technological choices are made and products sold, bought, and used, foreign technology is preferred because it is better. Better for the consumer because it works better than indigenous technology. Better for the investor because it is more profitable. That there are larger economic and political costs in continuing technological dependence may then be conceded, but when consumers, investors, and entrepreneurs are given an unfettered choice, so this view maintains, they will opt for foreign technology and the products based on it.

The Indian tractor industry provides an opportunity to examine the basis for this conventional wisdom through actual performance, side by side, of foreign and indigenous technology. Comparisons are difficult, because, as usual, data are incomplete and evidence is preliminary. The Indian tractor industry is relatively young (and indigenous tractor technology even younger) so that time periods for comparison are limited. Notwithstanding these limitations, a picture can be created, indistinct in some details, but clear in broad outline. That picture suggests that even in the real world of the factory, boardroom, and market place, indigenous technology can measure up. The picture also suggests that foreign technology inappropriate to local conditions or inadequately transferred

* I am indebted to Alan Heston, Acqueil Ahmad, Sekhar Chaudhuri, and K. K. Subrahmaniam for their comments and suggestions, although the analysis and conclusions presented are entirely my own responsibility. This chapter is part of a forthcoming study, *The Political Economy of Science and Technology in North–South Relations: A Study of U.S. Indian Relations*, a preliminary version of which is available from the National Technical Information Service, Springfield, Virginia. A portion of the chapter in significantly different form appeared in the *Economic and Political Weekly* (20 December 1980).

can be a powerful stimulus to indigenous technology generation because of the demands of the real world.

This study reveals as well some of the advantages and disadvantages of foreign technology in a Third World country with a still incomplete but rapidly developing industrial infrastructure like India. Among the advantages of foreign technology are the saving of time in getting into production and diminished risk to the local entrepreneur in using proven production technology from abroad. For the consumer, it also means the possibility of obtaining a well-established product with a wide international reputation but not at a cheaper price, as indigenously designed Indian tractors are no more expensive than equivalent models based on foreign design (and in one instance, significantly less).

The disadvantages of foreign technology in this particular industry are related to the higher social and economic costs to the society as a whole. They are reflected in considerably greater capital and foreign-exchange costs and the general lower level of interest (and in some cases, capacity) that Indian entrepreneurs using foreign technology have in manufacturing newly designed products with wider social application, such as small tractors for small farmers.

An historical view of the Indian tractor also underscores the indispensability of foreign technology to its establishment and present evolution. The critical questions for a country like India, however, lie not in the past but in the future. Here our analysis indicates that indigenous technology is quite capable of standing up to the competition from enterprises based on foreign technology if it is given a chance.

That the performance of indigenous technology can measure up to foreign technology may seem like an unexceptional point to observers in industrially advanced countries who are used to technology choices based solely on product performance and price, with the nationality of the technology largely irrelevant. For a developing country struggling to create a viable scientific and technological capacity effectively linked to the productive sectors of the economy, however, the actual demonstrated ability of locally generated technology to measure up is crucial to establishing the credibility of indigenous technology as a valid means of meeting economic and social needs, in addition to the heretofore exclusive reliance on foreign technology.

But creating the capacity for generating indigenous technology, is like opening up Pandora's box. Once created, it can be used for good or for ill. What is the social merit, sceptics would ask, of using this indigenous capacity to design and build self-propelled job destroyers such as combine

Table 1 Tractor manufacturers in India

Name of Indian Firm	Make/Model	bp	Source of Technology	Retail price (Rs)*
1 Escorts Ltd, Faridabad	E3036	35	Motoimport of Poland	53050
	E335MDC	35		55624
	E335ADDC	35		
2 Escorts Tractors Ltd, Faridabad	Ford-3600/3000	46	Ford Motor Co. of USA	68681
3 Eicher Tractors Ltd (I), Faridabad	Goodearth	26.5	Eicher of West Germany	36780
4 Punjab Tractors Ltd, Chandigarh	Swaraj 720	19	Indigenous	32050
	Swaraj 724	24		50865
	Swaraj 735	35		54250
5 International Tractor Co. of India Ltd, Bombay	B-275	35	International Harvester of UK (and parent company in USA)	53400
	444/431	45		58450

Company	Model	HP	Supplier	Price
6 Tractors & Farm Equipment Ltd, Madras	MF-1035	35	Massey-Ferguson of UK	57802
	TAFE 504	50		67525
7 Hindustan Machine Tools Ltd, Pinjore	Zetor/HMT 2511	25	Motokov of Prague, Czechoslovakia	49350
	HMT 3511	30		53400
	HMT 5711	55		72382
8 Harsha Tractors Ltd, New Delhi	T-25	25	Pommash Export of USSR	50157**
9 Hindustan Tractors Ltd, Baroda	Super-50	50	Motokov of Prague, Czechoslovakia	64490**
10 Pittie Tractors, Poona	4000	35	Indigenous	55215
11 Kirloskar Tractors Ltd, Nasik	D-4006K	43	Klockner Humbolt Deutz of West Germany	75500
	D-6006K	75		189889**

Source: Adapted from *Indian Farm Mechanization*, October, 1976, *Agricultural Engineering Today*, various issues, and industry data.
  * As of 1 January 1980. Retail prices include excise duty and dealer margin.
** Ex-works price.

harvesters in the labour-surplus Indian economy? Yet that is exactly what has occurred and forms an integral part of the unfolding story of the Indian tractor industry to which we now turn.

TRACTOR MAKING IN INDIA

A profile of the industry

The Indian tractor industry produced by the end of the 1970s about 60 000 agricultural tractors a year, in a horsepower range from 20 to 75. The industry is characterised by a dozen producing units, of which seven account for over 90 per cent of all production. These units, the models they manufacture, and the source of their technology are indicated in Table 1. As can be seen from this table, technology has been drawn from a variety of foreign sources – Poland, United States, West Germany, Czechoslovakia, United Kingdom, and the Soviet Union. There are also two units making indigenously designed tractors, of which only one – Punjab Tractors Ltd – can be characterised as a principal producer among the top seven.

Tractors were imported into India from the major industrialised countries until the early 1960s. Since, then production has risen steadily from 880 in 1961–62 to about 20 000 a decade later, and to figure in the neighbourhood of 60 000 at the start of the third decade of tractor manufacturing in India. Most of the major manufacturers are currently engaged in expansion of production, with industry forecasts suggesting a production level of 100 000 by the mid-1980s.

At its present level of production, the Indian tractor industry is still not large by US standards.[1] In 1978, 197 000 tractors were produced in the United States, where the number of units produced has been declining since 1973 (237 000), as farm sizes and tractor sizes have both increased.[2] However, if anticipated growth materialises, India will not be an insignificant producer in the world by the middle of the decade, and in number of units (not horsepower), it is already within the top five countries. (See Table 2 for tractor production since the mid-1960s.)

As can be seen from Table 3, seven of the eleven manufacturers dominate the industry with 92.8 per cent of the output (1979 figures). The three largest have almost 50 per cent of the market (62 per cent, if one takes into account the circumstances that one parent enterprise – Escorts – makes the largest in units of production, based on Polish technology, and the fourth largest through a subsidiary joint venture with Ford, the US source of the technology).

Another important characteristic is that market shares have also been

Table 2 (Part I) Tractor production in India from 1966–67 to 1974–75 (units produced)

	1966–67	1967–68	1968–69	1969–70	1970–71	1971–72	1972–73	1973–74	1974–75
1 Escorts Ltd, Faridabad	2133	2556	5569	7835	8770	3831	3418	4863	5819
2 Escorts Tractors Ltd, Faridabad	–	–	–	–	–	1609	1804	2882	3572
3 Eicher Tractors Ltd, Faridabad	92	204	349	378	859	789	854	1082	1226
4 Swaraj Tractor, Chandigarh	–	–	–	–	–	–	–	–	578
5 International Tractors Co. of India Ltd, Bombay	1301	2901	4011	4403	6494	9186	10210	9601	8263
6 Tractors & Farm Equipment Ltd, Madras	3397	4087	3275	2828	2768	2823	1459	1889	2746
7 Hindustan Machine Tools Ltd, Pinjore	–	–	–	–	–	–	2508	3393	6800
8 Harsha Tractors Ltd, New Delhi	–	–	–	–	–	–	–	–	41
9 Hindustan Tractors Ltd, Baroda	1893	1646	2218	1665	1193	342	549	435	781
10 Pittie Tractors, Poona	–	–	–	–	–	–	–	–	43
11 Kirloskar Tractors Ltd, Poona	–	–	–	–	–	–	–	25	731

Source: Adapted from *Indian Farm Mechanization*, October, 1976.

Table 2 (Part II) Tractor Production in India, 1975–79 (units produced)

	1975	1976	1977	1978	1979
1 Escorts Ltd, Faridabad	4786	5211	7211	10375	12233
2 Escorts Tractors Ltd, Faridabad	4701	4850	5660	6671	7404
3 Eicher Tractors Ltd, Faridabad	1461	2940	3476	5158	7021
4 Punjab Tractors Ltd, Chandigarh	1470	2711	3561	4569	5888
5 International Tractor Co. of India Ltd, Bombay	6960	6915	1854	7131	8425
6 Tractors & Farm Equipment Ltd, Madras	3278	4963	5795	6193	4819
7 Hindustan Machine Tools Ltd, Pinjore	6161	3281	6929	8801	8115
8 Harsha Tractors Ltd, New Delhi	921	691	1017	736	930
9 Hindustan Tractors Ltd, Baroda	797	1500	2105	2486	1915
10 Pittie Tractors, Poona	—	100	114	307	309
11 Kirloskar Tractors Ltd, Masik	781	500	267	577	1036
Total	32016	37662	38889	53003	58095

Source: Industry data.

shifting significantly in the past five years. Thus, International Harvester, which had 21.7 per cent of the market in 1975, dropped to 14.5 per cent in 1979, even though its production increased from 6000 units to 8425 units. Similarly, the Hindustan Machine Tools (HMT) Tractor Division decreased its market share from 19.2 per cent to 14 per cent. By contrast, Eicher (based on West German technology) increased its market share from 4.6 per cent in 1975 to 12.1 per cent in 1979, and Punjab Tractors Ltd

Table 3 Market share of tractor manufacturers in India 1975–79 (per cent of units produced)

	1975	1976	1977	1978	1979
1 Escorts Ltd, Faridabad	15.3	15.5	19.0	19.6	21.1
2 Escorts Tractors Ltd, Faridabad	15.0	14.4	14.9	12.6	12.7
3 Eicher Tractors Ltd, Faridabad	4.7	8.7	9.2	9.7	12.1
4 Punjab Tractors Ltd, Chandigarh	4.7	8.1	9.4	8.6	10.1
5 International Tractor Co. of India Ltd, Bombay	22.2	20.5	4.9	13.4	14.5
6 Tractors & Farm Equipment Ltd, Madras	10.5	14.7	15.3	11.7	8.3
7 Hindustan Machine Tools Ltd, Pinjore	19.7	9.7	18.2	16.6	14.0
8 Harsha Tractors Ltd, New Delhi	2.9	2.1	2.7	1.4	1.6
9 Hindustan Tractors Ltd, Baroda	2.5	4.5	5.6	4.7	3.3
10 Pittie Tractors, Poona	–	0.3	0.3	0.6	0.5
11 Kirloskar Tractors Ltd, Masik	2.5	1.4	0.7	1.1	1.8
Total*	100.0	100.0	100.0	100.0	100.0

Source: Industry data.   *May not total exactly due to rounding

(the only principal manufacturer based on indigenous technology) moved from 4.6 per cent to 10.1 per cent during this period.

Also significant is the distribution of horsepower sizes in the tractor industry, which has important implications for the social and economic impact of the industry on farming. Table 4 gives the distribution over the

Table 4 Horsepower distribution of tractor production in India, 1975–79

Horsepower range	1975		1976		1977		1978		1979	
	No. of tractors	Per cent	No. of tractors	Per cent	No. of tractors	Per cent	No. of tractors	Per cent	No. of tractors	Per cent
19–27	9913	31.05	7505	19.9	11845	30.5	13915	26.3	16082	27.7
35	14564	45.5	21470	57.0	18450	47.4	27029	51.0	29579	50.9
45	6271	19.6	7055	18.7	6195	15.9	8175	15.4	9788	16.8
50 and over	1268	3.9	1632	4.4	2399	6.2	3884	7.3	2646	4.6
Total	32016	100.0	37662	100.0	38889	100.0	53003	100.0	58095	100.0

Source: Industry data.

last five years. This distribution, which has not changed significantly during this period, stands in marked contrast to the situation in the major industrialised countries, where the distribution of horsepower sizes is at substantially higher levels and horsepower size has been increasing.[3] (The average American agricultural tractor today is 125 horsepower.) Whether this trend will change with increasing fuel costs remains to be seen. But at least at the present time, the trend upward in horsepower size in industrialised countries has been so substantial that several of the international farm-equipment manufacturers with joint ventures or licensed producers in India no longer make, elsewhere in the world, the smaller horsepower sizes being manufactured in India.

Getting and generating technology

Much has been said about how and why developing countries do and should make technological choices, but examination of the Indian tractor industry suggests that these choices, although certainly influenced by prevailing government policy at the time, are likely to be highly enterprise or situation specific. Thus, when HMT, a large public sector enterprise making machine tools, watches, and lamps as well as tractors, was confronted with a marked decline in the market for machine tools and a substantial deficit, its management, under considerable government and parliamentary pressure to improve its profitability as a bellwether publicly owned company, decided to diversify with an eye to technology acquisition which would yield early production and quick profits. Therefore, after considering foreign and Indian designed tractors, it opted for the foreign which was a proven production model, having been made for a number of years in its country of origin, while the Indian designed tractor was still in the prototype and testing stage.

The wisdom of the decision to opt for foreign technology, given HMT's problems and its management's objectives, is revealed in Table 5. HMT moved quickly into a position of profitability on its tractor operations (which actually began with simple assembly of imported components from its collaborator in Czechoslovakia). However, its profitability has declined as it has indigenised production and been compelled to increase capital investment.

By contrast, the indigenous technology option which HMT rejected but which was taken up by an enterprise especially formed for that purpose — Punjab Tractors Ltd — did not even begin significant production until three years after HMT was under way and was not able to realise a profit until five years later.[4]

The case of Punjab Tractors Ltd was obviously quite different. Here,

Table 5 Comparison of production, investment and profit levels for HMT and Punjab Tractors Ltd

	1971–72	1972–73	1973–74	1974–75	1975–76	1976–77	1977–78	1978–79
Production (no. of tractors)								
HMT	1600	2508	4000	6800	7000	4500	6457	8503
Punjab Tractors Ltd	–	–	80	650	1790	3340	3486	4859
*Level of Investment (Rs crores cumulative)**								
HMT III Tractor Division*		0.2	0.5	5.84	10.5	11.89		
Punjab Tractors Ltd.	0.12	1.4	3.2	3.7	3.7	3.7		
*Net Profit/Loss (Rs crores)***								
HMT III Tractor Division (estimated)	0.9	1.0	1.1	0.9	0.5	0.6		
Punjab Tractors Ltd	–	–	0.6	0.9	0.06	0.9		

Source: Adapted from Patricia Blatt, *Self-Reliance or Rediscovering the Wheel?: Case Studies of Technology Transfer and R & D in the Indian Tractor Industry* (MA Thesis. Department of Political Science, University of Melbourne, Australia, June 1979), with some production figures from *Agricultural Engineering Today*, January–February, 1980.

*Total investment was Rs118.9 million (at 1972 prices). This was largely made between 1974 and 1976. A further investment of Rs74 million is being made on a foundry to produce tractor castings in-house.

**One crore = 10 million

the choice of technology dictated the creation of the enterprise when those involved in developing the technology were unsuccessful in selling it to any existing enterprise, such as HMT. The existence of government-created and supported applied research laboratories without strong links to industry is often deplored in countries like India because of the difficulties in translating research done in such laboratories into actual production in industry. This is one instance, however, when R&D work in a government research laboratory (the Central Mechanical Engineering Research Institute — CMERI — in Durgapur) did get translated into productive activity, largely because of the entrepreneurial drive of the then Director of the Institute and the leader of the original design group (who has since become the Managing Director of the enterprise making the tractor in question). This indigenously designed tractor, known as Swaraj, has since established itself in the Indian tractor market in competition with tractors based on technology from some of the world's leading manufacturers of agricultural machinery, but because it was the first indigenously designed tractor, many hurdles had to be overcome.[5]

A very different picture of technology choice is found in the instance of Escorts Ltd, now a diversified mechanical engineering enterprise. The first involvement of Escorts in the tractor field was serving as importer and agent for the Massey-Ferguson tractor. On the strength of the good performance qualities of that tractor, Escorts had built up an effective dealer network, especially in North India. With relatively little advance notice, Massey-Ferguson decided to enter into a joint venture for the manufacture of its tractors in India with another concern in South India, leaving Escorts with its dealer network high and dry.

The Escorts Management responded to this crisis by seeking collaboration on terms that would enable them to get some product into the hands of their dealers as soon as possible, for without a product to sell, their dealers would either leave them or go out of business. The result was a Polish collaboration, leading to the manufacture in India of the Ursus tractor, and subsequently, a collaboration with the Ford Motor Company of the US through a joint venture, which is now manufacturing the Ford tractor in India. Here, enterprise survival in a very real and immediate sense was the overriding motive.

While these technology choices were all enterprise and situation specific, there is a correlation with changing government policy towards the import of technology. All of the technical collaboration agreements of the six principal tractor manufacturers using foreign technology were negotiated and approved in the 1960s (or very late 1950s, in a couple of cases), when prevailing government of India policy was to permit importation of such 'conventional' technologies as those involved in making tractors on the ground that the requisite knowledge and skill did not exist within the country. The seventh principal producer is the exception.

That exception is the only major tractor manufacturer based on indigenously generated technology, namely, Punjab Tractors Ltd. While the earliest beginnings of PTL occurred in the mid-1960s when R&D work began at CMERI in Durgapur and when Indian policy toward the import of technology was starting to change but was still ambivalent, many of the critical stages of decision-making on PTL, particularly its financing, did not occur until the turn of the decade. By that time, government policy had begun to shift, in fact, in the direction of greater technological self-reliance, at least in more traditional sectors of industrial activity such as tractor manufacture. Launching an industrial enterprise based entirely on indigenously generated technology in the modern industrial sector was, none the less, a sufficient innovation that PTL's promoters had a difficult time establishing the credibility of their technology and gaining the necessary support. But in the final analysis they did succeed.[6]

It seems unlikely today that the government of India would approve a *major* industrial project in the manufacture of tractors and related equipment unless some revolutionary advance in technology should occur elsewhere in the world and not otherwise be available in India. The word 'major' has been underscored because even today, established manufacturers do go abroad for additional collaborations (thus, one leading manufacturer is just now getting into production with earth-moving equipment, based on collaboration with a British enterprise) or for specialised components not made in the country (e.g. fuel injection systems).

Nor does it seem necessary for a country like India, in its present stage of industrial development, to depend on additional imports of technologies as 'matured' or stable as those involved in making tractors. The dilemma of technology choice today for India is quite different than it was a decade and half ago, when government decision-makers and the HMT management were weighing in the balance foreign collaboration or indigenous technology. The problem is also very different today in advanced and volatile technologies such as microelectronics. In such situations, India either tries to develop its own technology, usually remaining one or two generations behind the most advanced state of the art internationally, or it goes abroad for the most advanced technology, perpetuating its dependence on external sources for a vital factor of production.[7]

After the initial choice of technology has been made, the next critical question is how additional technology is acquired since, even in a relatively 'mature' field of industrial activity such as tractor manufacture, the technology does not stand still nor do the requirements of individual enterprises seeking to survive and, if possible, prosper in the market place. Conventional wisdom among advocates of indigenously generated technology holds that the initial importation of technology has an inhibiting impact on the capacity to generate technology indigenously, causing enterprises to go back again and again to the well of foreign technology rather than trying to develop their own. The experience in the Indian tractor industry suggests that this is partly true but not invariably so.

Most major tractor manufacturers in India today have some kind of R&D unit or establishment (in some cases associated with the parent mechanical engineering company when a separate joint venture has been created to make tractors with foreign collaboration). The spread of these R&D units, not only in the tractor industry but in other sectors of India's modern industrial economy, during the decade of the 1970s may be as much attributable to government incentives as to any 'felt need'. And in some cases, these units engage in little more than quality control and production trouble-shooting rather than any real governmental work.

How seriously R&D is taken appears to depend in considerable measure, on the mode of acquisiton and the character of the original technology. In at least two instances of Indian tractor production based on foreign technology, the technology proved to be inadequately transferred (i.e. without sufficient back-up training and consultancy services) or inappropriate to Indian conditions. The result was a powerful stimulus to these enterprises to create some kind of *de facto* design and development activity because of their need to survive in the market place, where repeated design failures of their products were causing them to lose ground rapidly. In one of these cases, furthermore, the technical collaboration agreement was hurriedly arranged and apparently included not much more than acquisition of the design drawings and other technical specifications with little back-up consultancy from the source enterprise or opportunity for training of the Indian company's production engineers by the source of the technology.

In another instance involving foreign collaboration with a leading multi-national, the position is quite different. There, in the view of the MNC management its Indian collaborator is making a world tractor which must conform exactly to the standards and specifications set down by the MNC for the same tractor wherever it may be manufactured throughout the world. Even though this collaboration is a decade old, the MNC continues to station a quality control engineer at the Indian plant with authority to shut down production (an authority which is said to have been exercised at least once) if there is any significant deviation from standards established by the MNC. In such circumstances, obviously, there is little stimulus to local technology generation; indeed, it seems to be specifically forbidden under the terms of the collaboration agreement, at least as long as the particular product carries the brand name of the source company for the technology.

A sharp contrast exists between this kind of situation, where the technology is hermetically sealed off from the local environment, and the one enterprise among major tractor manufacturers in India based on indigenously generated technology. By the very nature of things, Punjab Tractors Ltd, being based on technology of its own generation, has an active R&D unit and has made its capacity for technology generation a central element in its overall corporate strategy.

Thus, when the initially designed small Swaraj tractor (in the 25-horsepower range) proved not to be competitive in the market with tractors only slightly more expensive but considerably more powerful, in the 35-horsepower range, PTL quickly put its R&D group to work in designing and putting into production a 35-horsepower tractor.

It then decided to take a gamble on a segment of the tractor market all but abandoned by others in the industry (with one exception) — namely, a truly 'small' tractor (i.e. at or below 20 horsepower) at a significantly lower price which would be affordable by smaller farmers with land holdings with 2 to 4 hectares or even less (The number of tractor owners in this category of land holdings is growing through the increasing practice of custom-hiring to other small farmers in order to make the investment in the tractor pay off.) Again, PTL's R&D unit went to work and in relatively short order, came up with a newly designed tractor (the Swaraj 720 or Sartaj), which is the lowest-priced tractor on the market (approximately Rs32 000, or about $4000, in contrast to the next least-expensive tractor, the Eicher 25 horsepower, which is RS36 000 or approximately $4600). The PRL small tractor thus far appears to be doing quite well in the market.

As part of its overall corporate strategy to survive and grow in what will probably become an increasingly competitive market by the middle of the 1980s, the PTL management has concluded that it would be in a stronger position if it could offer prospective customers a wide range of models in horsepower sizes. Its R&D unit has, as a consequence, begun work on design of a 50-horsepower tractor, which the PTL management claims will give it the widest range of models in the market of any manufacturer (19 horsepower, 25 horsepower, 35 horsepower, and 50 horsepower).

Of course, other tractor manufacturers have not been idle. One of PTL's major competitors, with probably the largest R&D establishment in the industry, has designed a small tractor of its own but has not put it into production because it does not believe (nor do most of the others in the industry) that there is a real market for a small tractor in India. If PTL should establish in a truly convincing way that there is, this company might well go into production.

But in terms of overall enterprise strategy, PTL appears to have banked most heavily on its own capacity for generating technology. That may indeed be its comparative advantage over its competitors in the industry because of the very nature of its origins. But creating the capacity for indigenous generation of technology is a little bit like opening up Pandora's box. Once created, this capacity may be used for social good or ill, and is likely to prove to be difficult to control. Indeed, it is one of the perversities of technological self-reliance that PTL, under commission from the Punjab State government, has proceeded to embark upon a crash development programme to design and make combine harvesters which have been dubbed by critics of extensive mechanisation of Indian agriculture as 'self-propelled job destroyers'.

That PTL should have accepted the challenge of such a complex developmental task as designing and building from scratch a relatively complicated piece of mechanical equipment such as a combine harvester is a reflection of what may well be the greatest consequence of encouraging industrial development based on indigenously generated technology. Once PTL succeeded in designing, building, and selling a tractor based on indigenous technology, which competed effectively with tractors based on technology from some of the leading farm equipment manufacturers in the world, PTL engineers acquired considerable self-confidence in their ability to solve technological problems. This self-confidence has grown as they have surmounted additional challenges put before them — first, the 35-horsepower tractor, then a genuinely 'small' tractor, and now the combine harvester. It is also reflected in recent PTL initiatives to tackle what is clearly going to be a major constraint on agricultural mechanisation in India in the decades ahead — namely, the rising cost of petroleum-based fuels. The PTL R&D unit is beginning work, initially in collaboration with a microbiology research group established with their support at a neighbouring university, on alternative fuels based on biomass.

Other tractor manufacturers using foreign technology have also been active in generating their own technology, some more than others. Escorts and Eicher stand out as having made determined efforts to overcome defects and limitations in the foreign technology they originally acquired. In many ways, it might be said that such enterprise started out not with the intent of creating an R&D capacity but with having to cope with some serious design problems. Having successfully adapted the foreign technology, these enterprises find they have acquired a capability for technology development which can then be put to other uses.

One of the major lessons of the Indian tractor industry is that while initial dependence on foreign technology does not require indigenous effort to generate technology, it does not prevent it. Perversely, if the technology transferred is significantly inappropriate to Indian conditions and the terms of the transfer sufficiently disembodied (essentially the blueprints with little back-up technology consulting and training), external acquisition of technology may actually encourage indigenous effort.

Enterprise performance

The significance of the varying modes of technology acquisition and generation lies in the performance of enterprises in the industry and the social efficiencies and consequences of technology utilisation. Comparing enterprise performance in the tractor industry, seemingly a simple and straightforward proposition, is in fact tricky and elusive. Even trickier and more elusive is the task of isolating technology as a key variable in enterprise performance. The latter cannot be done with any substantial degree of analytical rigour because other key variables in determining organisational effectiveness such as enterprise leadership, production and marketing skills, and financial management and access to resources cannot be held constant. None the less, a picture of sorts can be created by looking at various indicators and factors.

One of the more obvious is market position, figures on which for the past five years have been given in Table 3. Among the seven principal producers, the Escorts' 35-horsepower tractor (a mixture of the original Polish technology and substantial indigenous modifications) has steadily advanced during this period to become the market leader with 21 per cent of the market (in terms of units sold). The indigenous option — Punjab Tractors Ltd — has also done well, moving from less than 5 per cent to slightly more than 10 per cent of the market during this period, as has Eicher (original West German technology with substantial indigenous modifications), with an even more impressive climb from the same level to slightly over 12 per cent.

It may be noted that both Punjab Tractors Ltd and Eicher have given considerable attention to the lower end of the tractor market in terms of horsepower size, although the smaller horsepower ranges as a group have remained, with minor fluctuations, more or less constant in relation to the total tractor market (see Table 4). Both PTL and Eicher were at relatively low levels of production at the beginning of this five year period, albeit for different reasons (PTL because it was just starting production, Eicher, which started production a decade and a half earlier, because of persisting design, production, marketing, and financial problems only finally overcome by the mid-1970s). In a sense, therefore, they had no place to go but up, although other manufacturers not among the major seven were also at a low level of production at the beginning of this period and did not go up.

Because the Indian tractor market has been, for the most part, a sellers' market, with demand (determined in substantial measure by the availability of agricultural credit) being ahead of supply, changes in market position are as much a reflection of resourcefulness in securing the inputs for production (including capital resources for expansion) and managing the production process efficiently as they are a reflection of product quality and marketing skill. None the less, tractors which consistently perform poorly will not sell as well, even in a sellers' market (not all purchasers are so desperate to have a tractor that they will take any one), and marketing difficulties typically cause manufacturers to cut back on production in order not to build up too large an inventory. As we have suggested, in at least two instances the Indian manufacturers had serious teething problems in both design and quality control with their imported technology in the 1960s, although they had largely surmounted these problems by the middle of the 1970s.

Another conventional financial measure of enterprise performance is profitability. This is a measure of limited significance because profit margins are subject to too many internal manipulations and external influences (power cuts, strikes, raw material shortages etc.).

These limitations should be kept in mind in looking at some of the profitability ratios given for a cross section of tractor manufacturers in Table 6. It will be observed, however, that there is a rough correlation between relative profitability and market shares. Certainly no clear pattern emerges with respect to source of technology in relation to this measure of enterprise performance. Some enterprises based on foreign technology have done fairly well, as has the one based on indigenously generated technology; others with foreign technology have not fared as well.

The other measures, harder to quantify but perhaps more meaningful, are what might be called the vitality and adaptability quotients. The first

Table 6 Profitability ratios for selected Indian tractor manufacturers: Pre-tax profits/capital employed (Capital employed = net fixed assets + (current assets − current liabilities))

Year	Manufacturer (source of technology in parentheses)					
	International Tractor Co. of India Ltd (US/UK)	Kirloskar Tractors Ltd (West Germany)	Punjab Tractors Ltd (Indigenous)	Escorts Tractors Ltd (US)	Hindustan Tractors Ltd (Czechoslovakia)	Escorts Ltd (Poland/Indigenous)
1965	0.01	—	—	—	—	—
1968	0.24	—	—	—	0.21	0.34
1970	—	—	—	—	—	—
1971	0.09	—	—	—	(1.02)	0.16
1973	0.10	—	—	—	—	—
1974	0.02	—	(0.15)	0.21	0.22	0.38
1975	(0.45)	(0.11)	(0.21)	0.13	0.18	0.44
1976	0.30	(0.21)	0.01	0.12	(0.90)	0.61
1977	—	(0.31)	0.22	0.26	0.22	0.37
1978	—	(0.66)	0.29	—	—	—

Source: Company balance sheets and other industry data

(Figures in parentheses are negative numbers)

is a reflection of the ability to generate resources internally for expansion and diversification, and a demonstration of initiative in developing new products and services — in short, the capacity of an enterprise to remain viable.

A high vitality quotient is manifest in the way in which Punjab Tractors Ltd, the one major manufacturer based on indigenously generated technology, has internally generated the resources needed for its current expansion (approximately doubled) of production capacity. Yet another manifestation would be its initiation of long-term R&D work on alternative fuels, looking to the possibility of providing integrated energy systems (tractors, together with stills, to make fuel from biomass).

But enterprises based on foreign technology have also, at different times, demonstrated a substantial vitality quotient. Thus, Escorts has developed over the past two decades into a diversified mechanical engineering goods industry and continues to add new product lines such as its current collaboration to manufacture earth-moving equipment. It seems more likely that a high vitality quotient would be linked more closely to the character of management in an industrial enterprise than to the source of its technology, but with the qualification that an enterprise based on indigenous technology in an industry dominated by those with foreign technology will, in all probability, have to possess a fairly high vitality quotient simply in order to survive.

The adaptability quotient may be more closely connected with the mode of acquisiton or generatio of technology. We have already commented on PTL's exploitation of its capacity for generating technology by quickly developing and putting into production a 35-horsepower tractor when it was clear that the market for 25-horsepower tractors was not sufficiently strong for PTL to be able to survive. A similar manifestation can be found in its design and manufacture of a 'truly' small tractor — the Sartaj or Swaraj 720 — in an effort to open up a new market of tractor purchasers among smaller farmers.

All other things being equal, continuing reliance on foreign technology, save under special circumstances where inappropriateness or other limitations of foreign technology compel an enterprise to create a capacity for technology development, is less likely to generate a high adaptability quotient or to put the matter conversely, may even inhibit its emergence. Thus one major manufacturer with European technology faced a major crisis when its technology supplier abruptly stopped supplying the hydraulic systems. Even though by this time most of the content of the tractor in question was 'indigenised' (i.e. made in India — not to be confused with indigenously generated technology), the Indian enterprise had not yet tackled the hydraulic system because it is a relatively more difficult part of the tractor to make, and hence, was totally dependent upon its European collaborator.

In sum, in the experience of the Indian tractor industry, the source of technology does not appear in and of itself, to be a critical variable in determining enterprise performance. To the extent that superior enterprise performance can be regarded as a measure of the relative efficiency of various technologies in a narrow and explicit economic sense, the picture which emerges is mixed. The one major enterprise based on indigenous technology has done well but so have enterprises based on foreign technology. Nor does the geographical location and dominant economic system of the technology supplier seem to matter much, as we have examples of a range of enterprise performance based on technology supplied from East Europe, West Europe, and North America.

One further and important point in assessing enterprise performance in relation to the larger social costs and benefits to the country concerns the factor of time with regard to indigenously generated and foreign industrial technology. It can best be demonstrated graphically as in Figure 1. Foreign technology-based enterprises start with a substantial

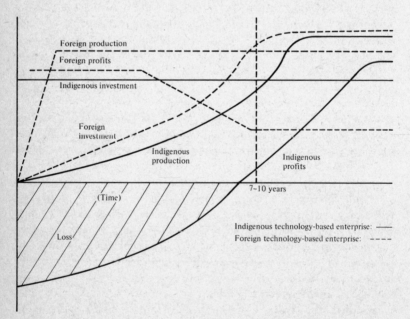

Figure 1 Comparison of levels of production, investment, and profit of indigenous and foreign technology-based industrial enterprises during the 'start-up' phase

cost advantage. The level of investment is low in the earlier stages because the operation is primarily one of assembling components imported from abroad, but the investment increases as the manufacturing operation becomes more indigenised and machine tools and other costly production facilities must be installed. Likewise, costs tend to go up since imported components (produced in huge quantities abroad) are likely to be less costly, even when imported and subject to transfer pricing, than indigenously made components in very small quanities. The result is that profits, which start at a high level, begin to decline after a few years.

By contrast, in enterprises based on indigenous technology, investment is high from the beginning and their costs are relatively high until production can be expanded and economies of scale in production, servicing, and marketing are realised. In the first few years, they will almost certainly operate at a loss while increasing their production, but the cross-over point for profits, investment levels, production volume, and costs usually comes after five to ten years. Beyond that point, the cost advantage of the foreign technology-based enterprise should disappear, and with generally lower capital:output ratios (at least in the case of Punjab Tractors Ltd in relation to its principal foreign technology-based competitors) and lower foreign-exchange requirements, the indigenous enterprise, if it is well managed and based on good technology, should move ahead, as measured by most standard indicators of economic performance.

The picture presented in Figure 1 is found in comparing the performance of, say, PTL with HMT (see Table 5) but not necessarily other enterprises in the industry. Comparisons are, however, difficult for all the reasons we have already mentioned, together with the different starting times of various tractor manufacturers in India. Time is, therefore, itself an important consideration in trying to compare enterprise performance.

TECHNOLOGY SOURCE AND SOCIAL EFFICIENCY

The picture which emerges when we look at the relationship of technology to social efficiency, although not conclusive, offers somewhat more contrast between foreign and indigenous technology. By social efficiency we mean, simply, that the factor or input proportions in the production process should correspond more, rather than less, to the relative availability of these factors of production in the economy. Thus, in economies like India which are endowed with abundant labour but limited capital, it is presumed to be socially more efficient to use less capital per unit of labour and output.[8]

Following this definition of social efficiency, the more units of output for each unit of capital in a capital-scarce economy the better, all other things being equal. Or conversely, the less capital required to achieve the given level of output the better, as it makes scarce capital resources available to meet other social needs, reducing the social opportunity cost of the productive activity in question.

The capital:output ratio is a very rough measure of capital efficiency and has been calculated for selected enterprises in the Indian tractor industry in Table 7. It will be observed that Punjab Tractors, the enterprise based on indigenous technology, shows up well in comparison with other tractor manufacturers, its ratio improving rapidly as is customary with any newly established enterprise. In all probability, when its current expansion programme is completed (doubling its output capacity with relatively marginal increases in capital cost), its ratio will improve still further, assuming it can maintain output at a level somewhat near capacity.

PTL was topped in 1977 (when, however, it was still a relatively young enterprise) by one other competitor — Eicher. Eicher is distinctive in the industry because of the continuing efforts it has made to conserve capital by adopting as many cost-cutting devices as possible. These included purchasing some second-hand machinery at bargain rates from its West German collaborator and using basic machinery from nearby small-scale producers at far less cost than machine tools from established manufacturers like HMT or Kirloskars. The management was no doubt making a virtue out of a necessity as its capital resources at the time were extremely limited but the result shows up in the best capital:output ratio in the industry.[9]

One critical variable which limits the significance of capital:output ratios is capacity utilisation. Obviously, if an enterprise is producing at or near full capacity, its ratio will be substantially improved. Data on capacity utilisation, however, are extremely difficult to obtain. Hence the figures presented in Table 7 must be used with caution. None the less, the capital:output ratio is a better indicator of the relative social efficiency of a given technology than, certainly the profitability ratios given in Table 6.[10]

Labour:output ratios have also been calculated in Table 7 and present a picture not dissimilar to that of capital:output ratios. Here again, Punjab Tractors Ltd shows up well in relation to other firms in the industry with the lowest ratio in the industry in 1977–78. Also with a low ratio is Escorts Tractors (based on US production technology, which gives great emphasis to increasing labour productivity because of substantially higher industrial wage levels in US industry). None the less, when we look next at capital:labour ratios and find that PTL is already at least

Table 7 Capital:output, labour:output, and capital:labour ratios for selected Indian tractor manufacturers

		Capital: output	Labour: output	Capital: labour
Eicher Ltd (West Germany)	(1976–77)	0.48	30.80	0.02
Punjab Tractors Ltd (Indigenous)	(1976–77)	0.91	24.33	0.04
	(1977–78)	0.61	21.39	0.03
	(1978–79)	0.59	22.73	0.03
Harsha Tractors Ltd (USSR)	(1975–76)	0.80	36.20	0.02
Escorts Tractors Ltd (US)	(1975–76)	0.69	22.95	0.03
Kirloskar Tractors Ltd (West Germany)	(1977)	8.60	107.80	0.08
International Tractor Co. of India Ltd (US)	(1975–76)	1.49	NA	NA
Hindustan Tractors Ltd	(1976–77)	0.66	35.62	0.02

Source: Company financial statements and industry data.

Notes: Figures in parentheses indicate time period for which calculation has been made.

Capital = net fixed assets

Output = value added (sales less net materials consumed after adjusting for year-end inventories)

Labour = number of employees at year end

marginally more labour intensive than Escorts/Ford — carried to one more decimal place, PTL's ratio in 1978–79 is 0.026 as against Escorts' 0.030 — (and in all probability will become even more so when its current expansion programme is in place since its workforce is being increased far more rapidly than the relatively modest additional capital investment required), then it seems reasonable to conclude that the indigenously generated technology is socially more efficient.

This argument becomes more compelling when comparing PTL with the HMT Tractor Division by examining levels of output and investment given in Table 5. The comparison is more appropriate also because the two enterprises began producing at more or less the same time. (HMT's production in the early 1970s was largely the assembling of parts made in Czechoslovakia, with significant indigenisation not occurring until the mid 1970s when PTL went into production.) HMT's capital investment is more than three times that of PTL up to 1976–77, while production is less than twice as much. The production gap has further narrowed since then, with PTL achieving, in 1979, almost three quarters of the output of the HMT Tractor Division. (Precise figures are not available for HMT's cumulative investment, but it almost certainly will have increased still further and by a substantial margin with the completion of the foundry mentioned in the footnote to Table 5, far more than the limited amount of additional investment which occurred by the end of 1979 with PTL's current expansion programme. Thus, the comparison is almost certainly that much more favourable to PTL by now than two or three years ago.) Labour:output ratios are not in and of themselves very meaningful unless linked to capital.

Conventional economic wisdom argues that factor proportions should bear some correspondence to factor endowments. In the Indian context, this suggests that a technology which uses more labour in relation to capital for an equivalent output is more socially efficient than one which uses less, since labour is relatively abundant and capital scarce. We have computed capital:labour rations in Table 7. Here once more Punjab Tractors Ltd appears to show up reasonably well, although not necessarily the best in relation to enterprises with foreign technology. Part of the explanation for PTL's failing to show up even better than it does may be attributable to its relatively young age. Yet again, when the current expansion programme is computed, PTL's numbers are likely to change significantly and its capital:labour ratio improve correspondingly because employment is expected to increase more rapidly than capital investment.

Eicher's greater labour intensity is a reflection of its very limited capital resource noted above. Harsha only began production in 1975 and was primarily an assembly operation in 1976, characteristically a more labour-intensive, capital saving phase of production. The ratio for Hundustan Tractors is an aberation, reflecting a huge write-off in capital assets from 1976 to 1977 (almost ten times).[11]

These measures, even though very approximate and rough, do generally support the proposition that in the Indian tractor industry, indigenously generated technology has a greater degree of social efficiency than foreign technology. The case becomes stronger when comparing two enterprises of roughly comparable age such as PTL and HMT. But there is also evidence to suggest that foreign technology varies considerably in social efficiency and that some foreign technology may turn out to be considerably more socially efficient than other foreign technology. In principle, if technology with a higher level of social efficiency in the Indian context could be identified before a decision is reached regarding one among several alternatives, it would improve the quality of technology choice. But in fact, our examination of the experience of the Indian tractor industry suggests that technology choice is much more likely to be determined by the specific needs and objectives of the importing enterprise than by any abstract analysis of the relative social virtues among alternatives (if indeed alternatives exist). Furthermore, the social efficiencies of a given foreign technology may well change markedly, depending upon the mode of technology transfer, how tightly it is controlled by the supplier, and the manner in which it is translated into an actual productive activity in the recipient country.

Given all these imponderables and uncertainties, a policy seeking to maximise the social efficiency of industrial production should, all other things being equal and assuming a viable indigenous alternative is available, opt for that alternative. At least, that is the picture which emerges from the experience in the Indian tractor industry. The extent to which that experience may also be applicable to other fields of industrial technology is, as we have suggested earlier, a matter to be discussed with some caution.

THE SOCIAL MERIT OF INDIGENOUS TECHNOLOGY

The preceding discussion of the relative social efficiency of different technologies for making tractors in India rests on an implicit assumption — namely, that tractors are socially desirable in India. If tractors are not socially desirable, then the whole question of social efficiencies of alternative technologies becomes irrelevant.

Of course, in the real world, these issues are never so starkly posed. No one would presumably argue that India should not have any tractors under any circumstances. The question rather is what kinds of tractors to perform what functions for whom at what prices. This brings us to the complex issue of the social utility of tractorisation — or more broadly, mechanisation — of Indian agriculture.

Debate over this issue has waxed and waned through three decades of Indian agricultural development since independence. Notwithstanding numerous attempts to provide one, there appears to be no simple, clearcut, universally applicable answer to the problem. This issue is in fact a complicated one, and discussion of it in sufficient detail to be meaningful would greatly expand the length of this chapter. But it clearly is an important consideration in considering the social merit of indigenous technology generation.

The issue has been thrown into high relief with the recent and the seemingly perverse application of the capacity for indigenous technology generation in the Indian tractor industry to the design and manufacture of 'self-propelled job destroyers'. What is the social merit of using this capacity to make combine harvesters which have such an immediate labour-displacing effect in an environment characterised by chronic and massive unemployment and underemployment?

It must be said that on the face of it, the technological achievement of Punjab Tractors Ltd in designing and building combine harvesters in record time (31 months from the first developmental work in late 1977 until the combine harvesters began to roll off the production line in April 1980) represents a socially perverse use of this capacity. Certainly there are many in the government of India who must think so, for the PTL achievement effectively circumvented a national policy prohibiting any further import of combine harvesters. In fact, the project was begun in secret by PTL (with active financial support and encouragement from the Punjab State government) because of fear that the central government would intervene.

While the combine harvester story is of sufficient complexity that it requires separate telling, suffice it to say that there is a connection between the choices in agricultural technology made in the 1960s (primarily by the central government, although state governments played a key role in implementing the high-yielding varieties strategy, perhaps especially in the Punjab) and this application of the capacity for indigenous technology generation a decade and a half later.[12] The impact of that strategy on the labour market in the Punjab during this period has been nothing short of transformational, one aspect of which has been the emergence of serious agricultural labour shortages at harvest time in the Punjab by the mid-1970s. These chronic and repetitive shortages led to increasing political pressure on state government from Punjabi farmers to do something.

Initially, the principal response was to encourage the importation of 'guest workers' from the neighbouring states to the east — Uttar Pradesh and Bihar, to which the Green Revolution had not spread in any thing like the same degree it had engulfed the Punjab and where the numbers of small and marginal farmers and landless agricultural labourers were very large and the opportunities for work very limited. But these workers not unnaturally view migrant labour as a court of last resort. If the crop were good and they could find a demand for their services closer to home, they would not come.

Thus, from the point of view of the Punjabi farmer and regardless of the social merit of providing seasonal employment to migratory labour from less developed regions of the country, the issue was in major part one of risk containment or minimisation. Add to that factors of timeliness in getting in the harvest (in order to permit optimal planting of the next crop), and the case for combine harvesters becomes compelling to Punjabi farmers, and by extension, to much of the rest of the state's economy and workforce which depend on the continued prosperity of Punjabi agriculture.

What this latest episode in the Indian tractor story does demonstrate is that the existence of this indigenous capacity for technology generation increases the availability of options of groups of economic and political actors in the society. Whether it leads to greater *net* social benefit is another and vastly more complicated question to which no definite answers are yet possible.

The overall picture which thus emerges from this study of the Indian tractor industry suggests that indigenous technology measures up well to foreign technology in performance and cost but takes more time to develop. Its social efficiency appears, on balance, to be greater than most, but not all foreign technologies, a conclusion, however, based on very time-limited data which prevents more substantial analysis.

On the issue of the social impact of tractorisation as such, the evidence is certainly not all in, but conventional wisdom about its adverse impact on employment is clearly subject to question. Assuming that there is net social benefit from tractorisation, or more broadly, mechanisation, then the evidence suggests that indigenous technology-based enterprise, with its greater capacity and disposition for generating technology more responsive to local needs, appears to be more sensitive to those needs than most, but not all, foreign technology-based enterprises.

But it is also clear that creating the capacity for indigenous technology generation such as has occurred in the Indian tractor industry is like opening Pandora's box. While it may solve some problems such as excessive dependence on foreign sources for a key factor in production, it also renders much more difficult the role of national policy makers in developing countries who believe that technology choices should be consciously and deliberately made for socially meritorious ends.

NOTES

1 See Robert T. Kudrle (1975). *Agricultural Tractors: A World Industry Study*, Ballinger, Cambridge, for an account of the international tractor industry.

2 *Implement and Tractor* (42nd Annual Statistics Issue), November 7, 1979, p. 66.

3 An exception is Japan, where smaller garden-type tractors are widely used in intensive cultivation of small plots.

4 See G. S. Aurora and Ward Morehouse (1972). 'The dilemma of technological choice — The case of the small tractor', *Economic and Political Weekly*, Special Number, pp. 1633–44; and (1974). 'The dilemma of technological choice in India: The case of the small tractor', *Minerva (London)*, October, for a discussion of the conflict over indigenous and foreign technology involving PTL and HMT.

5 For an account of these hurdles, see Aurora and Morehouse, ibid.; V. V. Phatt (1978), 'Decision making in the public sector: Case study of Swaraj tractor', *Economic and Political Weekly* (Review of Management); S. Bhaskar, Swaraj revisited: Problems and prospects, cyclostyled paper (Administrative Staff College, Hyderabad, 1977).

6 Aurora and Morehouse, *op. cit.*, described some of the struggles which PTL's promoters encountered in trying to sell 'unproven' indigenous technology.

7 Sumit K. Pal and B. Bowonder in a paper on R&D in the electronics industry (High technology and development in India, *Futures: The Journal of Forecasting and Planning*, August 1978, pp. 337–41) have discussed this dilemma for a country like India in an advanced and rapidly changing field of technology such as electronics.

8 This definition of 'social efficiency' should not be confused with 'social profitability' used in social cost-benefit analysis. The latter defines social profitability as the profitability of a project when costs and benefits are valued at social or accounting prices — i.e. prices supposedly reflecting the social opportunity cost of resources used and the social benefits of the production. While a measure of social profitability would tend to favour labour-intensive techniques, in a labour-abundant economy, this is not invariably the case. For a discussion of some of the limitations of social cost-benefit analysis in relation to anticipating longer-term social consequences of investment decisions and technology choices, see Frances Stewart (1978). 'Social cost-benefit analysis in practice: Some reflections in the light of case studies using Little–Mirrlees techniques', *World Development*, 6, 2.

9 Sekhar Chaundhuri (1980) *Acquisition and Assimilation of Technology in the Tractor Industry in India: The Strategic Perspective* (Dissertation submitted to the Indian Institute of Management, Ahmedabad), mimeo, pp. 81–105.

10 Another indicator of the relationship of capital to output, presumptively less crude, is the incremental capital:output ratio which concentrates on the relative efficiencies of additions to capital investment over specified periods of time. Unfortunately, meaningful time series data are not available for the Indian tractor industry, reflecting the young age of a number of firms in the industry.

11 The same can be said of incremental capital:labour ratios as was observed in note 10 regarding incremental capital:output ratios. An attempt was made in the present study to calculate production functions for enterprises in the Indian tractor industry, but the very limited data and number of cases did not yield statistically significant results.

12 I am at work on another paper on this subject entitled 'The dilemma of technological choice revisited: the case of the combine harvester in India'.

10 Institutions and decision-making in agricultural research*

STEPHEN D. BIGGS

INTRODUCTION

Recent literature on agricultural technology innovation has focussed on two major theories. On the one hand there is the induced innovation theory as developed by Ruttan, Hayami and Binswanger.[1] On the other there is structuralist theory, as I would describe the broad approach of such people as Griffin (1974) and de Janvry (1977). The induced innovation school argues that broad changes in national relative factor proportions lead to a change in relative factor prices, which in due course induces cost-reducing technologies. More recently they have argued that new institutions are also induced by changes in factor prices (Binswanger and Ruttan 1978). The structuralist argues that it is the relative power of different interest groups, as reflected by socio-economic structures and their interaction with the political-bureaucratic structures, which determine what new technologies are generated. While both schools of thought have appeal, and certainly both agree that relative factor endowments are critical determinants for the use and generation of technology, it would appear that both broad theories have a major limitation for policy makers and administrators concerned with planning the generation of new technologies to reduce rural poverty. So much of what is at the centre of analysis for research resource allocation is left to the 'hidden hand' of market forces in the case of the induced innovation theory. While agreeing with the structuralists about the need to analyse the influence of special interest groups on technology generation, neither theory looks inside and analyses the decision-making processes of institutions and of people who generate new technologies and new R&D institutions and research methods.

A third approach for analysing rural technological change looks inside

*This chapter was presented in a different form to a Workshop on 'Room for Manœuvre in Public Policy', Institute of Development Studies, University of Sussex, Brighton, December 1980.

formal and informal institutions which generate technology (Biggs and Clay, 1981; Clark, 1980). Emphasis is placed on understanding the institutional environments and the decision-making processes of researchers (whether they be formally trained in scientific methods or not). It is this approach which enables us to explore further the scope within R&D for benefiting poor people in rural areas. Having said this, one has to ask what type of R&D system, what types of institutions, what priorities, what programmes and which people are to be the main beneficiaries over what period of time.

R&D IN THEORY

Diagram One represents a simplified 'ideal' model of different levels of scientific investigation.[2] At the local level some innovative farmers and village artisans etc. are always experimenting and developing new technologies, as well as testing and adapting any materials or processes emanating from formal R&D systems (Biggs, 1980a, Brammer, 1980). Although these farmers are not generally trained in 'scientific methods' they apply at least one fundamental principle of formal science, namely the application of criteria in order to try out or retain one thing rather than another.

At the national level there are formal R&D institutions, such as Agricultural Research Councils, Rice Research Institutes, Appropriate Technology Institutions and Institutes of Irrigation and Water Resources. To complement and back up the work of these national programmes there are international organisations such as the International Rice Research Institute, and other institutions under the umbrella of the Consultative Group for International Agricultural Research (CGIAR, 1976). Also at the international level there are other organisations with a specific mandate to conduct R&D and technology promotion on matters relating to the reduction of rural poverty in low income countries, such as the UK-based Tropical Products Institute (TPI) and the Intermediate Technology Development Group (ITDG). To link up these different levels of scientists[3] one-way arrows denote organisational linkages and flows of information.

Linkage A

In the 'ideal' model, scientists appraise new technologies coming from local informal systems as well as diagnose producer problems so as to define priorities and programmes for national R&D institutions.

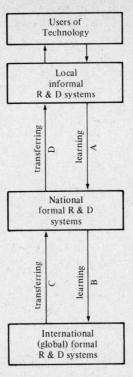

Notes: 1. The formal systems in this diagram relate to
             public sector systems and not to formal R&D
             in national and transnational corporations.

          2. The arrows denote linkages, communications,
              monitoring and feed-back systems.

Diagram One Linkages between informal, national and international agricultural
and rural R&D systems

Linkage B

This represents the linkages between national and international R&D
programmes, a process whereby international scientists learn from and
respond to the problems of national R&D systems. In the 'ideal' model,
international R&D institutions are dependent upon the existence of
strong national systems, because without them they cannot obtain empirical information on which the international scientists can base their priorities and programmes.

Linkage C

This linkage represents one of the flows in the other direction.[4] One example is the distribution of a 'finished' variety, IR8, from IRRI in the early days of the institutionalisation of the international agricultural research system. Another example is the international distribution of germplasm for trials and crossing in national programmes.

Linkage D

Finally we have linkage D, the transfer of technology and knowledge to rural areas. This linkage is *not* the extension linkage. Linkage D is still within the R&D process. It includes the activities of formally trained scientists who conduct their own research with farmers in village environments to develop and then to test whether new varieties and other technologies from research stations are relevant to or viable in the normal environment of the client group for whom the formal system is working. Extension is not the conern of this chapter. However, although it would appear (from claims by scientists in formal systems) that the laçk of adequate extension resources for the transfer of technology from the research station to the cultivator is one of the constraints on the adoption of their technologies, this may well be a smokescreen to prevent one asking whether the technologies they generate are relevant and viable for extension promotion. There is clear evidence that farmer-to-farmer exchange of information is the most important channel for the diffusion of new technologies and that economically dominant new technologies rapidly diffuse.[5]

In summary there appears to be an 'ideal' international R&D system for benefiting poor people in rural areas which looks like a circle. At the centre are international institutions, which cooperate and interact with national programmes. These national programmes then exchange information and have strong linkages with rural areas, whereby they interact with local informal systems. This 'ideal' scientific R&D system is to some degree already institutionalised and justified on the grounds of its relevance to reducing rural poverty. We now turn to factors which, in reality, determine the priorities and programmes of national and international R&D institutions, and see that the formal applications of scientific methods and ideas behind the type of 'ideal' system just described are only one set of many factors which influence the behaviour of research people and R&D systems and the technologies they produce.

R&D IN PRACTICE

Diagram Two represents five major sources of influence which determine the priorities and programmes of agricultural and rural R&D institutions in many developing countries. These five major sources are:

1. Professional objectives of national scientists.
2. Interests of international donors and scientists.
3. National development goals.
4. Special interests and problems of different client groups.
5. International commercial interests.[6]

At any given time one set (or part of a set) of influences may be more important than another. Moreover, while appearing to justify an R&D priority or programme on scientific grounds, institutions or scientists may well have a different primary goal in mind. For example, being the director of a large national research institute, with the attendant power and status, may be more important to a scientist than the personal satisfaction of correctly diagnosing a problem of a client group and then seeing the results of subsequent R&D rapidly spread. In addition, irrespective of international mandates (for example, for helping small farmers) the relevance and effectiveness of research resource allocations to national goals or to the problems of different client groups, may not be the operational criteria for the disbursement of donor funds. Commitment to the disbursement of funds, or the promotion of the ideas of specific scientists or a group of scientists, may be more important criteria for actually determining what actions are taken.

No one experienced in R&D operations would disagree that the application of scientific methods is often only a small part of the complex process of decision-making in formal R&D systems. Unfortunately, however, other influences (for example, political influence, lack of resources) are often looked upon as minor 'imperfections' of the ideal system, which are to be expected and lived with as part of the normal process of research. Even the most elementary of scientific criteria may no longer be applied to the appraisal or planning of public-sector research at the national or international level of decision-making. One purpose of this paper is to investigate some of the costs and consequences of these 'imperfections' and to explore ways of reducing the impact of those influences which give rise to them.

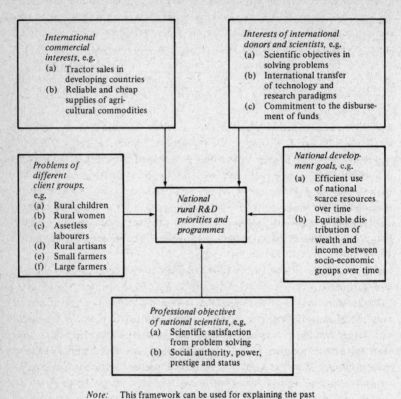

Note: This framework can be used for explaining the past
(ex-post) and for planning (ex-ante) analysis.

Diagram Two Determinants of national rural R&D priorities and programmes

COSTS AND CONSEQUENCES OF 'IMPERFECTIONS'

I have outlined an ideal model of R&D and briefly categorised some of
the factors which, in addition to the principles of the scientific method,
influence what scientists and research institutions actually do with their
time and resources. We are now in a position to investigate what happens
when 'ideal' R&D models and plans are implemented and institutionalised
in developing countries.

The type of imperfections which can occur will be illustrated by looking at the development of the Land Grant Colleges in the United States,
as these have had a persuasive influence on the character of agricultural
research systems in Asia.

The 'ideal' US system epitomises the application of rational science to the solution of problems. However, without even analysing the successes and failings of the 'ideal' model in the USA, one would expect certain imperfections to occur when it is applied in developing countries where there are anyway fundamental differences. As Stavis (1979) illustrates, the Land Grant Colleges and their public-sector research stations were created because farmers had recognised the strengths and weaknesses of their own informal R&D. Farmers were a major influence for the establishment of research stations to meet their perceived needs. In other words the Linkage A in Diagram One (scientists' understanding of farmers' problems) was very strong and effective. Consequently research priorities and programmes were oriented towards solving clients' problems. In many developing countries, however, scientists and donors have often decided *a priori* what are the clients' problems and set up research systems with little reference to Linkage A or any attempt to ensure an ongoing dialogue with the declared clients either when the new R&D institution was founded or as the clients' environment changed and the research institution starts to put down roots and starts to acquire its own set of vested interests.

While some critics of the green revolution technologies argue that they were specifically designed for the agro-economic environments of farmers with larger holdings, I would suggest that in many cases there may have been fortuitous benefits to the larger farmer because their resource conditions happened to be similar to the resource endowments of research stations. Consequently some of the technologies generated by the research stations were adopted because they were found to be more appropriate for larger farms. Looking at the physical location of some national and international research stations and sub-stations trials, we find that they are far from ideally sited, even with large farmers' interests as a primary goal. In fact, because the sites are not sufficiently representative even of agro-climatic and pest and disease conditions, it may be as much by chance as by research planning and design that useful technologies are generated.[7] In other cases, where sites may have been chosen on sensible, scientific criteria, there is the problem that 'results' are either not reported or that the management of the trials is (or is thought to be) unreliable, when low yields are reported, and the findings therefore rejected (Biggs, 1982).

In such a situation, though, analysis often continues as if the ideal institutional model has been used. Besides not generally recognising that the results are invalid, researchers are often reluctant to stand back and pragmatically redesign their programmes in the light of observed management and organisational problems. It is often easier to try and adopt R&D institutional designs from elsewhere and blame 'lack of resources etc.' for inefficiencies than to develop a local system which, while applying scientific principles, is country specific as regards its institutional form and mode of operation.

REDUCING 'IMPERFECTIONS'

The problem for some research administrators in developing countries is not so much recognising that there are many 'imperfections' in the R&D system, as deciding which are the most serious imperfections and finding institutional ways of dealing with them.[8] In this section, I list a number of points which, if taken into account, could reduce the chance of fundamental imperfections either not being recognised or being so institutionalised that nobody dare make elementary, scientific objections.

Criteria for reducing imperfections in national R&D systems[9]

Justifying research against national development goals

In agricultural and rural technology R&D programmes in developing countries it is instructive to note how seldom there is a national policy to guide the allocation of research funds to national priority problem areas. For example, in Bangladesh irrigation and water management is perhaps one of the areas most in need of technological and institutional innovation. However, there is no formal R&D system to cover this and there has been comparatively little work on it or on consolidating the lessons of experience (Biggs *et al.*, 1978). A National Rural Research Policy and Plan would have identified this priority area and would, perhaps, have drawn attention to the social costs of allowing other influences to determine the allocation of scarce research funds.

Client group oriented research

Agricultural research is generally justified on the grounds that it addresses the problems of farmers, but there is often a failure to specify which socio-economic group of farmers in which part of the country. While, for reasons of survival, an institution may not want explicitly to omit a client group from its broad mandate, it is difficult to draw up work programmes or to assess the usefulness of a programme when no specific group of clients has been identified as being the direct beneficiaries. A simple reference to the declared national goals as set out in the National Plan of most developing countries would set the stage for scientists wanting to work on the problems of poorer groups of clients in rural areas.

Specific problem-solving research

Although applied scientific research (according to the ideal model) is supposed to be problem solving, much research in developing countries is in fact descriptive, or is merely an investigation and sometimes an arbitrary shift of some technical production frontiers. Hypotheses are not set up nor are implications drawn which could be applied to identified problems. While it may legitimately be claimed that the criteria of 'basic' research (knowledge for knowledge's sake) should be the scientists' criteria, when public sector funds have been allocated to solving the problems of clients this is a questionable stand.

Rewards to scientists on the grounds of their technologies being adopted

How often is the widespread adoption of an innovation one of the normal criteria for a scientist's promotion rather than, for instance, the publication of journal articles or the acquisition of a higher degree?

Application of interdisciplinary analysis

For social scientists, multidisciplinary institutions often mean a group of economists with some political scientists and anthropologists associated. For a crop improvement programme, multidisciplinary can mean a group of plant breeders with associated agronomists and pathologists etc. While both groups of social and applied natural scientists agree that interdisciplinary analysis within R&D decision-making is important implementing this idea is difficult. Interestingly, when a new technology has proved itself and has spread, one finds that even if it was developed and planned in a formal institution with no participation by social scientists, the applied natural scientists involved were often aware of, and took into account socio-economic as well as technical issues throughout the R&D process.

Integrated field and experiment station programmes

On-farm surveys, experiments and field workshops are a fundamental part of any public research programme. It is a sure sign that an R&D programme may not be in touch with its clients, and that other factors are determining the allocation of R&D funds, when field trials are turned over to an extension department, or top plant breeders and agronomists are not themselves interviewing farmers in the course of selective special-purpose agro-economic surveys.

Communication between scientists

While field research programmes help to ensure that scientists keep in touch with the real problems of clients, steps need to be taken to ensure they keep in contact with each other. The dearth of professional articles for local consumption (compared with articles for an international audience), and the lack of local and national workshops to which outspoken and possible critical international and local scientists are invited, is a sure sign that non-scientific factors are probably having a major impact on the allocation of research resources and that there are considerable imperfections in the ideal model.

Evidence of monitoring for replanning and changing R&D programmes and priorities

While the ideal scientific method emphasises experimentation and hypothesis testing to generate new technologies, scientists are often reluctant to monitor their own institutions and research methods and change them when it becomes clear that the 'software' technology is not viable or appropriate. Empirical evidence of a system changing, in order to move closer to the ideal scientific model and reduce major imperfections would seem an important criterion of whether the system is an asset or a liability to the public sector.

Evidence of the rationalisation of research resources

When imperfections occur in an R&D institute, one reaction by administrators is to decide that it has become so plagued by 'problems' that a new institution should be set up. However, the new institution may well fall victim to 'problems' in the same way as the old one. In addition, considerable staff time and effort can evaporate in inter-institute rivalry, with no benefits accruing to the declared client groups of either.[10]

These are the characteristics which, if incorporated in a national R&D system, would reduce the risk of public-sector funds being allocated in sub-optimal ways according to national development goals. We must now ask where ideas for viable institutional changes are likely to be found to address the problems inherent in the process of institutionalising science.

The most important source of innovation is in the developing country itself. A second and less important source may be societies with similar cultural and socio-economic characteristics. And the last and least important for contemporary problems are the institutional forms, organisational arrangements and research methods in developed countries — irrespective of whether they are based on apparent current practice or historical events. This might seem to over-emphasise the importance of endogenous forms. But the fact that they are endogenous means they are more likely to have passed the acid test of being viable to some degree in the society where they are evolving. It seems relatively insignificant whether some part of the institutional form or method has been used in another society. What is of overriding importance is the presence of an open-minded local scientist or research administrator who is able to screen a wide range of institutional forms or methods from outside and from within the society and, with a specific context in mind, to select parts which might posssibly, with a great deal of adaptation, be relevant to the current and future local environment. One of the inherent problems for scientists and researchers in formal R&D systems is the fact that the wealth of scientific knowledge has been generated in, and lies in, the rich countries. It is unwittingly easy to assume that the institutions and methods which may have been used to generate knowledge there are — more or less — the approximately correct institutions and methods for R&D systems in developing countries. In spite of the 'imperfections' of rich country transplants it does not seem that enough emphasis in the past has been put on developing and promoting endogenously generated R&D systems. I would suggest, in the context of improving the welfare of rural poor people in developing countries, a change of emphasis from looking outside the local environment to looking within it for cost-effective R&D methods.[11]

The most important place to look is towards practitioners. While the literature is full of horror stories, lists of the biases of scientists and lists of constraints and obstacles preventing scientists from doing their work, we are often overlooking the cases where, often under difficult conditions practitioners have identified problems and already come up with solutions. It appears sometimes that people who get on with their work in an innovative and cost-effective way are not seen as sources of innovation. Or sometimes they get told of 'new methods' they have been using for years, after they have been recycled through the international arena. A two-month survey in 1968 by a local District Commissioner, Mr S. K. Chakravertty, documented the problems faced by small farmers in Bihar and their causes. It was a critical, timely input to the creation of the 'target group' small farmer development agency programme in India and must be a salutary example of indigenous ability to conduct rapid research and develop viable projects in rural areas (Bihar, 1969; 1970). The exploratory surveys of the new agricultural and rural technology innovations by interdisciplinary groups of researchers from the Bangladesh Agricultural Research Council in 1974 showed that senior administrators have certainly been aware of the importance of such methods (BARC, 1975).

220 Stephen D. Biggs

The new interest of the international agricultural research centres in on-farm and farming systems research, and the way to link the work of experiment stations with field surveys and trials, follows the path already laid out by Indian scientists in Tamil Nadu in the early 1960s (Gaikwad, 1977). The research planning procedures of the Philippines Natural Research System in Agriculture and Natural Resources, has a lot in it which would be of relevance, with modification and adaptation, to many international and rich-country R&D systems (Madamba, 1976).

Other important examples of 'appropriate' research institutions and methods developed within the local environment, include the R&D process for a landless labourer credit scheme in Bangladesh (Yunus, 1978) and a women's co-operative project in the Bangladesh Ministry of Rural Development and Co-operatives (Zeindenstein, 1977 and Abdullah, 1974).

CONCLUSION

For many scientists in developing and developed countries administration is often seen as a major constraint on their ability to get a job done well. They think many of their administrative problems are very special to their work, whereas in fact, there are often principles and problems that cut across all public sector administrative activities (Schaffer and Wen-hsien, 1975). It would appear that there is a considerable pay-off to the rural poor in developing countries, if professionals trained in, say, plant-breeding research or economic research, were to turn to professional colleagues trained in administrative research, in order to help reduce the impact of normal and predictable problems where there are high administrative loads. Unfortunately I suspect this suggestion would not go down well with most natural scientists, or even economists, in large-scale public-sector R&D systems which could be most cost effective.

NOTES

1 For example see Hayami and Ruttan (1971) and Binswanger and Ruttan (1978).
2 In this and later contexts, I am using the term 'scientist' to cover all areas of professionalised activity. Consequently, a scientist (or researcher) may be a plant breeder, an engineer, an economist, an anthropologist or a trained professional in public administration.
3 The importance of looking at different levels of decision-making and at the linkages between different levels for planning rural technologies has been discussed elsewhere (Biggs, 1978). Recently Timmer (1980) has noted the lack of analysis of decision-making people and groups who operate in the linkage (interface) areas. In the anthropological literature, Bailey (1966) describes the critical nature of linkage 'brokers' and how extension agents' behaviour, for very good reasons, is different from their formal terms of reference.

4   I have used separate arrows to denote the flows of technology and information in different directions, rather than double headed arrows ↔, because of the inherent ambiguity of double headed arrows for an understanding of the direction of causation and the relative importance of different directional flows. It is interesting to note, in the context of our institutional behaviour theory of technology generation, that the most spectacular and significant green revolution technology to date (Mexican dwarf wheat) emanated not from an international institution, but from a national (Mexican) R&D programme, and that the key linkages and exchanges arose from transactions with the US and Japanese national research systems. It was only after the pioneering work on dwarfing wheat varieties that the International Maize and Wheat Improvement Centre (CIMMYT) was created with an international mandate.

5   Almost all adoption studies show that farmers learn of new technology from other farmers. For a recent review of Indian studies, see Singh, 1978. The very rapid spread of wheat in Bangladesh (Razzaque and Hossain, 1979) and of small machine hullers in Java (Timmer, 1974) amply demonstrate the result of introducing a technology which is dominant in the specific local environment

6   These important sources of influence are not discussed in this chapter as we wish to focus attention on sources of influence which have been less analysed in the past.

7   Documentation of some of these issues may be found in Darling (1976); G. B. Pant University (1978 and 1979); Biggs (1980b and 1982). Unfortunately there is little written of an analytical nature about reconciling the scientific management problems of the location of research stations.

8   The damaging implications of major institutional problems and the existence of caste behavioural characteristics in the Indian agricultural research system are described by Sivaraman (1978). Drilon (1977) describes major organisation and management problems recognised in different Asian programmes.

9   Clark (1980) uses a similar 'check-list' approach and similar procedures and methods are being thought about and developed in Bangladesh (BARC, 1979 and Moseman *et al.* 1980). Harriss (1980) has recently addressed the problem of establishing relevant and feasible research for a part of ICRISAT's R&D programme.

10 For example, in Bangladesh the Soil Fertility and Soil Testing Institute have had a programme of on-farm research trials for all the major crops since 1957 (Government of East Pakistan, 1967). The objectives of the programme are very similar in many respects to the philosophy about contact with farmers of the on-farm trial and farming systems research of the International Agricultural Research Centres. However, in the building up of the Bangladesh Rice Research Institute, with the support of and significant input by the International Rice Research Institute, emphasis was placed on the development of a new pilot project area around the research station for field testing of varieties and for contact with farmers. No mention was ever made of the in place country-wide SFSTI programme. The contact with farmers of BRRI staff is still relatively minor and the SFSTI programme has had few scientists interested in the feedback of information from its trials. The current sudden awareness of a major zinc deficiency problem in the country (Roy and Shahjahan 1979) could almost certainly have been picked up by the SFSTI programme if it had been properly implemented according to its original terms of reference, and the BRRI programme had been integrated with, and been responsive to, research signposts coming out of the SFSTI programme. Klepper (1980) has recently looked at the implications of institutional behaviour on agricultural research in Zambia and stressed the importance of analysing the determinants of research priorities.

222   *Stephen D. Biggs*

11   Recently Clay (1979, 1980) has documented technological and institutional
     changes occurring in North-East India and suggestions for ways to monitor and
     use these have been discussed elsewhere in the context of river-basin planning
     (Biggs; 1981). Other work on learning from practitioners about viable regional
     planning methods is being conducted by Belshaw and Douglass (1980).

REFERENCES

Abdullah, T. A. (1974). *Village Women As I Saw Them*, Bangladesh Academy for
    Rural Development, Comilla, Bangladesh.
Bailey, F. G. (1966). The peasant view of the bad life, *Advancement of Science*,
    23, December, p. 114.
Bangladesh Agricultural Research Council (1975) *Proceedings of the Workshop
    on Agricultural Technology*, Dacca.
Bangladesh Agricultural Research Council (1979). *National Agricultural Research
    Plan*, Dacca, December.
Belshaw, D. and Douglass, M. (1980). Leading issues in rural regional planning in
    less developed countries, School of Development Studies, University of East
    Anglia, November.
Biggs, S. D. (1978). Planning rural technologies in the context of social structures
    and reward systems, *Journal of Agricultural Economics*, xxiv(3).
Biggs, S. D. (1980a). Informal R & D: Farmer resistance to new technology is not
    always a sign of backwardness, *Ceres*, 13(4), pp. 23–6.
Biggs, S. D. (1980b). Priorities for maize improvement from on-farm research (Re-
    port to the International Maize and Wheat Improvement Center (CIMMYT),
    Institute of Development Studies, Brighton, June.
Biggs, S. D. (1982), Generating agricultural technology: triticale for the Himalayan
    hills, *Food Policy*, February.
Biggs, S. D. (1981). Monitoring for re-planning purposes: the role of R & D in river
    basin development, in *River Basin Planning: Theory and Practice*, ed. S. K. Saha
    and C. J. Barrow, John Wiley. Chichester, pp. 325–42.
Biggs, S. D. and Clay, E. J. (1981). Sources of innovation in agricultural technology,
    World Development, 9(4), pp. 321–36.
Biggs, S. D., Edwards C., and Griffith, J. (1978). Irrigation in Bangladesh, *Discussion
    Paper No. 126*, Institute of Development Studies, University of Sussex.
Bihar, Government of (1969). *Problems of Small Farmers of Kosi Area (Purnea and
    Saharsa Districts)*, Bihar Secretariat Press, Patna.
Bihar, Government of (1970). *A Pilot Project on the Agricultural Development of
    the Small Farmers of Patna District*, Bihar Secretariat Press, Patna.
Binswanger, H. P. and Ruttan, V. W. (1978). *Induced Innovation: Technology,
    Institutions and Development*, Johns Hopkins Press, Baltimore.
Brammer, H. (1980). Some innovations do not wait for experts: a report on applied
    research by Bangladesh peasants, *Ceres,* 13(2).
CGIAR (1976). *Consultative Group on International Agricultural Research*, New
    York.
Clark, N. (1980). The economic behaviour of research institutions in developing
    countries – some methodological points, *Social Studies of Science*, 10, pp. 75–93.
Clay, E. J. (1979). Technical innovation and public policy: agricultural development
    in the Kosi area 1969–79, typed report, School of African and Asian Studies,
    University of Sussex. *Agricultural Administration.*
Clay, E. J. (1980). The economics of the bamboo tubewell: dispelling some myths
    about appropriate technology, *Ceres,* 13(3), 75.

Darling, H. S. (1976). Memorial to cotton research, review of *Agricultural Research for Development: the Hamulonge Contribution*, (Ed.) M. H. Arnold, *Nature*, 264.

de Janvry, A. (1977). Inducement of technological and institutional innovations: and interpretative framework, in T. M. Arndt *et al.* (Eds.) *Resource Allocation and Productivity in National and International Agricultural Research*, University of Minnesota Press, Minneapolis.

Drilon, J. D., Jr. (1977). *Agricultural Research Systems in Asia*, SEARCA, Laguna, Philippines.

Gaikwad, V. R., Desai, G. M., Mampilly, P., and Vyas, V. S. (1977). *Development of Intensive Agriculture: Lessons from IADP*, Indian Institute of Management, Ahmedabad, India, pp. 149–53.

G. B. Pant University (1978). *Maize On-farm Research Project 1978 Report*, G. B. Pant University of Agricultural and Technology, Uttar Pradesh, India.

G. B. Pant University (1979). *Maize On-farm Research Project 1979 Report*, G. B. Pant University of Agriculture and Technology, Uttar Pradesh, India.

Government of East Pakistan (1967). *Technical Report of the Scheme for Rapid Soil Fertility Survey and Popularisation of the use of Fertilisers in East Pakistan for the Period from 1957 to 1962*, East Pakistan Government Press, Dacca.

Griffin, K. (1974). *The Political Economy of Agrarian Change*, Macmillan, London.

Harriss, B. (1980). *Relevant and Feasible Research for ICRISAT's Research Program in Agricultural Markets*, ICRISAT, Andra Pradesh, India.

Hayami, Y. and Ruttan V. W. (1971). *Agricultural Development: an International Perspective*, Johns Hopkins Press, Baltimore.

Klepper, R. (1980). The determinants of agricultural research priorities in Zambia, Institute of Development Studies, University of Sussex, August.

Madamba, J. C. (1976). Goals, implementing programs and projections of the Philippines National Research System in agriculture and natural resources, Philippines Council for Agriculture and Resources Research, Los Banos.

Moseman, A. H. *et al.* (1980). *Bangladesh Agricultural Research System*, Report of the Review Team, Ministry of Agriculture and Forests, Dacca. (Printed by and available from the International Agricultural Development Service, New York.)

Razzaque, M. A. and Hossain, A. B. S. (1979). Wheat production in Bangladesh – an effective research and production approach, Paper for the International Wheat Conference, Madrid, May 22–25, BARI, Dacca.

Roy, A. C. and Shahjahan, A. K. M. (1979). Zinc deficiency – a new problem for irrigated rice in Bangladesh, *IRRI Newsletter*, October.

Schaffer, B. and Wen-hsien, H. (1975). Distribution and the theory of access, *Development and Change*, 6(2), pp. 13–28.

Sivaraman, B. (1978). Address to the meeting of Vice-Chancellors of Agricultural Universities, New Delhi 16 October 1978.

Singh, K. N. (1978). Factors affecting adoption behaviour of farmers, Paper for the Seminar on the Economic Problems in the Transfer of Agricultural Technology IARI, New Delhi, November 9–10. Forthcoming Indian Agricultural Research Institute publication on seminar proceedings.

Stavis, B. (1979). Agricultural extension for small farmers, *MSU Rural Development Working Paper No. 3*, Michigan State University.

Timmer, C. P. (1974). Choice of technique in rice milling on Java, Research and Training Network Reprint, Agricultural Development Council Inc., New York.

Timmer, C. P. (1980). Public policy for improving technology choice, revised version of a paper for the Workshop on Appropriate Technology: Macro Concepts and Micro Applications, Harvard Institute for International Development, February 29.

Yunus, M. (1978). Bhumiheen Samiti (Landless Association) and Mohila Samiti

(Women's Association) in Jobra and other villages, Paper for the National Seminar on Rural Development, Ministry of Local Government, Rural Development and Co-operatives, Dacca, April 24–29.

Zeidenstein, S. (1977). A Bangladesh project for rural women, Paper presented at a Population Council Seminar, New York, June.

PART IV   PRODUCTS

11   New products: A discussion of the welfare effects of the introduction of new products in developing countries*

JEFFREY JAMES and FRANCES STEWART

INTRODUCTION

One of the most important ways in which advanced countries have changed poor countries is through the impact of new products. Products designed in industrialised countries have transformed consumption and production patterns, culture and society. The significance of new products is widely recognised at a popular level and forms a central part of much informal discussion: 'good' products (vaccination, new seeds) are contrasted with the notoriously 'bad' (powdered baby milk, high-tar cigarettes, sophisticated and expensive weapons). But while the effects of new products are recognised as of enormous importance at a popular level, economists have generally neglected the question. Discussions of technology transfer are mostly framed in terms of the costs of the transfer and of the production characteristics of the techniques.

The neglect of the effect of new products in LDCs in large part follows a similar neglect in advanced countries. Tens of thousands of new products are produced and marketed each year and as many more 'old' products are changed in significant respects.[1] Indeed, the very dynamic of oligopolistic competition requires adherence by firms to the maxim of 'striving to render obsolete everything you have done before'.[2] Yet most discussion of economic welfare ignores new products, or changing characteristics of old products.[3] For example, in neither of two classic works on welfare economics, Little or Graaff, is there any substantive discussion of new products. In so far as new products are discussed in traditional consumer theory, the most that is said is that — by increasing choice — consumers' welfare is potentially increased. A significant reason for this lacuna is that the traditional theoretical framework is unsuited, perhaps incapable, of dealing with the question of new products.[4] But the 'new' theory of consumer demand, associated with Lancaster, which treats products as

* This chapter is reprinted from *Oxford Economic Papers*, **33**, 1 March 1981.

bundles of characteristics, lends itself far more readily to dealing with the question.[5]

The aim of this chapter is to suggest a more systematic framework in which to assess the impact of new products on poor countries. To do so we consider the general conditions according to which new products are likely to increase/decrease economic welfare, looking both at 'absolute' effects and also distributional consequences. We consider the likely direction of effects when products from advanced countries are introduced into poor countries. We briefly describe and analyse eight case studies. Finally we consider some of the policy implications of our findings.

THE LANCASTER FRAMEWORK AND NEW PRODUCTS

Each product is regarded as being a bundle of characteristics, combined in a certain ratio, so that each product may be represented as some vector q, representing a certain combination and quantity of characteristics, i.e. $q = (ia, iib, iiic . . .)$ where a, b, c, describe the characteristic of the products (such as nourishment, beauty, etc.) and i, ii, iii, the quantity of each characteristic embodied in the product. It is assumed that consumer preferences are ordered for *characteristics* rather than for products in themselves. A new product — represented say by some vector, r — then consists in a changed bundle of characteristics. Since the consumer ordering is for characteristics, not products, the new bundle of characteristics may be compared with the old, without requiring a new consumer ordering. In contrast, in traditional theory, since consumer preferences are assumed to be for products not characteristics, a new product must involve a new ordering. Since a reordering leads to non-comparability between the two situations being considered it rules out welfare consideration of new products. This is the fundamental reason why traditional theory cannot deal with new products, but the new theory can. It should be noted that the new approach does not distinguish between changed characteristics of old products and 'new' products — both would be represented by a different vector involving a changed bundle of characteristics. This lack of distinction seems reasonable in the light of the gradual spectrum of changes which may occur, so that any classification of changed products into 'old' products with changed characteristics and 'new' products is somewhat arbitrary. In what follows, therefore, we phrase the discussion in terms of the impact of 'new' products, although the discussion also encompasses what might more normally be described as minor changes in old products. This means that the discussion has a much wider application — empirically — than a discussion of new products confined to major product innovations, such as the motor car, the ball point pen or the microwave oven. Indeed it could be said that in modern societies, almost all products change in some way in a quite short time — the exceptional products are the ones that *do not* change.

While, as we show in some detail below, the framework is much more amenable to handling the question of new products, there remain problems of non-comparability when new products involve entirely *new* characteristics. Of course if characteristics are very broadly defined — e.g. nourishment, warmth, entertainment etc. — it might be possible to avoid this problem, since at the broadest level human needs — basic and base — and therefore product characteristics, remain similar over time. But with such broad definitions it may be difficult to pick up various subtle changes in product characteristics which are of significance: 'washing whiter', or 'speeding up calculations' *can* be classified under very broad categories such as 'satisfaction in appearance' or 'efficiency of operations', but something is lost in so doing. Thus where a new product involves a new characteristic we may be back to the problem of non-comparability, associated with the old approach. But this is likely to happen in a much smaller range of cases, and may be largely avoided by a broad classification of characteristics. In what follows we ignore this problem. For simplicity of presentation, we consider products with just two characteristics.

With the new approach problems of comparison arise if the introduction of a new product directly, or as the result of associated promotional efforts, alters tastes and hence consumer ordering. To start with we assume that changes in consumers' welfare are solely a function of an individual's own consumption, and that tastes are unchanged as a result of the introduction of new products. In such a situation, a new product will unambiguously improve economic welfare if it extends the range of efficient choices by creating a new bundle of characteristics, containing more of at least one characteristic for a given cost while leaving the existing range of products unaffected, in both availability and cost.

Figure 1 portrays a situation of two characteristics, 1 and 2 and two initial products, X and Y. AB represents the price ratio between the two goods. New product Z represents a combination of characteristics previously obtainable by combined consumption of X and Y. The price of Z is such as to extend the efficiency frontier from AB to ADB. Z' represents another new good which embodies a previously unobtainable combination of characteristics and thus extends the range of efficient choice. Since neither X nor Y is displaced, the introduction of either (or both) of these new goods represents a Pareto improvement irrespective of the preference pattern of consumers. However, the preference pattern of consumers will

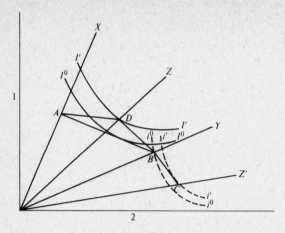

Figure 1

determine the *distribution* of gains from the new products. With the preference pattern shown in the diagram as $I'I'$ and $I^{\circ}I^{\circ}$, consumers gain by the new good Z, but are not affected by Z'. However, consumers with preference pattern $i'i'$ and $i^{\circ}i^{\circ}$ would gain by Z' but are not affected by Z.

In many situations, the introduction of a new product either totally displaces existing products, or leads to altered production and cost conditions for them. If the new product involves the same ratio of characteristics as the old product, but a greater quantity for any given cost, then its introduction is likely to lead to the displacement of the old product as 'rational' consumers will no longer consume it: since consumers will be able to consume more of both characteristics for the same cost, in a Pareto sense welfare will have improved.

But if a new product involves a *changed* combination of characteristics for a given cost (more of some characteristic and less of another), *and* alters the production cost and/or availability of existing products, its welfare impact is more ambiguous. Generally speaking, this is likely to happen in three types of condition. First, where the existing and new products compete in using the same (scarce) factor of production, and the production of the new product raises costs of production of the old product. For example, the introduction of mechanised methods of textile manufacture may have raised the price of raw cotton to traditional spinners. At a more general level, the vast array of new products (and technology) introduced over the past 200 years has raised the price of labour to producers of

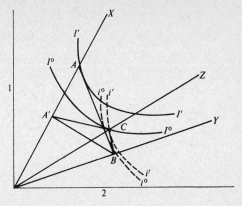

Figure 2

existing products, increasing their costs of production. Secondly, where there are economies of scale, and diseconomies of small scale, so that if the demand shifts away from existing products to new products, costs of production of existing products rise.[6] Thirdly, where markets are dominated by a few very large firms, these firms may withdraw their old products (and/or raise their price) when they introduce new products. They may do so because costs have risen, for one or other of the reasons just mentioned, or because their marketing strategy requires it. The latter is probably the most usual reason with firms withdrawing old models so as to ensure that demand is switched to the new products. Changes in fashion with respect to clothing and automobiles are obvious examples here.[7]

If, for any of these reasons — competing use of scarce resources, indivisibilities or marketing strategy — the relative costs of old products rise, or they become non-available, then the introduction of the new products may lead to a deterioration in welfare, for some groups in society, or even for whole societies.

In Figure 2, the initial efficiency frontier was represented by AB. The introduction of a new product, Z, leads to a rise in the cost of production of X, such that the new frontier is represented by A'CB. Whether consumers are made better or worse off by the change will depend on whether their indifference map is represented by the set of II, or by ii. Consumers with indifference curves ii will be better off; those with the II map worse off. Any situation in which the price of existing products is increased, or their production withdrawn, may make some consumers worse off, if the new products involve a changed bundle of characteristics (for a given cost).

If all consumers had identical indifference maps, then they would either *all* be of a II type, or all of a ii type. If they were all of a ii type then they would all be better off. If all were of a II map, then presumably the new product would not be introduced. Hence, for new products to involve a deterioration in welfare, consumer preferences must differ, and while the welfare of some consumers may go down, that of others goes up. As one would expect, the group of consumers whose preferences are most directed towards the characteristics combined in the old product, whose price has risen (or which has been withdrawn), are most likely to suffer a deterioration in welfare, while those whose preferences are most directed at characteristics embodied in the new goods are most likely to gain. In a commonsense way we can say something about the likely causes for people to be in one group or the other:

1. People with 'conservative tastes' who dislike change are likely to be among those with preferences weighted towards the old product characteristics, and are therefore more likely to be losers.
2. In so far as economies of scale are of significance in determining the change in costs, then those with the tastes of the majority are likely to be among those who gain, those with minority tastes among those who lose. One should add that 'minority'/'majority' is here defined with reference to total effective *monetary* demand, not with respect to felt needs. With an unequal income distribution, the majority of the people may represent the minority of the purchasing power.
3. One of the most significant sources of differences in tastes is that of differing income levels. As consumers get richer, the product characteristics of the goods they consume change towards more high-income types — i.e. better quality, more uniform standards, more luxurious etc. (see Stewart, 1977). In so far as new products are directed to satisfy the needs of those with rising incomes, then each new set of products will embody more high-income characteristics and less low-income characteristics. Hence the higher-income consumers will tend to be among those who gain, the low income among those who lose.[8]

Suppose characteristic 1 represents low-income characteristics, characteristic 2, high income. Then a new product, Z, is likely to be to the South East of Y representing more high-income characteristics. Where the new product leaves existing products unaffected, no group of consumers will lose, but the gains from the new product will be concentrated among high-income consumers. Suppose high-income consumers have indifference map II in Figure 3. With the introduction of new product Z, they will move

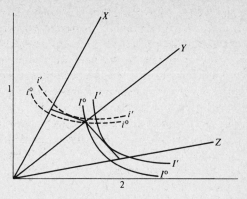

Figure 3

from $I^{\circ}I^{\circ}$ to the higher indifference curve $I'I'$. But the poor consumers with indifference map ii will remain on the same indifference curve, $i'i'$. Thus while no-one will lose, the relative gains will be concentrated on the rich consumers. If as a result of the new product, one of the old products, X, is withdrawn from production, then poor consumers (indifference map ii) will suffer a loss of welfare moving to a lower indifference curve $i^{\circ}i^{\circ}$. A similar consequence would follow for an increase in cost of the old products. If the new product represented a more *efficient* product (i.e. involving at least as many of each characteristic as some existing product, at lower cost) the old product would be eliminated as inefficient. *All* groups of consumers would gain. However, unless each characteristic was reduced in cost by the same proportion, relative gains would be concentrated among the consumers who most prefer the characteristic most reduced in cost.

Over time, as incomes rise there is a systematic shift in consumer preferences towards higher-income characteristics, so that 'average' preferences shift as shown in Figure 4.

New products are designed — and old products withdrawn — in accordance with this shift in tastes. When new products are introduced into an economy for which they are designed (i.e. when technological change is endogenous) negative effects on consumers' welfare, of the type described above, are likely to be confined to certain groups within society, because if *all* consumers were made worse off, then it would be unlikely that the new products would be developed and introduced. This is generally the situation in advanced countries. Minority groups and poorer consumers may suffer welfare deterioration as new products are introduced but majority (in a monetary demand sense) consumers will gain: an obvious

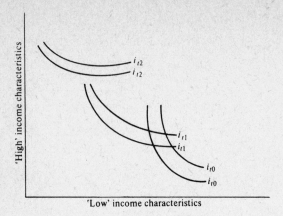

Figure 4

example is the way in which poorer consumers lose as private transport replaces public, and large-scale units of consumption replace small. To assess the overall welfare impact of new products in such cases requires weighting the gains and losses of different groups of consumers.

The situation is somewhat different when products from one (richer) society are introduced to another (poorer) society. New 'high-income' products are developed for the high- and rising-income societies, and consequently have increasingly high-income characteristics. While these new products tend to correspond to the consumer preferences of large groups in the rich societies — i.e. in terms of Figure 3 the ii map may represent all (or most) consumers in poor societies; the II map that of all (or most) consumers in rich societies. If that were so, then the question to be answered is why the new products should be introduced into the poorer societies at all, and why, if they are (e.g. to serve a minority elite with similar consumption patterns to those of the rich society), the low-income goods should be increased in cost or withdrawn. There are of course goods where this does not happen, and countries where the new products are not introduced. And in most poor countries there is some lag before new goods are introduced from rich societies. But there is some tendency for the new high-income goods to be introduced and old goods to be withdrawn even where the new goods do not correspond to the main consumer demand. This may happen:

1. Where monetary demand in the poor country is heavily concentrated among the rich, so that preferences expressed by monetary demand are similar to those of the rich countries. Some Latin American

countries provide well-known examples: it has been argued, by Furtado for example, that the maldistribution of monetary income and demand is a deliberate policy-induced strategy in order to create demand for the new products and therefore a market for those companies producing the new products. In this type of situation the negative welfare effects of new products arise from the distribution of income, rather than the introduction of new products as such (although the production technology associated with the new products — see below — may be partly responsible for the skewed income distribution).

2.   Where production of *all* goods — old and new — takes place in the advanced countries: the rise in price of the old goods/withdrawal of them that arises with switches to the new goods in the advanced countries then also affects consumption possibilities in the poor countries.

3.   Where production of both types of goods (old and new) takes place in the poor countries, using technology from the advanced countries, and the change in the advanced countries towards the new products changes the relative costs of production *in the poor country*: this could happen where products compete for scarce factors, or where there are world-wide economies of scale (e.g. in technology development, maintenance, inputs, advertising and so on), which affect the relative costs of production in the poor countries, even though the change in demand and production initially only takes place in the rich country. In many cases, for example, problems (including rising costs and non-availability) in securing parts and inputs persuade entrepreneurs in poor countries to switch to more recent techniques and products.

4.   Where the production of both goods, which takes place in the poor country, is dominated by particular decision-makers whose private interest lies in switching to more recent products. For example, a continuous switch in products may be the most effective way for multinational companies to prevent local competition.

5.   Where production of both goods takes place in the poor countries — or where production of the old good takes place in the poor country, and the new good in the rich country — and where some switch in demand away from the existing products raises their costs — because of indivisibilities. Such a situation (ignoring for the moment the impact of advertising) may occur so long as there are some high-income consumers whose tastes are more in line with rich-country tastes (i.e. a similar situation to (1) above, but less extreme).

In two of these cases (1) and (5), some distributional judgements are involved in assessing the impact of new products, since some consumers gain; however, in both the distributional judgement required is of a different kind from that involved in the rich-country case. In case (1) in monetary terms, the majority of consumers gain, but the majority of consumers, in terms of *numbers* of people, may lose. This is unlikely to be the case in the rich-country situation. In case (5), the gainers may be confined to a minority among monetary consumers. In the rich-country situation, it is likely that new products will only be introduced if a substantial proportion of consumers are likely to gain. In the other cases ((2)–(4)), new products may be introduced even though the *whole* society loses. It should be noted that this will only be the case on certain assumptions about consumer preferences, about the nature of new products, and of indivisibilities associated with production. Whether or not these assumptions apply will vary in different products/countries. But is is possible to generalise a little:

(a) Assuming consumer preferences are unaffected by the existence of alternative products and by promotional efforts (an assumption we relax below) poor-country preferences are likely to be towards low-income characteristics compared with rich-country products.

(b) If new products are first developed *for* rich societies — as for the most part they are — each new product is likely to embody more high-income and less low-income characteristics than existing products. However, because of technological advances in product design and technology, the cost per unit of each characteristics (including low-income characteristics) *may* be lower than that of old products.

(c) There is abundant evidence of economies of scale in much of modern technology — which is accentuated by even more marked economies of scale in marketing etc.[9] In so far as one 'modern' technology product replaces another — as in much of the changes in the modern sector — indivisibilities may be of significance. Indivisibilities are much less marked in traditional techniques/products, so that costs of production of these traditional products may not rise as new modern-sector competing products are introduced. But costs of traditional products may rise if the costs of inputs rise as a result of the new products. The established decline in traditional products over time may in part be due to the fact that they do not represent efficient alternatives; in part to policy changes which discriminate against them (e.g. standard setting, making low brewing illegal, etc). But part is likely to be due to rising costs. Traditional/old products may be more likely to survive in large economies, where even declining demand may still represent a sizeable market, than in small.

Taking these considerations together, whether or not new products benefit or harm poor societies is likely to vary according to the products. This is part of the explanation of why there are apparently 'good' and 'bad' products. But there are three other types of reasons, not allowed for in our framework so far: the effects of new products on tastes, learning by consuming effects, and indivisibilities and complementarities in consumption.

TASTE CREATION

Producer sovereignty type effects, associated with promotional efforts on the part of producers, mean that producers attempt (and often succeed) to change preferences. These attempts are systematically related to new products, so that expenditure to promote new products tends to increase preferences for new products as against old. This is particularly marked where the old products are traditional ones, normally associated with minimal promotion, but is also true where one new modern-sector product replaces another. One effect of the tendency for greater promotion of new products will be to accelerate the switch in demand away from old products and therefore to increase the tendency for these to rise in cost/be withdrawn. In a strict consumer-preference framework, it is not possible to compare a situation in which consumer preferences have been altered, with the preceding situation. But stepping outside this framework, it is reasonable to argue that promotional expenditure on one type of product is likely to lead to over-consumption of that product compared with the less-well promoted products. Consumers subject to such imbalanced promotional efforts will tend to spend a greater amount on the new products than they would in the absence of such expenditure. If we take expenditure patterns in the absence of promotion (or with 'equal' promotion, which may not produce the same results) as the 'balanced' pattern of consumption, then promotional expenditure on new products will tend to lead to an imbalance of consumption expenditure towards new products — which in the case of poor countries is likely to mean towards high-income products. Consumers will then spend too little on low-income characteristic goods. The results are likely to be insufficient expenditure on basic needs. It is plausible to argue that this has been the effect in relation to many goods consumed in poor countries.

It should be noted that the effect on preferences is not just a matter of formal promotional expenditure: all sorts of other influences also operate. For example, cultural dependency and the image of the sophisticated Westerner (which used to be described as 'demonstration effects') may have as much influence in promoting new products, as formal advertisements.

LEARNING BY CONSUMING

The formal theory of consumer preferences does not allow for learning by consuming. In practice this is a very significant element in consumption practices. Consumers become more efficient *qua* consumers as they consume — learning how the items consumed endure, how to use them, their effects in terms of the fulfilment of the needs for which they were demanded. These learning effects are a function of experience in consuming particular products: as a new product is introduced consumers tend to be inefficient in choice and in use once selected (i.e. secure less than the maximum possible combination of desired characteristics.) As time proceeds learning effects take place, and consumption efficiency rises. Since learning effects are related to the time for which a product has been available, the gap between efficient and actual consumption patterns is greatest for the most recently introduced products, least for the oldest products. In addition to this, there is a more general society-learning process, so that some societies are more efficient consumers than others, particularly in relation to certain types of products. In all societies, therefore, one can expect more efficiency in consumption of old products than new, and the gap in efficiency will be greatest where the difference in characteristics of products is greatest, and where the old products have been consumed for the longest period. One would therefore expect the biggest gap in efficiency between consumption of traditional products — which have been available for a long time and for which consumption efficiency is high — and modern newly introduced products. The observed fall in nutritional standards following the introduction of 'modern' processed goods is partly due to lack of learning experience with this type of product, as against the traditional products. The baby-milk case is an example of this. Rich societies in general put considerable effort into improving consumption efficiency — as a response to the steady introduction of new products, for which learning experience would otherwise be low. Children are educated to be discriminating consumers, consumer groups establish magazines etc. to inform consumers and the government intervenes to protect and inform consumers. The net result is a much higher degree of consumption efficiency in relation to new products than in poor societies. Lacking the learning experience related to many new products, social (including government) protection and information services, there is a systematic tendency for inefficiency of consumption of new products in poor countries.

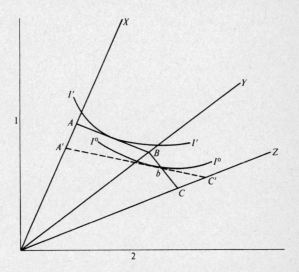

Figure 5

The combination of imbalanced promotional efforts and consumption inefficiency both concentrated on new products would tend to result, simultaneously, in an undervaluation of old products and an overvaluation of new products in relation to their true characteristics. This is illustrated in Figure 5. X and Y are existing products: Z is the new product. Because of differential promotional expenditure consumers underestimate the traditional products: whereas the actual combination of characteristics possible with a certain income is represented by ABC, and therefore the best position is on $I'I'$, consuming only X and Y, the potential of the traditional products is underestimated, because of lack of information/ advertising, while the potential of new product Z is exaggerated because of promotional efforts plus lack of learning effects. Consumers believe the efficiency frontier is represented by $A'C'$ and therefore consume at b, on a lower indifference curve than they might have done in the absence of new product Z, or with correct information about the alternatives.

INDIVISIBILITIES IN CONSUMPTION

Many products are more or less indivisible, the extent of indivisibility varying with the product. At one extreme, food grains may be perfectly divisible (although not the packages in which they are purchasable); at the other a modern aircraft or spaceship can only be purchased in very large units. The higher the income of consumers, the larger the unit in which they are prepared, and indeed may wish, to buy characteristics. This fact is reflected in the design of products – which tend to be increasingly indivisible[10] – in relation to any desired set of characteristics – the higher the income for which the products are designed. Indivisibility is thus a high-income characteristic. But it is sufficiently important to merit separate treatment. Products designed for high-income consumers tend to be more indivisible than would be appropriate for low-income societies. This means that new products will tend to benefit rich individuals more than poor.

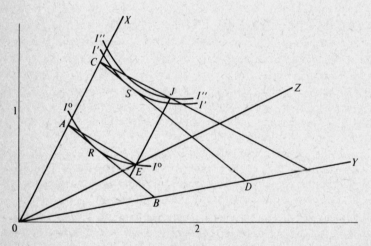

Figure 6

Figure 6 shows two individuals with different incomes (represented by AB and CD respectively) and identical tastes (represented by the indifference map II). Prior to the introduction of new good Z the two individuals consume at points R and S. Good Z is now introduced but cannot be bought in units less than OE. The result is that the low-income individual cannot improve his welfare (i.e. he can only move to E on indifference curve $I^{\circ}I^{\circ}$) while the second individual is able to combine OE of good

Z with AC (= EJ) of good X to reach J on the higher indifference curve I"I".

If the indivisible item is none the less purchased by the poorer consumer because he wants certain of the associated characteristics, then this involves disproportionate expenditure on that item as against other items of consumption. Consumption patterns in some underdeveloped countries illustrate the effects of indivisibilities. Consumer durables are outstanding examples of indivisible consumption items. Wells' survey of expenditure on consumer durables in Brazil revealed very widespread ownership of consumer durables, even among relatively low-income groups.[11] Increasing consumption of consumer durables was accompanied by a decline in nutritional standards. A survey in São Paulo found that between 1959 and 1969/70 'there was a significant rise in the share of household expenditure devoted to domestic appliances . . . an analysis of (physical) *per capita* food consumption shows that there was a downward trend, indicating that levels of nutrition among the working class deteriorated absolutely'.[12] Analysis of two family expenditure surveys in 1968 and 1974 showed that the share of expenditure devoted to food fell from 46.7 to 41.1 per cent between 1961/62 and 1971/72. This shift in expenditure was accompanied by an absolute deterioration in nutrition standards, with 2704 calories being consumed in 1961/62 (73.7 g proteins, 75.6 g fats) compared with 2531 calories in 1971/72 (80.2 g proteins, 70.5 g fats).[13] These trends in consumption expenditure are of course the outcome of a variety of effects, besides indivisibilities. Others include changing behaviour in response to the availability of new products, to promotional expenditure and to demonstration effects.

COMPLEMENTARITIES OF CONSUMPTION

For many consumer goods there are interdependencies, such that the enjoyment of one good depends on the consumption of some other good: tennis balls and tennis rackets; cars and roads; chairs and tables; and so on. Interdependencies in consumption may reinforce some of the other effects already discussed because they mean that a new product and/or the withdrawal of an old product not only has direct effects on consumers, but also affects the welfare gained from other items. Thus some existing products may be rendered obsolete by the replacement of a complementary new product. The initial replacement of one good by another might apparently benefit all consumers, leading to more of all characteristics than the replaced product; but the complementarity effect may render obsolete other products which are replaced by goods which make some consumers worse off. (Of course the reverse may also happen.) Alternatively, complementarities may, like indivisibilities in consumption, cause the benefits from new products to be out of reach of low-income consumers, who cannot afford all items in the package. Complementarities may also reinforce the effects of new products in causing imbalance in consumption. Absence of complementary goods and services is a major factor behind the harm done by powdered baby milk. The practice of feeding powdered milk to babies 'is being used by women with no knowledge of hygiene, no ability to read the instructions on the can, and no money with which to buy sufficient powdered milk. Thus, diluted powdered milk from dirty bottles and dirty teats is substituted for breast milk. This leads to malnutrition and dietary disorders such as marasmus, diarrhoea and vomiting'.[14]

Cars and roads provide another example of indivisibilities cum complementarities. Modern cars generally (despite the success of the East African Safari) require modern roads for efficient use. If the cars are provided without the roads, then serious inefficiencies result. If the roads are also provided, social expenditure is concentrated on the provision of roads to car-owners, indirectly depriving other consumers of much needed infrastructure.

SUMMARY OF EFFECTS

The analysis suggests that the impact of new products on economic welfare will depend on the particular circumstances and will need to be assessed separately for each product and for each country — since the effects vary according to consumer tastes and income levels, and the product characteristics and production technology of new and existing products. In general we may distinguish the following situations:

A   Where new products are likely to increase welfare in a Pareto sense. This occurs in two sets of circumstances:

A_1 where the new products are more efficient than the old — i.e. each characteristic is of lower cost;

A_2 where the new product does not displace nor add to the costs of existing products, and 'tastes' are not affected.

B   where new products are likely to decrease welfare for some or all consumers. This may occur:

B_1 where a new product displaces an old product or increases its relative cost;

B_2 where promotional expenditure on the new product leads to over consumption.

In all of these cases the new products will have distributional consequences. In general where new products are designed in rich societies and introduced into poorer societies, the distributional consequences can be expected to be inegalitarian. Gains will be relatively concentrated among high-income consumers; losses relatively concentrated among low-income consumers. Thus we may distinguish two alternative distributional consequences, C.

C_1 where the new product is egalitarian in its consumption effects;

C_2 where the new product is inegalitarian in its consumption effects.

In general, data for changes in income distribution over time do not allow for these effects, since they look at shares of incomes received by different percentiles, not at the purchasing power in terms of characteristics. Even estimates (which are rare), which take into account changes in prices of the main product groups consumed by different income groups, do not disaggregate sufficiently to allow for the effects of the introduction of new products.

EFFECTS ON PRODUCTION TECHNOLOGY

The discussion above has been confined to considering the effects of new products on consumers *qua* consumers. In practice, an equally – perhaps more – significant effect on welfare will result from the effects on production technology, and hence on employment and income distribution. New products developed in advanced countries in general involve a later vintage technology than older products: this normally means that the associated techniques of production tend to be more capital intensive, more sophisticated and larger scale.[15] The production of new products in poor countries, and the displacement of old products, will therefore tend to nudge the technology in use towards greater capital intensity and larger scale. This in turn will tend to reduce employment below what it might have been, increase technological dualism, and increase urban concentration.

Thus to complete our classification, we may distinguish between two types of production technology, D, associated with the new products:

D_1 where the production technology is more appropriate[16] i.e. labour intensive, small scale etc.) than that of existing products;

D_2 where the production technology is more inappropriate (capital intensive, large scale etc.) than that associated with existing products.

The total effects of new products on economic welfare will thus consist of the combined effects A → D.

EMPIRICAL EVIDENCE

Difficulties in handling changing product characteristics are notorious and this is one reason why the subject has been neglected. Most statistics classify products into such broad categories that many variations in product characteristics go unnoted. Another reason is the general reluctance of economists to incorporate changes in tastes into welfare analysis. It remains true, as Friedman pointed out in 1972 that, 'economic theory proceeds largely to take wants as fixed'. Lack of empirical attention reflects this theoretical bias. There is an abundance of evidence concerning production efficiency — almost none on consumption efficiency.

Ideally, what is needed are detailed microstudies into the history of product development/introduction in relation to some specified needs in a developing country, describing the changing product characteristics, changing costs per characteristic, the way in which different types of product are marketed and promoted, and the extent of reasons for product displacement over time. Some evidence is provided by existing studies of choice of technique, but mainly incidentally, since for the most part the studies aim to exclude product differences. In this section we summarise the findings of eight studies which throw some light on the question.

Sugar processing

The study by James highlights some of the important differences between the two major forms of sweetener consumed in India.[17] The traditional and unrefined product (gur) is shown to be more nutritious and cheaper than refined sugar although the keeping qualities of the latter are superior. Refined sugar is produced far more capital-intensively in factories. Production on a large scale, in India, began only in 1932–33 with the grant of protection to the industry. As a result, the number of sugar factories increased rapidly from 31 prior to the grant to 111 in 1933–34.[18] Despite the competition from sugar, the share of gur in total consumption of sweeteners has remained stable since then.

The Kenyan soap industry

Langdon's[19] study of the soap industry in Kenya focuses on the changes brought about by the introduction of multinationals (MNCs) in an industry, which until the Second World War, comprised entirely locally-owned soap factories. The product of the MNCs is more expensive than the hand-processed varieties in addition to being functionally inferior, i.e. it has lower quality ingredients and is less durable in cleaning. These facts notwithstanding, the new products have been highly successful. A major reason for this, in Langdon's view, is the differential promotional expenditures of the MNC subsidiaries and the local firms. The latter devote less than 1 per cent of annual turnover to advertising as opposed to the figure of 6 per cent for the subsidiaries. The shift to the high-income soap products has been at the expense of the growth and profitability of local firms which have been forced on this account to imitate MNC patterns of production. The initial displacement of local products has thus tended to become cumulative. This in turn has 'hurt most consumers in Kenya'.

Bread

Data from Chile on automatic baking revealed an unexpected but probably not unusual pattern: Sliced wrapped bread produced on automatic lines was displacing 'traditional' bread although its price per unit weight was considerably higher. The main advantages of the automatic bakeries were their capacity to advertise and, no doubt, influence consumer tastes, as well as the convenience of the product because of its longer shelf life. The automatic bakeries use very capital-intensive technology embodied in machinery systems which are imported *in toto* from abroad. The smaller bakeries use locally designed and fabricated equipment.[20]

Maize grinding

A study of maize grinding in Kenya[21] found that the product that resulted from modern methods of milling (first introduced into Kenya in 1935) differed considerably from ordinary posho, the output of older methods. The modern refined product was substantially less nutritious; costs of milling were substantially greater (prices charged were 3½ times as great) while methods of production were far more capital-intensive (ten times the investment per worker). None the less, the newer refined product has found a large and growing market. This is in part due to various superior qualities — it keeps better and the taste is preferred by many consumers. In part, it is due to heavy promotional expenditure, which is concentrated exclusively on the branded refined product. One enquiry suggested that promotional expenses added as much as one-third to production costs.

However, the introduction of the refined product has not displaced the old, which continues to be available, nor has it increased its costs.

Breakfast cereals in Kenya

Kaplinsky[22] finds a 90:1 price differential between the unit cost of the cheapest traditional staple and the most expensive imported cereal: the difference in cost per nutrient is greater because of the superior nutritional content of the traditional food. The differences among locally produced cereals are shown in Table 1.

Kaplinsky attributes the consumption of the manufactured breakfast cereals (which are taking an increasing share of the market) to the demonstration effect (consumption which started with European expatriates first occurs among the Kenya elite and then 'moves down') and to promotional expenditure, which is heavy and concentrated among the brand name products. 'Breakfast cereals with high nutrient costs are being aggressively marketed as an alternative to traditional foodstuffs.' The production technology of the advanced-country products is far more capital intensive than the traditional products. It is estimated that the same investment would create employment of 600 in maize mills compared with 15 in a Weetabix/Weetaflakes plant.

Cement blocks

A study of cement blocks[23] in Kenya found that cement blocks were stronger than the traditional clay blocks. If made with mechanised techniques they were of more standard quality. They cost more (at least twice as much) and used more capital-intensive techniques. There was little promotional expenditure associated with cement block sales — but mechanically produced cement blocks had replaced traditional clay blocks for urban use because of their superior qualities.

Footwear

A study of footwear in Ethiopia[24] found that moulded plastic sandals appear 'to offer much better value as simple covers for the soles of feet for peasant families' [than traditional leather shoes]. The price per pair is less than one-seventh of the hand-sewn leather shoe. The production techniques associated with plastic sandals are far less appropriate than those associated with the production of leather shoes. Fixed capital per employee is over three times as great; the materials are largely imported,

Table 1 Differential between unit nutrient costs for 100 per cent extraction maize flour and locally manufactured breakfast cereals

	Unit price differential	Carbohydrates	Protein	Fat	Ash	Fibre	Calories	Vitamins		
								Thiamine	Riboflavine	Niacin
Weetabix/maize flour	20	18	19	45	55	22	21	9	3	4
Weetaflakes/maize flour	25	22	30	64	68	29	24	12	3	5
Post Toasties/maize flour	27	22	36	225	164	100	27	18	3	10

while the scale of plant is much larger and employment is concentrated in the formal sector. In contrast leather shoes are often produced on a very small scale by families and use local materials. A study in Kenya,[25] where in 1975 70 to 80 per cent of shoe consumption was met by the Bata shoe company, found that 'The advantages of capital-intensive mass shoe production have rendered artisan shoe production redundant, because of its high production costs'.

Drugs

The drug industry provides illustrations of many of the points made in the discussion above.[26]

The development and promotion of new products forms a vital part of the marketing strategy of the large pharmaceutical firms. 'About half of the medicines sold on national markets are less than ten years old.'[27] Research and development into new drugs is concentrated in a few large companies in the developed countries. 'Pharmaceutical firms in developing countries do practically no research, with the possible exception of a few leading producers.'[28]

'Foreign firms are not interested in research on drugs for tropical diseases as the global demand for such drugs will not be sufficiently economic.'[29] The consequence of the nature of the industry, its competitive strategy, and the fact that research is concentrated in the developed countries, is that new products tend to be directed at diseases of the rich, rather than the poor, new drugs tend to be high cost, and product differentiation abounds. While the new drugs usually fulfill some additional benefit, as compared with the old, they often do so at a considerable increase in cost, as is illustrated in Table 2. For poorer countries (consumers) the additional benefits may not be justified in relation to the extra costs.

Table 2 Alternative costs of treating tuberculosis

Drug	Standard adult daily dose	Cost per year (US$)	Cost as percentage of lowest priced drug
Isoniazid	300 mg	0.90	–
Thiscetazone	150 mg	1.00	111.1
Paraaminosalicyclicacid	10 g	9.25	1,027.8
Streptomycin	1g	17.25	1,916.7

Source: H. Friebel, Therapeutic Needs and Production of Drugs, in UNIDO, *Establishment of Pharmaceutical Industries in Developing Countries: Report and Proceedings of Expert Working Group Meeting*, 1970 (ID/35), p. 33.

Heavy promotional expenditure in the industry – in the US for example expenditure on advertising exceeds expenditure on research and development by three to four times – raises the cost of each drug, and often misleads as to the relative efficacy of different drugs: 'the flow of essential information about the discovery of drugs, their relative efficiency and their relative cost is submerged in a deluge of glossy and persuasive advertising of particular products'.[30] Lack of official regulation and investigation means that the promotional efforts in LDCs are often potentially more harmful than those permitted in DCs.

Many of the new products do not contain new chemical properties, or therapeutic characteristics, but are differentiated with respect to packaging, presentation etc. Investigations have established huge cost differences between proprietary branded products and the generic equivalent – e.g. fifty to sixty times for antibiotics. In the US price differences of up to 1000 per cent have been established.[31] In India it was estimated that 116 drugs represented India's basic drug needs in contrast to the 15 000 drugs currently marketed.[32]

The net result has been drugs which are 'inappropriate in terms of price and therapeutic effects'.[33] 'The high price of modern drugs in developing countries, their heavy promotion and the training received by doctors all conspire with the unequal distribution of income and lack of free health provisions in developing countries to ensure that only a small minority of the population gain access to drugs.'[34] In India, it has been estimated that only 20 per cent of the population consume modern drugs.[35]

SUMMARY OF CASE-STUDIES

Table 3 summarises the effects of the introduction of new products in these studies. In only one of the eight – soap – did there appear to be substantial displacement of existing products. For the most part therefore (and this may have been true of the soap case too) the new products extended consumers' choice. Promotional expenditure, however, was probably responsible for over-evaluation of the benefits of the new products and over-consumption in at least six out of the eight cases. This may have had serious negative effects in the food and drug cases. In all the food cases, the nutritional content of the new products was lower than the old. In drugs, the substantial expenditure due to the consumption of expensive new products may have limited expenditure on other drugs. In seven of the eight cases, the new products had high-income characteristics compared with the old. In these seven cases the distributional impact was inegalitarian. Plastic sandals were the one case of a new low-income product whose

Table 3 Effects of new products

	Benefits some or all consumers		Negative effects on some or all consumers		Distributional consequences		Production technology	
	Reduces costs of characteristics	Increases choice	Displaces old product/increases cost	Promotion/over-consumption	Egalitarian	Inegalitarian	Appropriate	Inappropriate
	A_1	A_2	B_1	B_2	C_1	C_2	D_1	D_2
Refined sugar	−	+	−	+	−	+	−	+
Soap	−	−	+	+	−	+	−	+
Sliced, wrapped bread	−	+	−	+	−	+	−	+
Refined maize flour	−	+	−	+	−	+	−	+
Breakfast cereals	−	+	−	+	−	+	−	+
Cement blocks	−	+	−	−	−	+	−	+
Plastic sandals	+	+	−	−	+	−	−	+
Drugs	−	+	−	+	−	+	−	+

− indicates negative or zero effect
+ indicates positive effect

consumption impact was probably egalitarian. Production technology was inappropriate in every case, including sandals, as compared with the technology associated with the older products.

The net effects on welfare depend on the combined effects on consumption and production. In each of the cases considered there were both positive and negative considerations, so that the overall impact depends on how the various considerations are weighted. The chief positive effect lay in the extension of consumer choice and the benefits conferred on those consumers who prefer the new products to the old; the negative effects arose from over-consumption of the new products due to demonstration/ promotion, the inegalitarian consumption effects and the effects on production technology.

It must be emphasised that these products were not selected to be representative of products as a whole. Moreover more detailed and custom-designed research is required in each case to be confident about the results. But the direction of effects is broadly in line with what one would expect, given the historical circumstances. New products could, in principle, be designed for low-income consumers to be produced with appropriate technology. But the historical (and current) concentration of research and development into products and techniques in the advanced countries makes this a rarity at present.

SOME POLICY IMPLICATIONS

The introduction of new products that have been developed in and for developed countries into LDCs can have important welfare implications. In many cases, the distributional impact is likely to be inegalitarian, while in some cases, the new products may impose absolute losses on society. Our analysis suggests the need for countries to develop an active product policy. Elements of such a policy include:

1. Product development. There is a systematic tendency for product development in high-income countries to be inappropriate for LDCs, leading to products containing excessive characteristics. The development of appropriate products with low-income characteristics (including divisibility) and appropriate to the environment of poor countries would enable such countries to benefit from the increased efficiency of modern products, without being harmed by their high-income characteristics. The development of appropriate products should contribute to a more egalitarian income distribution. With an initial inegalitarian distribution, such product development might

need to correspond to 'felt needs' of poor consumers, rather than monetary demand. Even where modern products from advanced countries do confer benefits on consumers in poor countries — as in Figure 7 — the development of appropriate products would be likely to confer greater benefits.

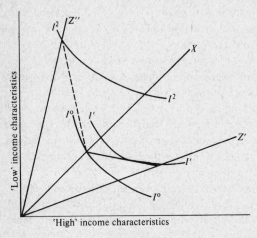

Figure 7

Suppose X is the initial product. The new product developed in a developed country, Z', enables consumer welfare in the LDC to rise from I^0I^0 to $I'I'$. But more appropriate product, Z'', leads to a greater rise in welfare in the LDC. Policies to develop more appropriate products require local research and development related to product (as well as technique) development.

2. Policies towards the import of products: a more selective approach is required towards the import of new products from advanced countries, while a more active search is needed to promote the import of appropriate products from other developing countries. More systematic research is needed to assess the benefits and costs of particular products in particular countries, but it seems likely that there is a strong case for a total ban on some products, and for differential taxation on others.

3. Government standards/specifications for products need revision. At present, in many countries they are either totally absent (e.g. no requirements for health warnings on cigarettes) or imitations of requirements in advanced countries, leading to 'too-high' standards

and over-specified high-income products. Government standards should be designed to see that basic needs–type characteristics are embodied in the relevant goods.

4. Policy towards advertising/promotional expenditure: the disproportionate concentration of promotional efforts devoted to modern advanced country products needs to be corrected. There is a strong case for limitations on promotional expenditure, which wastes resources and creates consumption inefficiency. Paradoxically, while the need for controlled advertising is greater in developing countries than in developed, in most LDCs there are no controls at all. A deliberate effort − of expenditure, organisation, publicity − needs to be made to provide accurate information about all available products. Taxation of private promotional expenditure could finance efforts in this direction. The system of trade-marks, which gives rise to much promotional expenditure, often leads to consumer adherence to well-established foreign products. Reform of this system is an important aspect of a products policy, as well as assisting local technological development, and reducing the price of imported technology.[36]

5. Taxes/subsidies and rationing may be used to encourage the production and consumption of more appropriate goods, and discourage that of inappropriate goods.

CONCLUSION

This paper has attempted to provide a more systematic framework for assessing the benefits and costs of new products. It presents a research agenda rather than well-established conclusions. We consider the conditions that are likely to lead to gains/losses in consumer welfare following the introduction of new products. We find, tentatively, that products developed in advanced countries are likely to have inegalitarian effects when introduced to poor countries and may, under certain conditions, cause losses among some or all consumers. These conclusions suggest the need for LDCs to have an active product policy.

We should emphasise that the paper uses a very conventional model of consumer choice and consumer welfare, as its point of departure − viz. it is assumed that consumers are isolated units whose welfare depends on their own behaviour alone and that individual consumer preferences are the ultimate determinant of economic welfare. If we were to introduce interdependencies of behaviour (see Sen) or of consumer welfare (Veblen), or a more sophisticated psychology of consumer welfare (as Scitovsky) we would have to abandon much of the framework presented here.[37] While we have not incorporated any of these approaches in any systematic way, each supports the need to challenge the usual assumption of the unquestioned benefits of new products.

ACKNOWLEDGEMENTS

We are grateful for comments on an earlier draft from Keith Griffin, Paul Isenman, Peter O'Brien and Howard Pack. Ruchira Chatterji provided valuable research assistance.

NOTES

1 According to Pessemier (1977), in 1970 17 per cent of all sales in manufacturing in the USA consisted of products less than four years old.
2 Midgley (1977) p. 180.
3 Notable exceptions are Veblen and Scitovsky – both have been treated with cold neglect by the profession. See Veblen (1899) and Scitovsky (1976).
4 As Lancaster puts it, 'Introduction of a new good requires that the preference function defined on n goods is thrown away and with it all the knowledge of behaviour based on it, and replaced by a brand new function on $n + 1$ goods, or the fiction that the consumer has a potential preference function for all goods present and future – Neither approach gets us very far'. Lancaster (1966) p. 20.
5 Helleiner (1975) has a summary treatment of some of the effects of new products, using Lancaster's approach on similar lines to those adopted in this chapter.
6 An article in the *Harvard Business Review* in 1965 advised the rapid phasing out of products in the final stage of the product cycle on the grounds that they have to be produced in short uneconomical runs and also demand a disproportionate share of scarce managerial and other resources. Kotler (1965).
7 'Apart from the few weeks at the end of the year when next year's models are already available but dealers also sell out their remaining stock of the old year's models, the consumer must buy his new car with its new design and new features whether he wants them or not.' Scitovsky (1976) p. 256.
8 Research and development on new products is directed at the biggest markets (in monetary terms) as indicated by these figures for the pharmaceutical industry:

New products introduced by revenue size of therapeutic market, 1969

Therapeutic class revenue parameter $ million	France		Italy		Germany		UK	
	No. of C	No. of P	No. of C	No. of P	No. of C	No. of P	No. of C	No. of P
0.0–0.5	18	3	17	1	23	2	23	5
0.5–1.5	30	13	34	17	36	19	20	5
1.5–2.5	18	13	19	10	13	14	9	10
2.5–5.0	23	23	29	22	28	47	20	44
5.0–10.0	31	45	27	68	21	41	10	39
10.0+	26	75	22	98	25	112	11	34
Totals	146	172	148	216	146	235	93	137

Therapeutic class revenue parameter $ million	Spain		Belgium		Holland		Austria	
	No. of C	No. of P	No. of C	No. of P	No. of C	No. of P	No. of C	No. of P
0.0–0.5	55	19	37	3	94	23	116	23
0.5–1.5	43	62	38	21	30	18	28	45
1.5–2.5	19	44	21	8	7	8	4	16
2.5–5.0	27	146	29	21	6	12	–	–
5.0–10.0	7	54	19	24	2	1	–	–
10.0+	6	156	9	21	–	–	–	–
Totals	157	481	153	98	139	62	148	84

C = classes; P = products

Source: D. Reekie, *The Economics of the Pharmaceutical, Industry*, Macmillan, 1975, p. 68. Even what relatively little R&D exists in and for poor countries appears to be directed largely to the high-income minorities in these countries. In Berg's survey of Indian firms more than half stated that new products were aimed at middle- and upper-income levels. Another study notes that in the case of processed foodstuffs very little interest has so far been shown in the lower-income segments of poor countries.

9 See, for example, Pratten (1971).

10 A study in the USA covering food and household goods shows for example a distinct trend towards packaging in larger sizes. See Stanton (1964).

11 See Wells (1977).

12 Ibid. pp. 269–70.

13 A similar phenomenon appears to be taking place in Trinidad and Tobago. One-third of households in the poorest four income classes spend less than 29 per cent of total expenditure on food despite the fact that there is 'considerable undernutrition and malnutrition among the population'.

14 See Hughes and Hunter (1972) p. 90.

15 See discussion in Stewart (1977).

16 There are well-known problems about defining 'appropriate' and 'inappropriate' technology. Despite these it is not difficult to arrive at a working definition (see Stewart, 1977; Morawetz, 1974).

17 James (1977).

18   Government of India (1965).
19   Langdon (1975).
20   Cooper (1976).
21   Stewart (1977), Chapter 9.
22   Kaplinsky (1978).
23   Stewart (1977), Chapter 10.
24   N. S. McBain (1977).
25   Swainson (1978).
26   This example is essentially taken from S. Lall, (1975).
27   DAFSA (p. 19).
28   Lall (1975), para. 30.
29   Hathi Committee, p. 93.
30   Lall (1975), para. 87.
31   Kefauver Committee.
32   Hathi Committee.
33   Lall (1975), para (VI).
34   Ibid., para. 74.
35   Hathi Committee, p. 194.
36   The question of trade-marks is explored in much greater depth in UNCTAD (1977) and Stewart (1981).
37   See Sen (1977), Veblen (1899) and Scitovsky (1976).

REFERENCES

Cooper, C. (1976). Policy interventions for technological innovation in less developed countries, Science Policy Research Unit, Sussex University (mimeo).
Documentation et Analyses Financieres S. A. *The Pharmaceutical Industry in Europe.*
Government of India (1965). *Report of the Sugar Enquiry Commission*, Delhi.
Hathi Committee on the Indian Drug Industry (1975). *Report of the Committee on Drugs and Pharmaceutical Industry*, New Delhi.
Helleiner, G. K. (1975). The role of multinational corporations in the less developed countries trade in technology, *World Development,* 3, April.
Hughes, C. C. and Hunter, J. M. (1972). The role of technological development in promoting disease in Africa, in *The Careless Technology*, (Eds, M. T. Farvar and J. M. Milton), Natural History Press.
James, J. (1977). Technology, products and income distribution: A conceptualization and application to sugar processing in India, ILO, WEP, November.
Kaplinsky, R. (1978). Inappropriate products and techniques in UDCs: The case of breakfast foods in Kenya, Working Paper No. 335 Institute of Development Studies, Nairobi, April.
Kefauver, E. (1966). *In a Few Hands: Monopoly Power in America*, Penguin, Harmondsworth.
Kotler, P. (1965). Phasing out weak products, *Harvard Business Review,* 43, March–April.
Lall, S. (1975). Major issues in transfer of technology to developing countries: A case study of the pharmaceutical industry, UNCTAD, TD/B/C.6/4.
Lancaster, K. (1966). Change and innovation in the technology of consumption, *American Economic Review*, 56, May.
Langdon, S. (1975). Multinational corporations taste transfer and underdevelopment: A case study from Kenya, *Review of African Political Economy*, Jan.
McBain, N. S. (1977). Developing country product choice: Footwear in Ethiopia, *World Development*, 5, September–October.
Midgley, D. F. (1977). *Innovation & New Product Marketing*, Croom-Helm.

Morawetz, D. (1974). Employment implications of industrialisation in developing countries: A survey, *Economic Journal*, **84**, September.

Pessemier, E. A. (1977). *Product Management: Strategy and Organisation*, Wiley.

Pratten, C. F. (1971). *Economies of Scale in Manufacturing Industry*, Cambridge University Press, London.

Scitovsky, T. (1976). *The Joyless Economy: An Enquiry into Human Satisfaction and Consumer Dissatisfaction*, Oxford University Press, London.

Sen, A. K. (1977). Rational fools: A critique of the behavioural foundations of economic theory, *Philosophy & Public Affairs*, **6**.

Speight, A. N. P. (1975). Cost effectiveness and drug therapy, *Tropical Doctor*, April.

Stanton, W. J. (1964). *Fundamentals of Marketing* (2nd ed.), McGraw Hill.

Stewart, F. (1977). *Technology and Underdevelopment*, Macmillan.

Stewart, F. (1981). International technology transfer: Issues and policy options, in P. Streeten and R. Jolly (eds) *Recent Issues in World Development*, Pergemon.

Swainson, N. (1978). The Bata Shoe Company: Types of production and transfer of skills, UNESCO, Division for the Study of Development.

UNCTAD (1977). The impact of trade-marks on the development process of developing countries, (TD/B/C, 6/AC.33).

Veblen, T. (1899). *The Theory of the Leisure Class*, Macmillan, London.

Wells, J. (1977). The diffusion of durables in Brazil and its implications for recent controversies concerning Brazilian development, *Cambridge Journal of Economics*, **1**, No. 3.

12   Product standards in developing countries

JEFFREY JAMES

Legal minimum standards below which products may not be marketed are widely used in developed countries. There is a commonly held presumption that these standards — almost all of which are imposed for goods endangering the health and safety of consumers — should also be adopted by the developing countries. In both groups of countries, for example, there is legislation prohibiting the marketing of drugs which are not approved in the United States.[1] The World Health Organization formulates international standards for drinking water and drugs,[2] while consumer groups urge 'that the United States support the development of international product safety standards'[3] and express indignation at the very idea that drugs which do not meet developed country standards should be available in developing countries.[4]

Perhaps because the policy is thought to be self-evidently correct, few advocates of uniform international product standards have found it necessary to provide any sort of justification for their views. At the same time, the competing idea that developing countries should adopt standards that differ from those in rich countries (or that they should have no standards) has not been pursued with much vigour. As a result, the important question of product standards in developing countries has occasioned remarkably little analysis or debate.

One approach to this problem is to consider the reasons why standards are adopted in developed countries. An appraisal of whether and how far these considerations also apply in the Third World can then be used as a basis on which to determine the requirements of developing countries. Consequently, the first part of the paper is devoted to a discussion of the rationale of product standards in developed countries; the second part will consider the problem from the contrasting standpoint of the developing countries and the final section deals with the policy implications of the analysis.

THE BASIS FOR INTERVENTION THROUGH STANDARDS IN DEVELOPED COUNTRIES

A fundamental assumption of Paretian welfare theory is that 'an individual should be considered the best judge of his economic welfare'.[5] This value judgment is often referred to as that of 'complete consumer sovereignty' and its rejection is perhaps the most basic reason for the adoption of standards in developed countries.

Paternalism

The need for government protection of particular groups in society — such as children and the insane — who are obviously unable to adequately assess their own interests has long been recognised. Some product standards, such as seatbelts for children, reflect this need for paternalism. Clearly, however, different reasons have to be adduced to explain why individual freedom of choice is abrogated in the case of standards (such as those relating to compulsory seatbelts and crash helmets) which are imposed on the *entire* population. One possible justification is the view that individuals tend to systematically underestimate the true risks of injury even when they are aware of these risks. It is well-known from research in social psychology for example, that individuals often use techniques of rationalisation (including the distortion of available information) to justify their own behaviour (smokers for example, underestimate the dangers involved in smoking compared to non-smokers).[6]

A similar type of argument, which may underlie some of the safety standards on housing, is that individuals need to be protected from harming themselves because they are typically short-sighted about risks occurring in the future — a form of Pigou's 'defective telescopic faculty'.

Externalities in consumption

In some cases standards which seem to be based on paternalism may also (or alternatively) be due to externalities in consumption: i.e. the effect of one individual's consumption on the welfare of others. The reason is that many of the risks undertaken by individuals are borne also by society. For 'even a person who harms only himself will often have to be rescued, patched up, nursed back to life, or buried with the aid of public services and partly or wholly at taxpayers' expense'.[7] And to protect the taxpayer, governments may restrict the freedom of the individual to decide what chances to take with his own safety. Legislation requiring that motorcyclists wear crash helmets, for example, may be due partly to paternalism and partly to a view that 'reckless' individuals should not impose their preferences on the rest of society.

In the presence of externalities product standards may also be required partly to *give effect* to individual preferences. As an illustration consider the question of speed limits and assume a situation in which for each individual in society the most desirable situation is one in which everyone except himself has to observe a speed limit. Provided that everyone else does observe the limit, however, he would prefer to have to adhere to it rather than have no speed restrictions. In this sort of situation, known in game theory as the isolation paradox, government intervention to enforce the speed limit is required not to overrule individual preferences, but rather to give effect to them through securing the collectively rational outcome. The requirement for minimum standards of roadworthiness for motor vehicles may also partly reflect this type of externality.

Imperfect information

The paternalistic and externalities arguments for standards apply even when it is assumed that the consumer is fully informed. When this assumption is dropped, an additional case for standards sometimes arises.

It is difficult to deal adequately with imperfect information in terms of the traditional theory of demand which assumes that goods as such are the immediate object of utility. The reason is that the scope for imperfect information about goods in this theory is limited to that about their existence and prices. The characteristics approach, in contrast, which views the demand for goods as a derived demand for the characteristics embodied in them, permits us to analyse a situation in which the consumer is imperfectly informed about any or all the relevant characteristics of a good.[8]

The fact that buyers are imperfectly informed in this sense does not of itself, however, indicate the need for product standards to be imposed by government. The 'first-best' solution to the problem of imperfect information is, of course, the provision of full information about product characteristics because it preserves freedom of choice. A zealous advocate of this approach to consumer protection is Milton Friedman, who argues that 'Insofar as the government has information not generally available about the merits or demerits of the items we ingest or the activities we engage in, let it give us the information. But let it leave us free to choose what chances we want to take with our own lives'.[9] The requirement that a health warning and statement of tar content be carried on cigarette packets and the compulsory labelling of many other categories of potentially dangerous products (such as flammable textiles and household appliances) in most developed countries indicate that the market mechanism, aided by the provision of information, is often thought to be superior to direct regulation through the imposition of standards.

In some cases, however, the provision of information is unlikely to contribute to more informed choices by consumers. Technical information about the safety of drugs for example, is unlikely to make much sense to the layman. Moreover, even if complex information can somehow be presented in a comprehensible way to individuals, the costs of doing so would often appear to be prohibitive. Where, for these reasons, information is difficult or impossible to communicate to consumers, reliance on the market mechanism becomes more difficult and product standards may be required to protect uninformed consumers. What has to be decided is whether the benefits to these consumers through the protection thus afforded by standards are sufficient to outweigh the costs imposed by the restriction on the range of products available. Following Colantoni *et al.*, the problem may be analysed with the aid of Figure 1.[10]

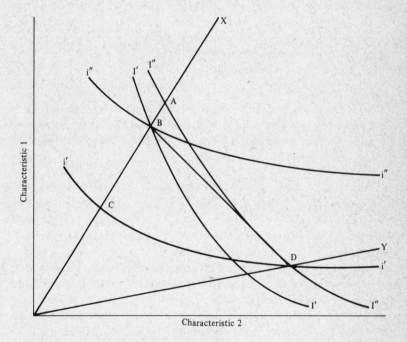

Figure 1 The welfare effect of product standards

Figure 1 portrays a situation of two goods X and Y. The prices of these goods are such that the slope of the efficiency frontier is given by BD. Two individuals, with the same incomes but different tastes are represented by the indifference maps ii and II. Possessed of perfect information the former would choose good X and the latter good Y. Let us assume, however, that the individual with the ii map overestimates the characteristics embodied in good Y to the extent that he chooses it in preference to good X. The effect of government intervention to remove good Y then implies that the individual with the ii map is made better off (because he is saved from making a mistaken choice) and the individual with the II map is made worse off, because his optimal choice is no longer available. In terms of good X the gainer could in this case compensate the loser and still remain better off, i.e. BC > AB. The effect of the withdrawal of Y on the distribution of income depends of course, on whether or not compensation is paid to the loser.

In any actual situation therefore, the argument in favour of the withdrawal of a particular good will be stronger:

1. the greater the extent to which individuals are misinformed about the characteristics embodied in it (or more specifically, over-estimate its positive characteristics and underestimate its negative characteristics) and the more serious are the risks associated with its consumption;
2. the fewer are those for whom the good is the optimal choice;
3. the more the change leads to a desired movement in income distribution.

While, of course, it cannot be said that governments actually calculate the relative size of these effects, it can be argued that they underlie in a rough way many of the decisions to ban dangerous drugs and chemicals that are made in developed countries.

DEVELOPING COUNTRY REQUIREMENTS FOR PRODUCT STANDARDS

The case for *some* standards in developing countries rests on the same grounds as those described above in relation to developed countries; namely, that because of paternalism, externalities in consumption and imperfect information, the unregulated market mechanism produces insufficient protection of consumers. But it does not follow from this that countries of the Third World should adopt either the same *number* or the same *level* of standards as the developed countries.

Where imperfect information is the problem underlying the need for product standards, it is understandable that in the case of many goods (some of which were described above), policy-makers in developed countries prefer modification of the market mechanism through the provision of information to direct regulation through standards. In these societies high levels of education and efficient communications networks enable much information to be provided, and assimilated by consumers relatively easily. The situation in most countries of the Third World however, is very different. Low overall rates of literacy (still below 30 per cent in Africa, for example) and educational attainment, and limited coverage of the mass media (especially in rural areas), make it much more difficult, and sometimes impossible to rely on the provision of information. The experience of nutrition and other mass education programmes in developing countries illustrates the difficulties of successfully conveying information to isolated and dispersed rural communities, many of whose members are illiterate. As a result of these difficulties, the role of standards in protecting uninformed consumers may need to be greater. But as we saw above, for the imposition of standards to be justified, the benefits afforded through protection have to exceed the costs incurred through the restriction of product choice. This, in turn, depends on the *level* at which the standards are set.

In choosing the level of product standards what needs to be established is the 'price' of additional units of safety on the one hand, and the evaluation of these units by the members of society on the other. The evaluation of safety by society will depend, among other things, on its level of affluence.

Safety and rising incomes

Income is a fundamental determinant of individual tastes. At the very low income levels that characterise developing countries, products are desired essentially (but not only) for the basic needs (for hunger, shelter etc.) that they help to meet. This was true also of the now developed countries when they were at a similar stage of development. But as societies grow richer the nature of the goods that they purchase changes in a systematic manner as has been described by Frances Stewart. Thus

> the same broad needs are fulfilled by a different set of products, em-
> bodying a different (on the whole more satisfying, more sophisticated)
> set of characteristics with higher standards. Rice tends to be replaced
> by wheat and by meat; medieval 'players' by movies and by radio; radio
> is replaced by television, first black-and-white and then colour. Cars
> take over from vehicles powered by horses or humans, and the cars
> become more sophisticated, faster and quieter.[11]

It is also true that as societies become richer they require increasing standards of safety from the goods that they purchase. New products developed in the rich industrialised countries often reflect this relationship. Cars and jets, for example, have both become safer over the years. In the case of drugs, 'The current trend of society in demanding quantitative increases in the quality of life has programmed itself, in terms of ethical pharmaceuticals, to accepting a lower level of risk.'[12] This is undoubtedly a major reason for the fact that 'the consumption of pharmaceuticals is now probably safer than at any time in pharmaceutical history'.[13] Indeed, a number of highly valued drugs in common use, such as penicillin and aspirin, would more than likely have failed toxicity tests by the current standards of a number of DCs.[14]

Product safety standards in these countries, such as those administered by the FDA (Food and Drug Administration) and the CPSC (Consumer Product Safety Commission) in America, reflect in a rough way the increased premium placed by these societies on safety as incomes rise. At the same time they are designed to fit in with the skills and other resources now possessed by these countries. For example, manually-operated X-ray machines are no longer approved in the USA because of the risk to patients of unnecessary exposure. But the introduction of complex machines that automatically limit the beams to the area to be X-rayed was made possible by the availability of technical skills needed to operate the new equipment.[15]

The safety of many new goods developed in and for DCs is not, however, achieved without a cost. Increases in cost (and price) take the form not only of additional characteristics of goods (such as seat-belts, padded instrument panels and energy-absorbing steering columns) but also more extensive product testing. Some early antibiotics, for example, were developed, tested, and approved within eighteen months to two years. Now a period of five to seven years is considered normal.[16] At the same time the cost of testing new chemical entities has increased dramatically and is currently of the order of $54 million.[17]

It is very likely that the individual consumer in the typical LDC will have a view of the extent to which additional safety should be 'bought' which is generally quite different from that of his counterpart in the DCs. A basic reason for the difference lies in the close relationship between incomes and basic human needs.

According to the psychologist Maslow, basic needs are hierarchical — as one need is satisfied, another emerges.[18] In his scheme the most basic of all needs (such as hunger) are described as physiological. It is only when these are relatively well satisfied that 'there then emerges a new set of needs, which we may categorize roughly as the safety needs'[19] (such as 'security', 'protection', 'need for structure', 'limits' etc.). Even if in practice needs do not appear to be strictly hierarchical (many of the poorest individuals for example, consume lower elements in the hierarchy before their most basic physiological needs are well satisfied), Maslow's idea seems to capture something of the truth about the nature of preferences. And since it is income which primarily determines the extent of satisfaction of the physiological needs, Maslow's hierarchy can be translated into the notion that low income consumers in LDCs will tend to evaluate safety needs as less important relative to members of rich societies. By way of an (all too common) example consider the situation of a head of a low-income household in an LDC who is taken ill and is unable to work. Deprived of any form of sickness benefit he is aware that even a relatively short period of loss of earnings can mean severe physiological hardship for himself and his family. In this situation he will almost certainly have a marginal valuation of the safety, efficacy and price of drugs which differs sharply from that implied by DC standards.[20]

Empirical evidence for our view of safety as a 'high-income' characteristic is difficult to find, but one experiment conducted by Jones-Lee concerning the safety records of two airlines offers some support.[21] Each of thirty-one respondents was presented with the fare and safety record of a given (hypothetical) airline. They were then asked to indicate the fare that would just induce them to travel with another airline which differs from the other only in terms of safety (measured in terms of fatal crashes per 500 000 flights).

When the sample of response is divided into two income groups (above and below an annual salary of £3500) the results support the view that safety is a characteristic whose value does vary with incomes. In particular, the 'high-income' group would, on average, pay more for a 'safer' ticket; conversely, they would require greater compensation in terms of a reduction in the fare before being prepared to travel on the more 'risky flight' (i.e. they are prepared to pay more than the 'low-income' group to secure a reduction in risk on the one hand, and require greater monetary compensation to accept higher risk on the other).

If the valuation of safety by the individual consumer depends on income in the way described above, then the *macro* consequences for a developing country of adopting developed-country standards would be as follows. First, if the standards are enforced the vast majority of consumers in these countries would be denied the opportunity to purchase the cheaper (albeit often less safe) varieties that best accord with their tastes and would be forced to purchase the relatively expensive brands that conform to the standard of those living in rich countries (see Figure 2 for illustration).

AB is the efficiency frontier for the 'average' consumer in the developing country, whose tastes are represented by the indifference curves IC_1

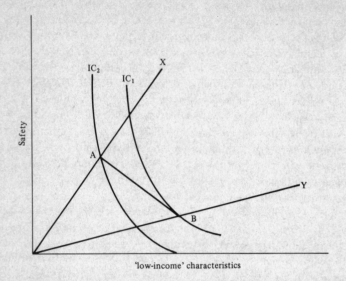

Figure 2 The effect of adopting developed country standards in developing countries

and IC_2. The effect of the imposition of developed-country standards is to render his preferred good Y unavailable, leaving him on the lower indifference curve IC_2. Consequently, the welfare effect of the change is that the minority of individuals with incomes and tastes similar to those prevailing in the developed countries gain at the expense of the majority. (Note that this conclusion is not altered if good Y is bought on the basis of imperfect information; because of the assumed nature of the relationship between preferences and incomes this good would remain the optimal choice for, and continue to be purchased by, most consumers even when they possess full information.)

A good example of the situation described by Figure 2 is to be found in the field of housing where: 'It is common for public agencies to build houses or flats to standards which the majority cannot afford, nor can the country possibly subsidize them on a large scale. On top of this, it is not unusual for governments to prohibit private building of the type of housing the vast majority can afford and are satisfied with.'[22] Purchase of the housing with 'too-high' standards involves a disproportionate expenditure on this item compared to other items in the household budget, i.e. it leads to imbalances in consumption (or to concentration of public expenditure on housing to the exclusion of other social needs). Alternatively, because unrealistically high standards are difficult to enforce, black markets may frequently develop. In Kenya, for example, cheap maize beer brewed by low-income households and served in oil cans is banned.[23] The same restrictions applies to the sale of gin distilled in the formal sector of that country.[24] As a result, the consumers of these popular products are forced to purchase them illegally. On occasion, the consequence of attempting to enforce unrealistically high standards in developing countries is that some consumers become even *less*-well protected. This paradoxical outcome has been observed in relation to standards for drinking water by Feachem who cites cases where health officials have closed down village tube wells because they were found to contain impurities slightly in excess of developed-country standards.[25] As a result, the villagers were forced to use irrigation canals that were far more polluted.

To avoid the undesirable macro consequences described above developing countries need, in general, to adopt lower product standards than those prevailing in the developed world. Recognition of this need does exist but mostly in rather fragmentary form in the literature on health issues in developing countries. For example, manually operated X-ray machines are no longer approved in the United States because of the risk to patients of unnecessary exposure (complex machines that automatically limit the beams to the area to be X-rayed are used instead). For the developing countries however, 'the benefits of having X-ray equipment available for use outweighs the potential risk of unnecessary exposure from manual operation'.[26] Similar considerations apply to the administration of oral contraceptives in LDCs. Given the shortage of medical manpower in these countries 'it is probably unreasonable to demand that every woman should be given all the warnings, or that she get a routine PAP smear'.[27] Though this is a less-safe procedure than that undertaken in developed societies, it is surely preferable from the point of view of safety itself, as well as other points of view to banning the drug or restricting it to those few who are able to have the more thorough treatment. Or again, expenditure of the government health budget on cheaper (if slightly older and perhaps more risky) drugs would allow a much higher proportion of the population of a developing country to enjoy the benefits of drug therapy.[28]

What is needed may in fact be described as *intermediate* standards, in the same sense and for the same basic reason as that which underlies the widespread advocacy of intermediate technology in the Third World. This should not be taken to imply a concern only for 'downgrading' developed country standards but also for 'upgrading' local norms where necessary. For example, drinking water from surface sources or open wells in developing countries often exceeds 1000 faecal coliforms per decilitre. Raising the standard to say, 500 faecal coliforms per decilitre is a long way from the WHO standards (of zero coliforms) but is none the less a significant improvement.[29]

Mortality rates, life expectancies and discount rates

High mortality rates and low life expectancies are common features of most LDCs. Like low incomes, they may also influence the way in which safety is evaluated in these countries relative to those that are more affluent.

High maternal mortality rates in LDCs may change the risk–benefit ratio associated with contraceptives because of the higher risks of an unwanted pregnancy[30] – a factor not, of course, taken into account in FDA decisions to ban or approve new contraceptive drugs for sale on the US market. (Depo-Provera, a contraceptive administered by injection has, for example, recently been banned.)

Moreover, in most LDCs average life expectancies are considerably lower than in DCs. On account of the differential probability of surviving another year in DCs and LDCs Eckstein has argued that time preference – the discounting of future benefits relative to the present – will also vary.[31] In particular, the greater uncertainty of survival for individuals in LDCs implies that they discount future benefits at a higher rate than members of DCs (i.e. they weight the present more heavily). The converse presumably applies to costs which are distributed over time. As a basis for different product standards this argument is weakened by the fact that life expectancy differences between rich and poor countries are most pronounced at birth – after just one year the gap narrows markedly. Still, it is often difficult to argue that long-term risks (of say drugs) should be discounted in the same way in Chad (where life expectancy at the age of 20 is 51) as in America (where life expectancy at the same age is 70.)

Differential incidence and severity of diseases

Many diseases occur with varying degrees of severity between DCs and LDCs. Almost always, the severity is more pronounced in the latter. Measles, for example, is very rarely a lethal disease in the affluent societies. It is most severe in infancy when combined with malnutrition and other diseases endemic to the poorest segments of the Third World. Since the benefits from treatment are on this account potentially greater in LDCs, reasonable decisions to ban the use of certain measles vaccines in DCs (such as that taken in the UK with the Beckenham-31 strain ten years ago) may make little sense for many LDCs.

The incidence of diseases also varies widely as between rich and poor countries. Many tropical diseases, for example, are virtually non-existent in DCs. Though this fact will not affect the risk–benefit ratio for drugs designed to treat such diseases in the case of a single patient, it does affect the net benefits calculated for society as a whole. Conversely, some diseases in DCs, such as those of the heart, are comparatively rare in the LDCs.

SUMMARY AND CONCLUSIONS

In both developed and developing countries the case for product standards rests on the failure of the unregulated market mechanism to provide sufficient consumer protection. However, the role of standards in developing countries may be expected to differ from that in developed countries in two major respects.

First, because of widespread illiteracy and the limited coverage of mass media, information is more difficult to convey to and be assimilated by consumers in the Third World. Consequently, provided that they lead to positive net benefits, product standards rather than warnings may be required to protect uninformed consumers in these countries. In the much publicised case of baby milk, for example, whereas the provision of information about the dangers of using these products may have only rather limited usefulness, the gains from a ban on their sale would be considerable. Not only could approximately 1 million lives a year be saved but also a vast amount of expenditure.[32] The losers from a ban would comprise those, such as working mothers and women who cannot breastfeed, for whom baby milk is the optimal choice. But these categories are likely to be small relative to those who would benefit from the banning of baby milk. Thus according to Jelliffe: 'Studies in most slum or shanty-town areas, in fact show that only a percentage (usually relatively small) are going away from the home to work.'[33] Moreover, 'recent research shows that only a minute percentage of mothers are unable to feed their babies, even among the badly under-nourished'.[34] (To ensure that these categories do not suffer from the ban, baby milk could be made available under prescription.)

Secondly, though a case can be made for the imposition of more standards in developing than developed countries, there are also good reasons to believe that the standards adopted in the former should differ from those prevailing in the latter.

Contrary to a popular view we argued that, because the premium placed on additional safety by the consumer in rich and poor societies will generally differ, rich country standards tend to have a negative welfare impact when introduced into most developing countries. In the long run moreover, when embodied in international regulations, such excessive standards may be inimical to the development of products which are suited to the needs of the majority of those living in the Third World.

In the case of bacterial standards for drinking water, for example, the WHO specifies international standards which, while reasonable in developed countries, 'may well have been responsible for retarding the development of water supplies in less developed countries'.[35] With respect to drugs as well, the legislation has until recently effectively exported US safety standards to the developing countries and, according to some commentators, this has hindered the development of new drugs which better conform to the needs of these countries.

Though there are proposals for amendment[36] US law prohibits the export of new drugs unless they are approved for marketing domestically.[37] Drugs may be sent abroad for clinical testing provided that they obtain an 'investigational new drug exemption' (IND), i.e. after the preclinical testing phase the manufacturer is required to file with the FDA for approval before human testing is initiated either in the USA or abroad. The effect of this system on the development of new drugs for tropical and parasitic diseases has been studied by DiRaddo and Wardell.[38]

'Of approximately 900 NCEs [new chemical entities] studied in man by United States-owned pharmaceutical firms from 1963 through 1976, 20 were candidates primarily for tropical or parasitic diseases. These 20 NCEs came from 11 of the 41 United States-owned pharmaceutical firms and affiliates from which data are currently available.'[39] Sixteen of the twenty NCEs obtained INDs and the remainder originated outside the US and were hence not required to obtain permission for testing in humans. Only two of these sixteen NCEs, however, were approved for marketing in the US while research on three of them is still proceeding. Thus, only two of the new drugs for tropical and parasitic diseases developed in the USA over the past fourteen years were allowed to be marketed in the Third World. Given the enormous financial costs required to obtain FDA approval for domestic sale, it seems clear that this regulation limits severely the incentive to market new drugs for tropical and parasitic diseases in LDCs. Moreover, even the requirement for obtaining a US IND prior to export is a 'deterrent that prevents more United States-discovered drugs from being studied abroad clinically at an earlier stage of their development'.[40]

DiRaddo and Wardell argue for less-restrictive standards for the introduction of new drugs into human testing — that these be determined by the LDCs themselves — and for the 'expedited international transfer of molecules discovered in developed countries to LDCs for clinical testing'.[41]

In conclusion, we advocate that developing countries adopt intermediate standards; standards which require upgrading local norms on the one hand and downgrading developed country standards on the other. It is true that efforts to formulate intermediate standards will incur costs, including those of an administrative kind, which need to be offset against the arguments adduced above in support of a different set of standards. But the burden of the costs involved could be substantially reduced through co-operation among groups of developing countries with respect to say, joint testing facilities, exchange of information and the formulation of standards.

ACKNOWLEDGEMENTS

Comments from Stephen Lister and Frances Stewart are gratefully acknowledged.

NOTES AND REFERENCES

1   We discuss this in detail below.
2   See WHO (1971). *International Standards For Drinking Water*, 3rd. edn., and A. G. Mathews (1972). The role of the World Health Organisation in the quality control of biological and pharmaceutical products, in M. S. Cooper (Ed.) *Quality Control in the Pharmaceutical Industry*, Vol. 1, Academic Press.
3   See *Consumer Reports*, September 1970, p. 564.
4   For instance, Martin Khor of the Consumers' Association of Penang, Malaysia objects to the use of Depo-Provera (a contraceptive banned by the FDA) on the grounds that it is 'grossly irresponsible' to 'distribute to our Malaysian women a drug which has been banned in the Western countries where it originated'. Quoted in the *Asian Wall Street Journal*, 10 April 1980.
5   S. K. Nath (1969). *A Reappraisal of Welfare Economics*, Augustus M. Kelley, p. 9.
6   L. Festinger (1957). *A Theory of Cognitive Dissonance*, Stanford University Press.
7   T. Scitovsky (1976). *The Joyless Economy: An Inquiry into Human Satisfaction and Consumer Dissatisfaction*, Oxford University Press, p. 221.
8   D. A. L. Auld (1971). 'Imperfect knowledge and the new theory of demand, *Journal of Political Economy*, LXXX, Nov.–Dec.
9   Milton Friedman and Rose Friedman (1980). *Free to Choose*, Secker & Warburg, p. 227.
10 C. Colantoni, O. Davis and M. Swaminuthan (1976). Imperfect consumers and welfare comparisons of policies concerning information and regulation, *Bell Journal of Economics*, 7, Autumn.
11 Frances Stewart (1977). *Technology and Underdevelopment*, Macmillan, p. 6.
12 B. G. James, *The Future of the Multinational Pharmaceutical Industry to 1990*, Associated Business Programmes, p. 119.
13 Ibid., p. 120.
14 F. H. Happold (1967). *Medicine at Risk: The Higher Price of Cheap Drugs*, Queen Ann Press.

15   Donald Kennedy (1979). Food and drug administration and pharmaceuticals for developing countries, in US National Academy of Sciences, *Pharmaceuticals for Developing Countries*, Washington.

16   Happold op. cit.

17   J. DiRaddo and W. M. Wardell (1979). Innovation and availability in the united states of drugs for tropical diseases, in US National Academy of Sciences, *Pharmaceuticals for Developing Countries*, Washington.

18   A. H. Maslow (1977). *Motivation and Personality*, 2nd edn., Harper and Row. The idea of using Maslow's approach in the context of risk analysis is to be found in W. D. Rowe (1977) *An Anatomy of Risk*, Wiley.

19   Maslow, op. cit., p. 39.

20   'In a poor country like Mexico it is very bad when the breadwinner of a family gets sick. To get such a man back to work quickly, many physicians take a chance and prescribe a treatment that is a little dangerous. But if the patient is away from work too long, his wife and children may go hungry.' The example in the text is based on this quotation by a Mexican cardiologist quoted in M. Silverman (1976). *The Drugging of the Americas*, University of California Press, p. 117.

21   M. W. Jones-Lee (1976). *The Value of Life: An Economic Analysis*, Martin Robertson.

22   J. F. C. Turner (1976). *Housing By People: Towards Autonomy in Building Environments*, Marion Boyars, p. 75.

23   N. Nelson (1979). How women and men get by: The sexual division of labour in the informal sector of a Nairobi squatter settlement, in R. Bromley and C. Gerry (Eds.), *Casual Work and Poverty in Third World Cities*, Wiley.

24   Ibid.

25   R. Feachmen (1980). Bacterial standards for drinking water quality in developing countries, *The Lancet*, 2 August.

26   Kennedy, op. cit.

27   A medical practitioner in an LDC quoted in Silverman, op. cit.

28   A. N. P. Speight (1975). Cost effectiveness and drug therapy, *Tropical Doctor*, April.

29   For a detailed discussion of standards of water quality in LDCs see R. Feachem, M. McGarry and D. Mara (1977). *Water, Wastes and Health in Hot Climates*, Wiley.

30   Kennedy, op. cit.

31   O. Eckstein (1961). A survey of the theory of public expenditure criteria, in J. M. Buchanan (Ed.) *Public Finances: Needs, Sources and Utilization*, Princeton University Press.

32   *Sunday Times*, London, 10 May 1981, p. 14.

33   D. B. Jelliffe (1972). Commerciogenic malnutrition, *Nutrition Reviews*, September, p. 201.

34   Sunday Times, op. cit.

35   Feachem *et al.*, op. cit., p. 87.

36   The proposed amendments to the existing legislation are embodied in the Drug Regulation Reform Act of 1978. Under the Act, 'Approved drugs in compliance with domestic requirements could be freely exported. Unapproved drugs or approved drugs *not* in compliance with domestic requirements could be exported only after an export permit had been approved by the Secretary. An export permit would be granted only when the exporter of an unapproved or noncomplying drug demonstrated that the importing government had assented to its importation after being informed of its legal status, and the basis for it in the United States. The scientific and medical data concerning the drug's unapproved status would be made available to the importing government to

assure an informed decision.' (See Kennedy, op. cit., p. 189.) While this proposal would, if approved, undoubtedly constitute an improvement, there is still the problem of the 'country of origin' rule in many LDCs in terms of which drugs can only be imported if approved in the country where they are manufactured in final dosage form. It is no doubt true, as Silverman (op. cit.) has pointed out, that this rule has not always been effective in the past, but it none the less obstructs the intentions of the amendment to the US export laws and should be abolished.

37   DiRaddo and Wardell, op. cit.
38   Ibid.
39   Ibid., p. 265.
40   Ibid., p. 276.
41   Ibid.

Notes on Contributors

Martin Bell is a Senior Fellow of the Science Policy Research Unit, University of Sussex. The paper in this volume was generated from research on technology transfer and industrial development in Thailand which was supported by the Ford Foundation. Current research is centred on issues about technical change and technological capacities in infant industries.

Stephen Biggs is a Lecturer in Agricultural Economics in the School of Development Studies, University of East Anglia. He has worked in Bangladesh and Northern India. He has been a home-based Fellow at the Institute of Development Studies, University of Sussex and has worked for the Ford Foundation and the International Maize and Wheat Improvement Centre (CIMMYT) and other aid agencies. Recently he has been involved in reviewing and assessing agricultural and rural technology research, development and promotion systems.

Charles Cooper was formerly a Professorial Fellow at the Institute of Development Studies in Sussex, and is now Professor of Development Economics at the Institute of Social Studies in The Hague. He has worked on problems of technology and development since the early 1960s.

Carl J. Dahlman received a Ph.D. in economics from Yale University in 1979. Prior to joining the Economics of Industry Division of the World Bank in the same year, he spent two years in Brazil studying technological change in the steel industry. His main areas of interest are the economics of technical change and the acquisition of technological capability by industrial firms, particularly those in developing countries.

John Enos is a Fellow of Magdalen College, Oxford, where he teaches economics. He has worked in India, Turkey and Chile. His publications include *Petroleum, Progress and Profits* (MIT, 1962) and *Planning Development* (with Keith Griffin), (Addison Wesley, 1970). His first degree was in engineering and he has always been interested in the interplay between economics and technology, especially in developing countries where he believes the game is rougher and the outcome more significant than in developed countries.

David Forsyth is a Reader in economics at the University of Strathclyde. He is presently working as consultant in Fiji. He has written widely on questions of foreign investment and technology choice. He has worked in Ghana and in Egypt.

Jeffrey James is Assistant Professor of Economics at Boston University. From 1978 to 1981 he was Research Fellow at Queen Elizabeth House, Oxford. He is co-author (with Keith Griffin) of the *Transition to Egalitarian Development*, Macmillan, 1981, and author of *Consumer Choice in the Third World*, Macmillan, in press.

Sanjaya Lall is Senior Research Officer at the Oxford University Institute of Economics and Statistics where he works on industrialisation and foreign investment in developing countries. He is presently on sabbatical leave in India conducting research on technological development and technology exports for the World Bank. His publications include *Developing Countries as Exporters of Technology*, Macmillan 1982.

Norman McBain is principal manufacturing engineer in Tube Investments Groups Services. He was previously a Senior Research Fellow at Strathclyde University.

Ward Morehouse is president of the Council of International and Public Affairs, Research Associate at the Columbia University School of International Affairs, and a Fellow of the Centre for International Policy in Washington. He has been a Visiting Professor at the University of Lund in Sweden and at the Administration Staff College in India, and consultant to the Ford Foundation. He was Director of the Centre for International Programs and Comparative Studies of the University of the State of New York. His works include *Science and the Human Condition in India and Pakistan* (New York: Rockefeller University Press, 1968), and *Science, Technology, and the Global Equity Crisis: New Directions for United States Policy* (Muscatine, Iowa: Stanley Foundation, 1978).

Howard Pack has taught at Yale University and is currently Professor of Economics at Swarthmore College. He has written about a number of issues arising during the process of industrialisation, including the choice of appropriate technology, the role of the capital goods sector, and the determinants of industrial efficiency.

Wit Satyarakwit is a Lecturer in Economics at the National Institute of Development Administration, Bangkok, where his current research is concerned with the demand for housing in Thailand.

Don Scott-Kemmis is a Fellow of the Science Policy Research Unit, University of Sussex, where his current research is primarily concerned with the development of industrial technology capability in developing countries.

Robert Solomon is senior economist with Dar Al-Handasah Consultants. He was previously a Lecturer in the Department of Economics at Strathclyde University.

Frances Stewart is a Fellow of Somerville College and Senior Research Officer at the Institute of Commonwealth Studies, Oxford. Her work includes *Technology and Underdevelopment* (Macmillan 1977) and *Framework for International Financial Cooperation* (with A. Sen Gupta) (Frances Pinter, 1982). She has been a consultant to many organisations including the International Labour Office, the World Bank and the United Nations Conference on Trade and Development.

Larry E. Westphal is Chief of the World Bank's Economics of Industry Division, where much of the Bank's research on industrial development and policy questions is concentrated. Before joining the Bank, he was on the facilities of Northwestern and Princeton Universities, and for a time served as resident advisor to the Economic Planning Board of the Republic of Korea. He has written extensively on industrial policy and development, on investment analysis under increasing returns, and on empirical analysis of production relationships and technological choice.

Index

for Latin America (ECLA), *Labour productivity of the cotton textile industry in five Latin American countries*, 85–91, 96–7, 103
United States: drug industry, 247, 256, 268

Value added per man, 40–5, 55
Veblen, T., 251

Wage rate and value added per man, 44–5; *see also* Real wages
'Walking-on-two-legs' strategy, 3, 29
Wardell, W. M., 268
Weaving, *see* Textile industry
Welfare: impact of new products, 14, 225, 242, 251–2; policy implications, 14, 236–7, 249–51
Wells, J., 239

Wells, L. T., Jr., 111
Wen-hsien, H., 220
Westphal, L. E., 7–10, 103, 111, 128, 134, 135
Winter, S., 103, 159
World Health Organization, 256, 266, 268

X-efficiency, 6–10, 99, 103; and concept of technological mastery, 7–8; differences in, at various levels, 92–101; in Latin American textile industry, 84–92; relation to choice of technology, 83–103

Yunns, M., 220

Zeidenstein, S., 220